new 3/98

DEFENDING
THE
SPIRIT

DEFENDING
THE
SPIRIT

A BLACK LIFE IN AMERICA

■■■

Randall Robinson

A DUTTON BOOK

DUTTON
Published by the Penguin Group
Penguin Putnam Inc., 375 Hudson Street,
New York, New York 10014, U.S.A.
Penguin Books Ltd, 27 Wrights Lane,
London W8 5TZ, England
Penguin Books Australia Ltd, Ringwood,
Victoria, Australia
Penguin Books Canada Ltd, 10 Alcorn Avenue,
Toronto, Ontario, Canada M4V 3B2
Penguin Books (N.Z.) Ltd, 182–190 Wairau Road,
Auckland 10, New Zealand

Penguin Books Ltd, Registered Offices:
Harmondsworth, Middlesex, England

First published by Dutton, an imprint of Dutton Signet,
a member of Penguin Putnam Inc.

First Printing, February, 1998
10 9 8 7 6 5 4 3 2 1

 REGISTERED TRADEMARK—MARCA REGISTRADA

LIBRARY OF CONGRESS CATALOGING-IN-PUBLICATION DATA:

Robinson, Randall.
    Defending the spirit : a Black life in America / Randall Robinson.
        p.   cm.
    Includes bibliographical references (p.   ) and index.
    ISBN 0-525-94402-8 (acid-free paper)
        1. Robinson, Randall, 1941–   .   2. Afro-Americans—Biography.
    3. Afro-American political activists—Biography.   4. Political
    activists—United States—Biography.   5. Transafrica Forum
    (Organization)   6. United States—Foreign relations—Africa.   7. Africa—Foreign
    relations—United States.   8. United States—
    Foreign relations—Caribbean Area.   9. Caribbean Area—Foreign
    relations—United States.   10. United States—Race relations.
    I. Title.
    E185.97.R665A3   1998
    973'.0496073'0092—dc21
        [B]   97-34052
                                                                  CIP

Printed in the United States of America
Set in Cheltenham Book
Designed by Leonard Telesca

This book is printed on acid-free paper. ♾

To my parents, Doris and Maxie Robinson Sr.,
whose inestimable gifts to me cannot be overvalued

For Hazel, my beloved wife and foreign affairs colleague,
and
For my children—Anike, Jabari, and Khalea

ACKNOWLEDGMENTS

I am extremely grateful to Roxie France-Nuriddin, who encouraged me to write this book and further facilitated its birth by bringing me together with Marie Brown, the exceptional literary agent, to whom I am equally thankful.

Early on, writer Tonya Bolden read the manuscript and rendered invaluable critical advice. Arnold Dolin cared enough about the project to find a home for it at Dutton and confer upon it the additional blessing of Anne Marlowe's meticulous editing.

My great appreciation to Mwiza Munthali and Satia Orange for their painstaking research assistance and to Deborah Harrod, who typed and retyped the manuscript with the patience of a saint.

The book, however would never have been conceived or written without the inspiration and substantive contributions of my wife, Hazel Ross-Robinson.

Contents

Everybody likes to go to Geneva. I used to do it for the Law of the Sea conferences, and you'd find these potentates from down in Africa, you know, rather than eating each other they'd just come up and get a good square meal in Geneva.

—Sen. Ernest F. Hollings (Dem., S.C.)
March 1994

Foreword

We should know a few things personal about those who tell us how we ought to think, feel, and behave. The regents of our civic values, the shapers of our public policy, the pundits of our democratic deliberations, all arrive to public discourse from distant and unseen beginnings which explain them as fully as their ideas. For public policy ideas, whether prudent or injudicious, broadminded or hidebound, seldom amount to more than the sum of their exponents' teachings and experiences.

One doesn't decide on bigotry or altruism the way one chooses a college major. The twig is bent early and keeps its shape throughout. There are of course exceptions, but I suspect, without benefit of survey data, that they are few.

Though it is no longer fashionable to say it, I am obsessively black. Race is an overarching aspect of my identity. America has made me this way. Or, more accurately, white Americans have made me this way.

They marred an otherwise unremarkable Southern childhood and, with the long-running effluvium of U.S. attitudes and policies toward the black nations of the world, preselected my adult career in global human rights advocacy. I can no more distinguish the beleaguered black self in me from my public advocacy than can untold many white American policymakers disengage their racist assumptions from the decades of multifaceted U.S. support for apartheid in South Africa and the corrupt dictatorships of Zaire, Liberia, Somalia, Sudan, and Haiti. The child is the father not only of the man but of the man's deeds as well.

After years of enduring America at home and watching her abroad, I am convinced that I will die in a society as racially divided as the one into which I was born more than a half century ago. This no longer appears to concern white Americans. They have virtually pushed domestic racial issues off the national agenda and tightly sequestered themselves and the rest of us from sight of the often painful consequences of America's foreign policies for blacks abroad.

African-Americans, perhaps still placated by the fool's gold of integration as an endgame achievement, seem not to have noticed our worsening condition with any alarm. At some point beyond the peak of the civil rights movement, we lost our bearings, as if sleepwalking. When we thought about it at all, we reckoned that we were forward of where we had been before. But if we had progressed, it hadn't been by much. Our longitude had changed but our latitude was virtually the same. If the new social terrain looked unfamiliar, it was only because we had drifted sideways, if not backward as well.

John Payton, an old friend and brilliant Washington lawyer, told me recently that UCLA Law School's large entering class for fall 1997 would likely include not a single black, owing to a general retreat from affirmative action. This is the new and disturbing national trend. In 1996 President Clinton signed a mean-spirited welfare reform bill that promised to push millions of children, black, brown, and white, into poverty. Months later the President, with much pomp and fanfare, called from a platform in Philadelphia for mass volunteerism as an answer to our nation's growing social ills. Sharing the platform with the President were former presidents Carter and Bush. General Colin Powell provided something of a black imprimatur for the idea of substituting volunteerism for federal assistance to the poor.

The black community has been slow to interpret the signs that are all around it. The Pentagon will not be touched by the current Congress's budget cuts although the Cold War ended six years ago. The cuts are to come significantly from the hide of the country's disproportionately black poor. Africa will continue to occupy the bottom rung of the State Department's ladder of priorities. The Agency for International Development has closed its Caribbean office and reprogrammed most of the aid that once went to the Caribbean to Eastern Europe.

The black community remains quiet, mystifyingly maintaining broad support for the President.

I am gripped with a feeling akin to the odd sensation one experiences while sitting in a stationary railway car as the train on the adjacent track slowly begins to move. Which train is moving? In which direction?

Thirty-odd years ago America with a massive exertion heaved itself from the swamp of de jure racial segregation. Domestically, it has done little since to facilitate racial equality. In its foreign relations with black nations over the same span, U.S. policies have been measurably less benign, resulting in the wreckage of much of Africa and the economic crippling of the democratic English-speaking Caribbean.

Although TransAfrica, my organization of twenty years, fought and won the U.S. policy skirmishes for South Africa and Haiti, it has not changed the variously indifferent and hostile face of American foreign policy toward Africa and the Caribbean in general. For policies are formulated by people who were once children and came ultimately to the world affairs table dragging behind them the baggage of an endemically racist society.

Fifty years ago I saw their faces across the great racial divide of the Old South. I see their faces now across tables in soft-spoken well-reasoned exchanges in well-appointed rooms. But the age-old racial divide is no less yawning than before.

Washington, D.C.
Summer 1997

PART ONE

Behind the
Race Wall

It is curious that I've never discussed it with any black person I've ever known. What exactly is hate, and has it to be returned in kind? Can it afflict its victim with a muted form? The kind that doesn't preoccupy, past which one can smile and function civilly? Can the tumor, enlarged and hardened over time by a weather of ceaseless slights, be benign? Normal, wouldn't you think, the injured angry soul's retreat inside behind an impenetrable wall of manners? What have I done with my pain? I am not eager to know. I can find no answer of which I can be proud. White-hot hatred would seem the proper reflex. But there is no survival there. In the autumn of my life, I am left regarding white people, before knowing them individually, with irreducible mistrust and dull dislike.

Spring 1995: Rural Virginia

I climb up on the loading platform in back of the small country hardware store somewhere off Route 13 near Nassawadox on the Eastern Shore of Virginia. I am looking for the proprietor. The air is cool in the shadows of the storeroom and redolent of fresh-sawn lumber. I hear voices behind me. The proprietor, middle-aged with skin leathered by the sun, is talking to two young white men in bib overalls. The young white men are leaning on a rusting 1962 Ford station wagon of indeterminate color. From the shadows of the storeroom, I move in their direction.

"A boy jus went in theah lookin fuh ya," one of the young men says to the proprietor.

It is two months before my fifty-fourth birthday. Twenty-five years have passed since I graduated from Harvard Law School. I have conferred with presidents and more than once altered the course of American foreign policy.

The "boy" to whom the semiliterate corn farmer is referring is I. And I have traveled a long way to nowhere.

My rage is complicated by the balm of comparative material success. I tell myself that I cannot be wounded by a red-faced hayseed. But I am. The child lives on in the man until death.

My father died in 1974 at the age of sixty-eight, of what the family now believes to have been Alzheimer's disease. Toward the end, and not lucid, he slapped a nurse, telling her not to "put her white hands on him." His illness had afforded him a final brief honesty. I was perversely pleased when told the story.

From slavery, we have sublimated our feelings about white people. We have fought for our rights while hiding our feelings toward whites who tenaciously denied us those rights. We have even, I suspect, hidden those feelings from ourselves. It is how we have survived.

Well-educated blacks have even been inculcated with the upper-stratum white distaste for excessive emotionalism. Black folk of my time talk about white people and their predilections at least once daily but never talk about or with anger. It seems unnatural. Where have we stored the pain and at what price?

The anger caroms around in our psyches like jagged stones. Hidden deep anger. We don't acknowledge it. We don't direct or aim it. But it is there.

Spin the cannon. When it points threateningly outward, even white liberals dismiss us to a perimeter of irrelevance or worse. When it points inward, white conservatives find in our self-hate praiseworthiness.

Best we just stow the cannon, hide the anger, and do the best we can. Without contemplation, this is the deal most of us are constrained to accept. A Nat Turner doesn't make it in America, but a Clarence Thomas frequently does.

■ Winter 1967: Cambridge, Massachusetts

I have arrived from segregationist Virginia to attend Harvard
Law School. Our first-year class of more than five hundred students is divided into four sections. My section is sitting through
a torts lecture given by young professor Charles Fried. Tall and
bespectacled, Professor Fried was born in Prague, Czechoslovakia,
in 1935, was educated at Princeton and Oxford and Columbia,
and will become Solicitor General of the United States under
President Ronald Reagan.

With what seems to me affected formality, Professor Fried is
holding forth from the well of the Austin lecture hall on the
notion of nuisance as an actionable tort. Among the listeners
are five black students, including Henry Sanders of Bay Minette,
Alabama, who will become an Alabama state senator, and
Rudolph Pierce of Boston, who will become a Massachusetts
judge. There are one hundred and twenty-one white students in
the large hall. Seated halfway up the ascending bowl to
Professor Fried's left is William Weld, a future Republican governor of Massachusetts. At eye level with Professor Fried and to
his right is Samuel Berger, who like Messrs. Sanders, Pierce, and
Weld will find his way into public service, eventually advising
President William Jefferson Clinton from the post of Assistant
to the President for National Security Affairs. To Mr. Berger's
right and two rows behind sits Mark Joseph Green, late of
Cornell University and Great Neck, New York. By the mid-1990s
Mr. Green will have nailed down a position as New York City's

public advocate and a statewide reputation as a liberal Democrat.

Professor Fried is superciliously droning on in a vaguely British accent about how the visitation of annoying or unpleasant conditions upon a neighborhood (grating noise or belching smoke, for example) can constitute a tort or cause of action for a civil lawsuit.

"Can anyone think of an actionable nuisance we haven't touched on today?" asks Professor Fried.

"What about black people moving into a neighborhood?" suggests Mark Joseph Green, liberal Democrat of Cornell University and Great Neck, New York.

A thoughtful discussion ensues. Henry Sanders looks at me. We five blacks in fact all look at each other. Our faces betray little. In any case, the privileged young white scholars are oblivious. There are legal arguments to be mustered, pro and con. The discussion of whether or not the mere presence of blacks constitutes an inherent nuisance swirls around the five blacks. We say nothing. We cannot dignify insult with reasoned rebuttal. The choice is between ventilated rage and silence. We choose silence.

Mr. Green does not prevail and is foreclosed from extending his argument. Encouraged, he might have made Harvard Law School a plaintiff in a theoretical nuisance suit against the twenty-five blacks admitted to its class of 1970.

Doubtless Mr. Green will not remember his attempt to expand the definition of nuisance as a tort. Thirty years later I will not have forgotten.

1949: Richmond, Virginia

Maxie Jr. and I sit in the living room on a late Sunday afternoon going through Daddy's scrapbook while waiting for Miss Washington to collect us in her black four-door 1948 Plymouth. Maxie Jr. is ten and I am eight. Miss Washington is my brother's spinsterish fifth-grade teacher at Baker Street Elementary School. On Sundays after dinner she sometimes takes the two of us for a ride in her polished sedan.

The couch is old and sags in the middle, causing us to lean together while turning the dog-eared pages. The couch, which sits astride the hearth and blocks the fireplace in the tiny room, is flanked by end tables atop which rest maroon ceramic lamps bearing the oval portraits of two Victorian white women whose faces are framed by tight coils of dark hair that reach from scalp to bodice. My sister Jewell won the monstrosities in a teen essay contest.

The floor is covered by a piece of linoleum with broken edges. The raw wood perimeter floorboards have been painted with dark brown deck paint by Mama.

The scrapbook rests on a coffee table that matches the lamp tables. The set is made of mahogany wood with inlaid leather tops. I am proud of our tables. We are careful not to score the leather surface with the plywood scrapbook covers.

Attached to the black pages by tiny paper corner frames are serrated black-and-white photos from the early 1930s. The yellowing news clippings are pasted directly onto the stiff paper.

The slight man in the football uniform does not look like my father. His helmet is nothing more than a leather skullcap. His jersey has no number and is decorated only by leather strip appliqués. He wears no shoulder pads and no thigh pads. Hip pads stick up out of his skimpy pants at unstylish angles.

MAXIE ROBINSON SCAMPERS FOR
AN 80 YARD TOUCHDOWN
IN VIRGINIA UNION VICTORY

This is the headline from the article pasted under the picture. Another picture on the page shows Daddy running with a ball that looks as much like a basketball as a football. I look hard for Daddy in the pictures of this lithe young athlete with blazing speed but cannot find him. The Daddy I know just waved to us on his way out. By 1949 he is forty-three years old, overworked, overweight, and suffering from high blood pressure, but he has remained a handsome man of forbidding countenance.

Daddy's mother and father married in Richmond in their adolescence and divorced shortly after he was born. His father left for Baltimore, remarried, and unburdened himself of his only child. His mother also married again, this time to a disengaged alcoholic who worked for the railroad and played the guitar alone in his bedroom.

Maxie Cleveland Robinson Sr., with a mother scarcely fifteen years his senior, largely produced alone the man he was to become—a highly principled teetotaler, unaccustomed to the social domesticities of family life and with small gift for intimacy.

Doris Alma Jones, my mother, grew up in Portsmouth, Virginia, in a large white shingled two-story house on Palmer Street between Effingham and Chestnut. She was the first of seven children born to Nathan and Jeanie Jones. One child, a boy, died in infancy. Six survived to great age, a boy and five girls including my mother, now eighty-three.

Mama and Daddy had met years before in Richmond at Virginia Union University, a small school with a large reputation for producing epic preachers (Sam Proctor, Wyatt Tee Walker, Walter Fauntroy). Mama had come one hundred miles up from

Portsmouth to prepare for a teaching career. Daddy, who had grown up in Richmond, was working his way through college by taking courses one year and a job the next. She was eighteen and he was twenty-six when they were introduced. He was as iron-willed and determined as she was naturally brilliant. Starring in every sport, he was the campus hero and a local legend. She was a straight-A student and beautiful. I suspect that Mama was smitten by him early on, for Daddy had an overpowering room-filling presence about him—heady stuff for a eighteen-year-old girl never before away from home.

Mama was twenty in the summer of 1933. Portsmouth was in the grip of a late July heat wave. Mama and her ten-year-old sister, Evelyn, moved back and forth in the bench swing on the front porch of the old family house trying to win a margin of comfort from the motionless hot air. In May, Mama had completed her first year of college and come home for the summer. Since arriving, her thoughts had been increasingly of Daddy. During the school term in Richmond, they had gone together to the movies and sorority dances. He had kissed her the first time on their sixth date. It was an age of reticence, and the term ended before they could properly reveal to each other a fraction of what they were beginning to feel. Daddy was working during the summer as a waiter in Virginia Beach. In the fall, he would leave for Atlantic City to work in a similar capacity until spring. She had no idea when she would see him again, if ever. She had said nothing to her family about this new man looming so large in her reveries. Premature talk might have jinxed hopes that were, at once, exciting and scary. He was not her first beau, even if she could possessively think of him in such terms, which she could not. Yet this feeling was new and very different.

It was noon. Evelyn's feet touched the porch floor but without purchase. Mama absentmindedly tugged at a loose string from the waist seam of her cotton house dress and moved the swing backward.

A half-block away, a battered city bus stopped at the corner, and a man stepped off. He wore a Palm Beach suit of beige linen, white shirt, dark tie, and bone-colored shoes. The bent brim of his panama straw hat shaded his eyes.

"Oh my God," Mama said in disbelief, her heart suddenly racing. Evelyn, alarmed, said, "What is it, Doris? What is it?"

"Evelyn, a gentleman is coming to see me."

Mama was out of the swing and at the door before Daddy could catch sight of her.

"Tell him, tell him, I'll be right down."

Daddy stood on the steps in the shade of the forest green porch awning and waited alone, Evelyn having delivered the message and disappeared into the house. Ten minutes later, Mama came through the screen door onto the porch. She was wearing a light blue, full-skirted voile dress and white summer sandals. She wore no jewelry. Her parents did not approve of lipstick. Save for a trace of blush on her cheeks, she wore no makeup at all. Daddy stepped up onto the porch, took both of Mama's hands in his and kissed her lightly on her forehead.

"You are looking beautiful," he said. Mama blushed. They sat in the swing and chatted.

"I would like to meet your parents," Daddy said.

"Papa's at work but Mama's here."

The discussion with my grandmother, though formal, went well.

"If it would be all right with you, Mrs. Jones, I would like to take your daughter to a movie this afternoon." Mama had never been anywhere on a date in Portsmouth unaccompanied by her eighteen-year-old sister, Hattie.

"Mr. Robinson," my grandmother said while moving with Mama toward the screen door, "if you would excuse us for a moment." In the foyer, she looked at Mama and came directly to the point. "I don't know this man."

"But he's a good man, Mama. He's a gentleman."

"Well, I guess you can go. After all, it *is* broad daylight."

They walked the mile down Effingham Street to the Capitol Theater, trailed much of the way by an incorrigible neighborhood rascal chanting, "Doris got a boyfriend! Doris got a boyfriend!"

On August 31, 1936, at noon, Mama and Daddy would marry on that same street at the home of Reverend Harvey Johnson before sailing in the evening from Norfolk on the *Washington Steamer* bound for the nation's capitol. It was on their honeymoon that Daddy presented Mama with her first tube of lipstick. "I don't want your mother to see me wearing lipstick," Mama said. "Don't worry," said Daddy, "she wears a little herself."

Mama had taught school in rural North Carolina for a short time before they married. He had already become a history teacher and all-sports coach at Armstrong, one of Richmond's two black high schools. She became a housewife, mother, and public speaker. Our household income would never exceed $11,000 per year.

Mama and Daddy were the only heroes I've ever had. Not that other, global figures I've come to know in adulthood aren't worthy. But hero appreciation should be born of a close and varied knowledge and must, when healthy, die with childhood.

▪

We hear the horn of a car. It is Miss Washington's Plymouth, we know. I close the scrapbook with care and return it to the coffee table. Soon Maxie Jr. and I will be heading out for our Sunday ride.

The dark flat is long and narrow. There are four units in the red brick building, two up and two down. All four units have long skinny backyards, but only the two ground-level units have front porches and front yards. We live in one of these. The porch is small with a gray-painted wooden floor. Five of the boards have been replaced by the landlord the month before and left unpainted. The yard, more flower patch than yard, runs beside the porch and to the sidewalk.

Mama is showing Miss Washington her flower garden, which is just beginning its annual show. The creeping red phlox has bloomed for weeks. The tall, elegant irises wait their turn. The thin, upright Miss Washington, who looks like anything but a gardener, seems to be enjoying herself although unable to identify any of Mama's flowers by name.

Mama is bending over and pointing. "This is called sweet william." I like the name more than the plant. Miss Washington smiles but does not bend. "And these are snapdragons." I do not like the plant *because* of its name.

Maxie Jr. and I sit on the porch glider and wait. On the floor beside us are four empty quart milk bottles. The milkman will retrieve them when he delivers fresh milk tomorrow before Jewell, Maxie Jr., and I begin the walk to school.

Today we are wearing our white Sunday shirts, which will be worn again to school tomorrow before Mama washes, starches, and hangs out the family's wash on Wednesday. We look well turned out in our stiff shirts, suit trousers, and clean shoes.

"Are you ready, young men?" asks Miss Washington.

"Yes ma'am," we answer in unison.

There is the scent of dung in the air. Weekdays, old Mr. Johnson brings a horse-drawn vegetable wagon through the neighborhood and sells his goods from wire and wood produce baskets that hang from the wagon's sides. Evidence of his route is piled on the street not far from Miss Washington's Plymouth.

Riding in a car is a rare treat, and Maxie Jr. and I do not disguise our joy as we pull open the heavy rear doors that swing away from the thick post in the sedan's middle. This is our first ride with Miss Washington since the fall. The route does not matter, and the ride never seems to last long enough. On Leigh Street we cruise past High's ice cream parlor where a two-scoop cone costs five cents and a three-scoop cone unaccountably costs ten cents. Up at the corner is Tony's confectionery where on my walk to school, unknown to Mama and Daddy, I often spend all thirty cents of my lunch money for six boxes of Raisinets. A. D. Price Jr. is standing in front of his funeral home. We think he must be very rich. A big hard-drinking man with a low gravelly voice, he is easily the most charismatic man in our neighborhood. He calls out to us as he prepares to step into his Cadillac convertible.

Farther along Leigh Street on the left is our barber shop. It is named, oddly, Your Barber Shop. A haircut costs fifty cents. Daddy takes us there every other Saturday. He likes it because Pop, the sixty-five-year-old proprietor, allows no profanity or blue talk.

Miss Washington turns left and drives down Broad Street, the city's main artery.

"You young men having a good time?"

"Yes, Miss Washington," we chime.

She drives with her eyes to the front and both hands high on the wheel. Her posture is sclerotic. We turn off Broad into Capitol Square where the governor's mansion is located.

"Boys, this is where the governor lives," she announces in a tour-guide voice.

"Yes ma'am," we say. She does not know that Maxie Jr. and I have been to the mansion several times before, banged on the front door and run. We do not like the governor. But we say nothing to Miss Washington.

■ 1950s: Richmond, Virginia

I spent the first fifteen years of my life at 521A Third Street, a ground-floor flat in the black section of downtown Richmond. Our small place housed six people and God only knows how many other living things. The long summer evenings we would spend on the porch talking until our bedrooms had cooled enough to allow sleep.

We were poor. I knew we were poor. I saw what others had and we didn't. We had no car—but then, neither Mama nor Daddy could drive. The monthly rent for our rodent-infested shotgun-style flat was thirty-seven dollars.

Daddy would trap the rats at night in a cage, and drown them (caged) the next morning in the claw-foot bathtub.

I remember believing as a little boy that a sign of wealth in a home was a wall-mounted light switch. In the room near the rear of our flat where Maxie Jr. and I slept, the light switch was in the center of the ceiling on a string. Entering the room after dark, I would stamp the floor, loudly, to announce my coming to the rats. Truce offered, I'd give them time to vacate my space before grasping blindly for the light string. After the light was out, I could hear the furry bastards moving inside the crumbling plaster walls.

No television, no telephone, no central heating. Only kerosene space heaters that had to be fueled every morning from five-gallon cans filled from two large tanks in our fuel shack toward the rear of an unlighted backyard. In the mornings, we would warm ourselves by backing against the open oven in our tiny kitchen.

Yes, we were poor and I knew it. And yet, while I was inconvenienced by poverty, I was never scarred by it, at least in no core sense. We were not pathologically bereft of resources. We were always clean, well clothed, and well fed. More important, we were always loved by two extraordinary people. Mama was solicitous to a fault and Daddy made us feel safe. He seemed fearless. I respected and feared him at the same time. He would teach us by word and example to take stands on moral principle notwithstanding the price. Self-respect was all. Life without it was pointless.

Daddy taught all day, coached his teams in the early evening, and ran the city recreation center until closing. His workday went from 9:00 A.M. to 9:00 P.M. Mama, academic success long behind her now, labored to make an uncleanable house clean, ugly rooms sightly. She taught me early on to wallpaper and paint. With tin patches she covered the holes gnawed through the three-quarter-inch-thick wooden baseboards by the furry bastards.

∎

On our block segregation compelled what would otherwise have been a very unlikely black unity.

Around the corner on Leigh Street, the Peterson family rented one side of a duplex. George Peterson was principal of my high school. His wife, Thelma, taught at the junior high I attended. Their two daughters were friends of my sisters. Theirs was one of Richmond's most prominent black families.

Directly across the street from us in a flat not unlike ours lived Margaret and Grace. Margaret and Grace worked at home. They were prostitutes. Margaret was thickly built and somewhat taciturn. Grace was slender, tall, and elegant. She was without doubt the brains of their pimp-free enterprise.

Next to Grace and Margaret lived Puss Owens, the flamboyant owner of the Esso service station at Second and Leigh Streets. Puss drove a fire engine red Hudson convertible. He put his Christmas tree up on his front porch in November and took it down in March. From that front porch you could smell the industrial strength fumes emanating from the nearby open windows of one of our community's most viable businesses, Shirley's Beauty Parlor.

In retrospect, Shirley's can only be seen as an indicator of black self-loathing. Black women with "bad" hair came to Shirley by appointment to have Africa fried out of their heads. The sickly sweet burning odor produced of grease and fry-level heat was repellent. Shirley's hands were off-putting: fingers gnarled, darkened, nearly burned to inflexibility. Up to four women would be in various stages of the wash-and-fry process, their necks scarred by errant hot pressing combs.

This is not to single out the Shirleys or the women who sought their services. We had all bought in. Everything around us instructed us of our inferiority and we believed it in every aspect. It followed that, if kinky hair and black skin were naturally characteristic of us, they too must be seen as ugly and inferior. Dutifully on Saturday nights I would wash my hair, apply Tuxedo Club Pomade to my wet hair, and don a stocking cap before going to bed. On Sunday I would be blessed with ersatz waves for church.

It never dawned on us that group success, whether the group is defined racially or otherwise, can only flower from the rich soil of self-acceptance and self-approval. Across the globe, reaching back over the centuries, slavery and colonialism had denuded us of an ancient and proud culture. We were pained victims of a stolen identity. We had become pitiably failed mimics of those arrayed against us, with no discernible memory trace of victorious Moorish forays into Spain and Portugal, the military feats of Hannibal, or the great African civilizations of Kush, Songhay, and Monomatapa. Blighted mirror. Forgotten glory. Looking for Senefer in black Richmond was as fruitless as searching for heirs to the awe-inspiring Mayan civilization in Guatemala. The footprints had long since petered out. We were lost.

In a rooming house next to us lived George Scott. Mama and Daddy told us never to look directly at him. We never spoke to him, and he never knew we knew his name. In our house, unbeknownst to them, we had given every neighbor a physically descriptive nickname. Ham Fat. High Pockets. But George Scott was too mean a man to ever play about. This man who regularly shot at people when he was drunk remained George Scott.

A moral counterbalance to the sinister George Scott lived on the other side of us: Mrs. Bolling. Sixtyish, upright, God-fearing, Mrs. Bolling owned a large well-maintained walk-up duplex in which she rented rooms to blacks shut out of white hotels. When I was thirteen, I rushed to her door with half of the boys in the neighborhood to meet Larry Doby, the slugging center fielder of the Cleveland Indians. Three months after Jackie Robinson's debut, Doby became the second black to play in the major leagues. He was the Indians' most valuable player. But when Cleveland came to town during its exhibition schedule, he wasn't allowed to stay with the team. He stayed with Mrs. Bolling. It is likely that he found her in the Green book, the travel guide that provided a comprehensive listing of places throughout the South that provided meals and lodging for "traveling coloreds."

At Second and Leigh were the offices of Dr. Charles Sutton, who was Mama's sister's husband. Uncle Charles, a solicitous and decent man, was a general practitioner whose patient load comprised largely poor blacks. His waiting room was always packed. I wondered why it was invariably overflowing when his patients saw him by appointment. It turned out that most of the unscheduled sick were the patients of white doctors who only saw black patients on Wednesdays. Those who had the misfortune of falling ill on a day other than Wednesday would try their luck in the waiting rooms of Uncle Charles and other black doctors. "I treat them successfully," Uncle Charles lamented to me on more than one occasion, "and then they go back to the white doctors who wouldn't see them on white days."

Our brides were never pictured in the *Richmond News-Leader.* Beyond tiny box scores, our high school teams were never covered in the sports section. Bucky Keller was a white high school basketball sensation famous statewide. "He can't play dead," Daddy said, meaning Bucky was inept. When my brother won second place in Virginia's "I Speak for Democracy" contest, the local papers ignored it. Black faces almost never appeared on television. Stepin Fetchit was one exception. Another was a forgotten baritone on the *Ted Mack Amateur Hour* singing, "I got plenty o' nuthin and nuthin's plenty for me." That a white person would sing such a lyric seemed unimaginable to me. Some did, I later learned. But I never heard it.

We had families, gardens, ladies' clubs, cotillions, reunions, christenings, picnics, commencements, recitals, funerals, baby showers, joy and heartache. In Richmond, as throughout the Southland, we had a community visible only to us.

Shut away and barricaded off from white Richmond, we made a world of our own with black service providers—teachers, doctors, lawyers, preachers, hoteliers. Adjusted for segregation's psychic cost and our persistent poverty, our community was quite viable and my childhood essentially happy.

The Southern white power structure apparently understood throughout the Jim Crow era that if this vicious system were to have any chance of surviving, we blacks would have to be made to some large extent willing co-keepers of our own prison. The corpus of unjust laws, the bottomless poverty, the psychological and physical color-coded ghettoizing of people, the relentless slanting of the available educational materials—all of these measures were designed to teach but a single lesson: that we were unfit, substandard, inferior. And indeed, if we could be convinced of it, we'd stay in our assigned places and everything would be fine.

■

From the edge of memory, I recall going with Mama to Montaldo's, a women's apparel store on Grace Street. There were at least a half-dozen white clerks behind their counters. Mama and I were the only customers. We stood there. No one would wait on us. I looked up at Mama. Mama of brilliance and academic achievement. Mama who lived an ethical and Christian life. Mama who loved her husband and children. Mama of grace and beauty. She who was everything to me had become invisible to every half-educated white clerk in Montaldo's.

I was six. All the people I loved and trusted were black. The people I was learning to facelessly despise were white. By then,

I had stood with Daddy in the packed back of a bus when seats in front were empty. I had trudged with Daddy up flights of wooden steps to the back door of the Golden Welcome restaurant for takeout chop suey. I had seen black teachers dither uncomfortably when white school officials from downtown deigned to visit Baker Street School. I had seen white fountains that gave cold water but drunk warm water from black spigots. I had regarded Mama, humiliated, covering her head with a beanie cap before trying on a Sunday hat at Thalheimer's department store. I had seen pictures of firelit white men, women, and children posing smiling before black bodies dangling from trees, wrenched askew at the neck, and burned crisp.

Race awareness is now a subtext of all encounters. My emerging personality has been pressed hard against the color-conscious society's rigid contour. When I was very young, before an impervious shell had been grown around me by both those who loved me and those who hated me, I thought grown-ups quite silly for making such fuss about a difference in human features that seemed no more important than any other. Tall. Short. Fat. Skinny. Black. White. A small child's logic soon to be crushed by an infectious malevolence that would make the color difference all-consuming and unique among human differences. The ancient unbridgeable difference that would shape and preoccupy me for the rest of my life. Make for me innumerable subliminal decisions. Choose my friends. Direct my course. Lay claim to my creative and intellectual energies. This is the subjugated's burden.

A few of us, when given a chance, will flee, chameleon-like, unconditionally into the pale arms of the pain bringers. Most will figuratively remain forever behind the race wall, proud, girding, fighting, always fighting, ever and relentlessly defending all that is really worth defending—the fountainhead, the dark hearth, the drawn bow string, the beleaguered last tenderness—defending the spirit.

I had seen the ornate outsides of movie theaters for whites and the shabby insides of those for us. Unlike other Southern cities where blacks in movie theaters were confined to balconies, in Richmond we were confined to our own cinemas. Max and I would be admitted without charge to the white-owned black Globe Theater because our uncle Jim operated the film projector. Occasionally, films with black themes would be shown. At those allegedly out of Africa, we would laugh: a kind of muffled, sniggering laugh in a desperate and unsuccessful effort to separate ourselves from the simpering fools on the screen. Bubble-eyed black characters created by white film-makers and held up to us like a mirror. We were being taught to understand that we fully merited the bottom rung on the American ladder, to come to terms with segregation. To some extent it worked. I believed we collectively were inferior. Hence, so too must I be. When we laughed at the screen, we laughed at ourselves. But our shame was our salvation. Our shame connected us to the people on the screen. Our shame was a feeble hedge against denial. Our sniggering was desultory, broken into bits and bursts. We wouldn't look at each other laughing at ourselves. We were profoundly ashamed, not so much of the buffoons depicted on the screen as of ourselves for willingly accepting this intended humiliation.

Africa, when mentioned at all in my childhood, was almost invariably in a humiliating context. Yet it was the fountainhead of our people. Like it or not, we were indissolubly bound up with it by blood and history. But every white reference to Africa—in films, books, newspapers, and television—was negative, grossly and meanly so. Edgar Rice Burroughs saddled us with Tarzan, D. W. Griffith with *Birth of a Nation*. A tortured and damned people from a ridiculed continent. This was the lesson of my childhood South.

Can you understand the disaggregating weight of duality this placed upon a child? Loved by ours for good reason, hated by theirs for none. Seen, known, appreciated, nurtured by ours, scarcely visible to theirs. Normalized and denormalized. Built up, torn down. Learning to love ourselves while being taught to hate ourselves. The double exposure of the emotional membrane to high praise and searing contempt. Small wonder the damage was direct and permanent.

I had little collateral knowledge of victims elsewhere. I had never heard the term colonialism. I must have heard of slavery but was too young to understand its meaning. Emmett Till, not knowing what awaited him in Philadelphia, Mississippi, was a happy black child growing up in Chicago. More than a half century before, Queen Victoria had given Kenya's Mount Kilimanjaro to Germany's future Kaiser Wilhelm II as a birthday present—a piece of Africa not rightfully hers to give, to a child who in any case wanted a pony and cried to show it. I knew none of this when I was six. But I knew about the mean blade of racism. By then I had been irreparably savaged by it.

■

Mama and Daddy loved books. Books were all around us, hers mostly religious, his political. Everyone read, and talked incessantly about what they'd read. Jewell, the eldest child, read her way from kindergarten through high school with a string of A's broken only once by a B in algebra in the eleventh grade. (The B to this day remains contested.) Upon finishing high school in 1955, she was awarded $5,000 in scholarships (a school record at the time) and a place at Goucher College as the first black student ever admitted. Two years later Maxie Jr., or Max as he would come to be known, broke Jewell's record, winning awards totaling $7,000. From there he went on to become the nation's first black news anchor on network television, with ABC's *World News Tonight.*

My own high school academic record was considerably less stellar (husbanding my intellectual energy, late bloomer, and all that). Young rebel that I was, I declined to answer the challenges on the faces of my teachers who had taught the foregoing Robinson prodigies. As a child would see it, you don't fail if you don't try. I did little or very close to it. With some embarrassment I would eventually head off to Norfolk State College on a basketball scholarship, transferring later to my parents' alma mater. More responsibly, Jeanie, the baby and five and a half years behind me, followed Mama and Daddy, becoming an elementary school teacher in Washington, D.C.

■

If Daddy feared anything he feared grays. Gray complicates a life that's already complicated enough. Daddy was a moral absolutist. Mama was active in the church. Daddy had not been seen in one after his eighteenth birthday. His rules for living were immutably stamped on a stone tablet he kept in a secret compartment of his walnut chifforobe.

Samuel Gladden unluckily said "motherfucker" within earshot of Daddy. He was banished forever from the Armstrong High School basketball team. People who said words like "motherfucker" were no good. Done. I was luckier than Samuel. Once, at age seventeen, I forgot in whose presence I was, and I said "shit."

Daddy, preoccupied with some other thought, said, "What did you say?"

Petrified (this is when I began to learn to think on my feet), I stuttered, "Sh-sh-sh-shift gears, Mr. Reed in Drivers Education is teaching me how to shift gears."

"Good," Daddy said and retreated to this thoughts.

I could hear my heart in my ears.

Max and I were corporally punished by Daddy infrequently and judiciously but very, very memorably. Jewell and Jeanie were exempted. Among other things, Daddy believed that a real man never strikes a female, a rule he suspended only once and deservedly in Jewell's case when early one Saturday morning she repeatedly ignored his order to be quiet by shouting non-stop, "I can't hear you, I have my fingers in my ears!"

Once Mama, after a long Sunday service, descended the stone steps of our impressive Fifth Street Baptist Church to find parishioners bunched tightly around a loud and mobile ruckus on the church steps. An onlooker turned to Mama with some embarrassment and said, "Mrs. Robinson, I think you'd better come and have a look." Max and I, aged thirteen and eleven, faces flushed, knees skinned, trousers torn, neckties askew, were down on the steps transported in battle.

"Mama, please don't tell Daddy. He will kill us. Can't you see we're sorry. We'll never ever do that again. Please, Mama, just this once. Just this once." We made this reasonable plea trailing behind Mama for the three-block walk home.

"Maxie Senior, would you step here, please." This the moment she opened the front door. I thought we would die that Sunday.

The conventional wisdom was that you should not whip a child in anger. But when else are parents going to beat the hell out of their offspring?

My strategy was always to be whipped first. Max calculated it wiser to go last. My thinking was that, by going first, I would avoid the added agony of having to watch what I was about to get. Max figured, I now think rightly, that Daddy would vent his anger and wear himself out on me before getting to him. This was a decision we would be faced with roughly once a year before reaching our mid-teens.

Daddy had further ground rules. He would not accept any of his children in his history classes lest he be accused of favoritism. When, in my sophomore year of high school, Geechie Reynolds and I competed evenly for the last slot on the varsity basketball roster, Coach Robinson/Daddy let the players choose by secret ballot. I made it. When I led the team in scoring and to a 21–2 record my junior year, Daddy explained to me why I could never be captain. I understood. His players respected him. I did as well. Deeply. He made my relationship with my teammates easier to manage.

■

"No son of mine will ever shine shoes, so forget it."

"But, Daddy, other boys are doing it."

He glared at me.

I checked myself. I should have known better than say to *him* what other boys, men, women, presidents, kings, queens—what another anybody anywhere was doing.

"Do you see what we have to tolerate from them? Do you feel what they are doing to us? I don't know when and if things will change. But I do know that no son of mine will ever shine a white man's shoes."

◼ Summer 1951: Portsmouth, Virginia

For as far back as I can remember, Daddy spent the summer teaching baseball school at Brookfield Garden, a city-funded sports complex for blacks. The complex, with its three baseball diamonds, two tennis courts, and swimming pool, was overseen by Arthur Ashe Sr., whose sons Arthur Jr. and Johnnie lived with him in a well-kept white clapboard bungalow nestled between the tennis courts and the baseball fields.

From pewee level at age six for as many as ten summers, Max, Arthur, Johnnie, and I were taught to play baseball by Daddy. (We had no inkling that Arthur was learning another sport on the other side of his house.)

At the end of the summer, all of the city playground students would go to Washington in a caravan of buses to visit the zoo and see the Washington Senators. Black playground children and white playground children on black buses and white buses. The playground teams had played against each other during the summer but never across racial lines. At Griffith Stadium, I saw the Indians' Larry Doby and Luke Easter. When I was ten in 1951, I saw Joe DiMaggio at the end of his career and Mickey Mantle at the beginning of his.

Ritually at midsummer Mama would take the four children to Grandma and Granddaddy's house in Portsmouth for a two-week stay. Daddy would remain behind to work. The poorly ventilated Greyhound bus would head south on Route 460 with roadside stops at Petersburg, Disputanta, Ivor, and Suffolk. At

Wakefield, the midway point of the three-hour trip, the white passengers would go into the bus-stop restaurant to relieve themselves and have lunch. We would go to a bathroom around back, then lunch in the rear of the bus on sandwiches Mama had prepared at home.

Grandma and Granddaddy had a substantial house with four bedrooms upstairs, a living room, dining room, kitchen, and a long entrance hall with a telephone beside a divan downstairs. The entrance hall gave in the rear onto a side porch on which Grandaddy had an old-style barber's chair. Granddaddy, past sixty and retired from the Navy Yard when I was born, would cut hair and sharpen saws on the side porch. I still have the manual scissors-action clippers with which he cut hair, including mine and Max's.

Behind the house was a pen for Granddaddy's six hunting hounds, and a grape arbor. There were side lawns with red roses I liked and blue hydrangeas I detested, then and now. A porch with a swing, a long cushioned glider, and striped canvas awnings spanned the front of the house. Granddaddy cut the grass every day, front, back, and sides, with a push mower. There were no sidewalks, concrete gutters, or curbs. None anywhere in Portsmouth's black community that I can remember. Granddaddy planted grass on the ditch bank and mowed that, too.

The house had floral wallpaper throughout. The large country kitchen was heated by a cast-iron potbelly stove, with the rest of the house relying on oil burners. In the living room was a console Dumont television set with a round picture tube that warped the people on the screen. Unlike the dangling strings at home, Grandma and Granddaddy had light switches on the wall with two buttons in a toggle plate. When you pushed one of the buttons in to turn the light on, the other button would pop out. This was the first place I had ever seen such a switch, and I was very impressed. I thought Grandma and Granddaddy must have been rich.

They had come to Portsmouth from rural North Carolina with Grandma's sisters Aunt Virginia, who lived around the corner on Chestnut Street, and Aunt Ethel, who at eighty-nine still lives around an opposite corner on Effingham.

Grandma never worked. On Sundays she baked bread from dough that rose during church and smelled like the best part of my childhood. Granddaddy did carpentry work during the day. In the evenings Mama would sit on the front porch with Grandma and other visiting siblings while Granddaddy played checkers with Uncle Gene in the side yard on his custom-made wooden inlaid checkerboard.

God-fearing country people on a sleepy street where one evening was much like the last and the next.

Jeanie, five, sat on the glider with Mama and Grandma trying to make the glider go faster than Mama and Grandma wanted. Jewell, fifteen, was around the corner at our teenage cousin Alva's house. Alva was Aunt Ethel and Uncle Marvin's adopted daughter.

"Boy." Granddaddy, slight of build at five foot nine and 135 pounds, spoke a language we called low-voice, one-word, no-nonsense.

"Yes, Granddaddy," Max and I said in unison. We didn't know which of us he was addressing.

"Stay out of my flower beds."

Max and I, thirteen and eleven, had been tearing around the yard chasing one another.

"Doris."

"Yes, Papa."

"Keep those boys out of my flower beds."

"Yes, Papa."

I always liked to hear Mama speak to Granddaddy. "Papa" was a much warmer title than "Daddy" or "Dad." "Pop" denoted cynical alienation and "Father" utter lovelessness. But "Papa" sounded loving, reverential, traditional. "Papa" felt like old red wine, big family dinners, and no divorces.

Mama's family was deep and eternal. Daddy's was small and patched. As a child, Mama had known her great-grandparents on both sides as I had known mine only on hers. She had many parents. Daddy had had only a young girl who was more a contemporary than a mother. This allowed Mama an openness that Daddy couldn't afford. He had made himself. She hadn't had to. Her inestimable strength was congenital and unapparent. His was worn like a suit of armor. Where she was mild of temperament, he was combative. Where she had little interest in politics and world affairs, he had interest, apart from sports, in little else. She was devoutly Christian. He was devoutly agnostic. She was *there.* He was very much here.

Max and I scrambled out of Granddaddy's flower bed.

All would grow quiet again as night fell and fireflies brightened. At nine o'clock sharp the nightly single cannon shot heard from the Navy Yard marked bedtime for most of Portsmouth.

■ Spring 1954: Richmond, Virginia

At thirteen I began making deliveries for Katz Groceries at Clay and Belvidere Streets. Mr. and Mrs. Katz were solicitous and patient with their new hire, and I was earnest if only marginally efficient. I worked from four until seven-thirty weekdays, seven to seven on Saturdays, and a half day on Sundays. The store was a mile's walk from our flat, a half block north to Clay and west to Belvidere. I earned thirteen dollars a week. Mama and Daddy allowed me to keep the money to manage as I saw fit. I opened an account at Consolidated, then one of the country's oldest black banks, whose president, Mr. Nickens, was a figure of considerable community stature.

With a portion of my earnings I bought clothes, partially relieving Daddy of the burden. From Julian's Fine Clothiers on Broad Street I purchased a white-on-white cloth Billy Eckstine dress shirt with the gull-wing flying collar. I accessorized the shirt with argyle socks and a tie whose width I tailored down severely to the black community's fashion tolerance of the time. My suit and pants remained those that Max had outgrown.

At 2:30 P.M. on the afternoon of May 17, 1954, I was sitting in Mr. Bland's eighth-grade science class at the battered desk on the outside row near a bank of open windows, wearing my Billy Eckstine classic. The school was Benjamin A. Graves Junior High, an imposing old colonnaded redbrick building situated on Lee Street halfway between Katz Groceries and home.

Mr. Bland was a big barrel-chested man with a booming voice

and a brush mustache. Unlike the diminutive but stern Mrs. Diamond who fixed her thirteen-year-old geometry students with "the look" before the lesson, Mr. Bland couldn't control his class. Well, in fairness, it was me and one or two others he couldn't control. Sometimes, even now, I feel a twinge of remorse about the stress I caused this large, kind man who taught science and played the violin.

"———— has just been handed down and it will change all of our lives." Mr. Bland was talking. I wasn't listening but everyone else appeared to be, which was unusual.

"What did he say?" I asked the girl in front of me. Mr. Bland heard.

"I said, Randall, that the United States Supreme Court has outlawed public school segregation. The schools will be integrated."

I was stunned. The class was quiet, reactions difficult to read. If this warranted a celebration, it got none from Mr. Bland's science class.

Within days, I thought, I'll be in another school with white people. I was trying to come to terms with this news, which was unsettling to say the least. I'd never expected such. Not in my lifetime.

Let me be completely honest about my memory of the effect on me of Mr. Bland's announcement. I did not want to go to school with white people. I wanted the right to go anywhere I wished to go. I also wanted the right not to go. And if the choice were mine, count me out. I'll concede that I was more than a little frightened. After all, white people had spent the better part of four hundred years conspiring to convince me of my innate intellectual inferiority. They had made some headway. And I hated them for that. At thirteen, I only sometimes thought I was smart. I secretly believed I was special. I even felt, well, yes, immortal, as I later discovered many thirteen-year-olds do. But the doubts about competitive ability had been well sown. Also by age thirteen, I had intuitively developed the cardinal guidepost for emotional health: the Never Wannabe Rule. Never want to be with people who don't want to be with you. Its derivative has served me just as profitably: Never like people who don't like you. There may be occasions when you are allowed to dislike those who like you. The converse proposition, however, is anathema.

The bell was about to ring, sending us back to our homerooms. Mr. Bland was asking us about the characteristics of cumulus clouds.

My mind wandered. I was thinking about how white students might be accepting the news at Hermitage, Highland Springs, and Thomas Jefferson. I couldn't visualize these schools. I'd never seen them. But I pictured white faces, some tear-streaked, some angry.

Don't flatter yourselves. I'm not coming to your school.

I needn't have troubled. Forty-three years later, Richmond's public schools are virtually as segregated as they were that spring afternoon of Mr. Bland's bombshell.

■ Summer 1955: Richmond, Virginia

I was fourteen and in the second year of my job life. Now I was working for Cohen's Grocery on the corner across from the Petersons, and I deposited every penny of my salary in my Consolidated account. In August, I gave it all ($208.68) to Jewell for school expenses.

Grocery store delivery bicycles, driven to eventual extinction by modern supermarkets, had an oversized carry basket over a tiny front wheel. Fully laden, they could easily prove unmanageable for a spindly teenager. I learned of this design defect on a snowy dark winter evening as I bounced off the curb on Leigh Street with a basket full of coal. The bike went end over end and I with it. The coal bags burst, sending chunks across four traffic lanes, slowing a rush-hour stream of cars, and earning a look of stern reproof from Mr. Cohen through the storefront window. I suffered the stinging embarrassment that adolescent boys often endure when they stumble and fall down the school steps with girls watching.

My deliveries to Margaret and Grace engendered embarrassment of a somewhat different quality.

Twice weekly without fail, Grace would call Abraham Cohen and order a twenty-four-bottle case of Richbrau beer. I, the delivery boy, at fourteen was still very much among the sexually innocent. Not surprisingly, it was with a mixture of nervousness and salacious anticipation that I would load the store bicycle with a cardboard case of Richbrau beer and ride the half block to the house of sin.

Their flat was arranged like a New Orleans–style shotgun house: narrow front, rooms in a line—living room, bedrooms, bath, and kitchen.

"Come on in," Grace called to me on one occasion from the bedroom. "The door is unlocked."

I put the beer down in an empty living room.

From the bedroom: "Come on in here, Randall, for the money."

The well-reared, Christian, virginal, fuzzy-faced fourteen-year-old delivery boy was now petrified. I edged through the bedroom door, half in, half out, to find Grace in bed with a client during a business hiatus.

"Your money's on the dresser, sugar." She winked. "The extra dollar is for you."

Grace gave bigger tips than any other of the store's customers.

"You gettin' to be such a big boy."

I was tall for my age.

"Christmas I'm gon give you a real special present." And she winked again.

My face heated up and arranged itself foolishly. I was struck dumb. Grace laughed a sisterly laugh. I fled to the relative safety of my unstable bicycle.

■

Mr. Cohen had driven me and a station wagon full of boxed groceries to a distant white residential neighborhood. It was dark. Had it been daytime, I would not have known where I was.

"Randall, the bill is taken care of. Just take these boxes in. I'll wait for you."

"This way." The man did not greet me. He turned and started away from me toward the rear of the brick ranch-style house. The carpet was deep and covered every inch of the floor. I sank in it. I had never seen this kind of flooring.

"There. Take the cans out and keep the boxes." He turned away from me and toward his wife and two daughters seated at the kitchen table. I had seen kitchens like this but only on television. I was struck by the oven that opened noiselessly out of a brick wall. The sleek refrigerator was four times the size of our single-ice-tray Frigidaire. The floor was marble, the likes of which I had seen only in the Virginia Museum of Art where Max and I had taken a Saturday art course for blacks.

The mother was speaking to the older of the two girls. "You will not ride with that boy in his car, young lady, until you are sixteen."

"But, Mother, I'm almost sixteen now."

"Did you hear your mother, young lady? The answer is no."

"But y'all are not being fair."

I hurried to unpack the box. My face was burning. I felt diminished, soiled. They were talking two feet away as if they had not registered my presence.

At the end of the summer of 1955, I caddied at the Country Club of Virginia. I stood on a putting green with a bag of clubs resting against my hip as the thirtyish white golfer whose clubs I had borne through twelve holes was addressing his ball. As he was about to strike the ball, the clubs shifted in the bag, making a disturbing clatter. The golfer looked up as if seeing me for the first time. "You do that again and I'll wrap this club around your neck."

I left the golfer and the bag of clubs on the twelfth green. I should have known better than to caddy. I never told Daddy.

▪

I don't know if the story is true or not. But it was widely accepted that Max was experimentally inoculating chickens in the basement of Armstrong High School in 1955. He was brilliant. Bronchitis caused him to hunch his shoulders in a scholarly fashion. His favorite piece of music was *Sheherazade* and he looked like a scientist at sixteen. While we moved in quite different social circles (my friends were largely pubescent jocks), I loved him. We were each other's best friend. He protected me from bullies as ably as any precocious sixteen-year-old scientist could.

Daddy had reason to be proud and contented as he taught his history classes that year. Max was on track to become a member of the National Honor Society. Jewell had been accepted on full scholarship as Goucher College's first black student. Jeanie was progressing nicely through elementary school. And I had not yet arrived at Armstrong to elevate his blood pressure.

I admired Jewell and felt to some degree intimidated by her. She was stunningly pretty. She was very smart. She had a natural savoir-faire and an instinctive taste for the arts, both aural and visual. (Inexplicably she loved the prize lamps and has the monstrosities to this day.) She was also one of those people who by divine authority selflessly tells rudderless lesser mortals what to do. But doesn't every fourteen-year-old think his older sister is bossy?

Fall 1955: Towson, Maryland

Mr. Harry Williams was the principal of Maggie Walker High School, the other black high school in Richmond. Mr. Williams and Daddy had coached together at Armstrong years before. During football season they would still travel to officiate black college football games on Saturdays. On one such occasion, when I was eleven, Max and I had gone with Mr. Williams and Daddy to Morgan State in Baltimore. I remember the trip because of Morgan's impressive stone buildings. Though Mr. Williams was Daddy's best friend, they addressed each other formally. It was always "Mr. Williams" and "Mr. Robinson."

Mr. Williams came to our flat on a Saturday to drive our family to Towson, Maryland. It was Family Day at Goucher College.

We were seated around tables for eight in an attractive dining hall. A crowd of hundreds included family members, students, and faculty. Our family and Mr. Williams were seated toward the center of the room. There were seven blacks in the room, all of them at our table. Everyone was keenly aware of Jewell's first-ness. I felt eyes on my back. Max's tweed suit was tight across my shoulders. I was drawing even with him in height, so hand-me-down days were nearing an end.

Although the Goucher staff had been warmly, if nervously, hospitable, I was uncomfortable. I was fourteen. Walking to the table, I concentrated on my legs, knees, feet, and muscles. There was something wrong with my gait. I had set short-term goals: get to my chair without stumbling and sit. I was seated between Jewell and Max. Next to Jewell was Mama, then Jeanie, Daddy, and Mr. Williams.

I had never been in a room full of white people. I had never eaten dinner in a restaurant or anything like one. I looked at Jewell. She smiled confidently. God! She always knew everything. I concentrated. I hastened to put my napkin in my lap. I then spied a two-inch-high block of lettuce before me. "Jewell," I whispered, "what do I do with the lettuce?"

"Cut it with the side of your fork," she instructed.

I attempted to do this. The lettuce block shot straight up, rising three feet before landing on the floor between Max and me. I looked at it. More eyes were on my back. The lettuce block on the floor appeared to glow and emit a beeping signal.

"Maxie, would you pick the lettuce up for me, please?" I implored desperately. With no hesitation, he picked it up.

1956: Richmond, Virginia

When Daddy's stepfather died, we used Grandma's insurance settlement to make the down payment on a house on Thirty-ninth Street, a modest three-bedroom red brick colonial with a side porch. It had a flower garden in which Mama would spend eternities and a side lawn on which I would later wash and polish a red Rambler that seldom ran.

The house stood across from down-sloping woods on the eastern edge of the city. We bought it from Mrs. Pritchard, a white woman, for $10,750. A few blacks had moved into houses directly behind us on Thirty-eighth Street, but we were the first on our street, which ran only one long block. We were told that Phil Bagley, a member of the all-white city council, had once lived in the house four doors down. Mr. Hoffman, whose Hoffman sandwich trucks were known to all Richmonders, lived just two doors away. He drove a pink Cadillac Coupe de Ville and in front of it was usually parked one of his tall green panel trucks with his company logo and name on the side. Mr. Hoffman wasn't famous, but his trucks were.

Daddy was ill during the weeks before and after we moved. Jeanie was too young to help very much, Jewell was at college, and Max, a senior in high school, had never been manually dexterous, so Mama put me in charge of the moving arrangements. I dealt with the movers, supervising the packing and unpacking and placement of furniture. Mama's confidence in me was vindicated. I was fifteen, and felt very much like a man as I cleaned the oak hardwood floors and painted the walls and woodwork with compulsive care. John Davis, a school friend, helped me paint the exterior wood trim of the house. The ladder would bow and bounce on the climb up to the high gable peak of the roof molding, so one of us would hold the ladder while the other painted. John appeared to like heights. I liked holding the ladder rather more.

After he closed on the house, Daddy seemed a different man, preoccupied and spiritless. The house was a vast improvement over the Third Street flat. But Daddy's thoughts were elsewhere.

Mama and I met with Mrs. Pritchard at the house a week before we moved in. Mrs. Pritchard looked around wistfully and said, "I sure hate to have to leave this house."

About as combative as I would ever know Mama to be, she asked, "Why did you sell it, then?"

Mrs. Pritchard, who had, in the time since we'd met her, comported herself decorously, gave no answer. But we all knew. Within six months of our arrival, the single long 600-block of East Thirty-ninth Street would be all black.

I saw Daddy crying once alone in his bedroom. I had never seen him cry and it frightened me. I asked Mama about it and she told me it was because he had gone into debt to buy the house. He had signed a twenty-year mortgage, committing himself to payments of fifty dollars a month. Daddy, our family's sole breadwinner, was mortally afraid of debt. He worked longer hours, doubled up on the mortgage payments, and paid off the loan in twelve years.

Fall 1958: Richmond, Virginia

Daddy didn't have a rule for cars. This may have been because he couldn't drive. I exploited this chink in his armor and asked him to co-sign a twelve-month $360 loan on a 1951 fire engine red Nash Rambler convertible.

"I can do this, Daddy, believe me. I can play ball, keep my grades up, and wash dishes at the hospital at the same time. You won't have to pay a dime. I am asking you to believe in me." How credible is a seventeen-year-old testosterone victim?

No good deed goes unpunished. Two months and five payments into my senior year, I tired of keeping my job, my grades up, and my scoring average high. I quit my job. Daddy now had seven payments left on a placebo convertible that looked good, started every third Tuesday, burned more oil than gas, stopped only with the assistance of the emergency hand brake, and once, through a driving rainstorm, ferried Mama the two miles home from the Safeway on Twenty-fifth Street with the top stuck in a half-up position.

I loved that car. My love was unrequited. In the first semester of my senior year, I, a former honor student, brought home three F's and a D. The D was a gift from my physics teacher, Ms. Eloise Bowles, a friend of the family.

I would now have to attend summer school to finish high school in 1959. I would not march with my class. And I would not play another game for Maxie C. Robinson Sr. Daddy bounced me from the team after we'd won the black Virginia State

Championship and just before the team left to compete for the national black high school championship in Nashville.

Through the second semester and summer school I made straight A's.

If Daddy appears from this rendering to have been inflexible and humorless, that was not the case. Even less so in retrospect. A red Rambler story will illustrate my point.

Less than a week after persuading Daddy to co-sign my car loan (co-sign is a bit of a stretch; I was only seventeen so he must have signed alone), I was tooling across the Marshall Street viaduct going toward Churchill and home when I looked in my rearview mirror and noticed I was being dangerously tailgated by a high-riding black truck. I asked of my red Rambler a margin of safety and floored the accelerator. The rubber-band engine coughed and responded by enveloping the four bridge lanes in a cloud of black smoke.

As I surged ahead I looked again in my rearview mirror. Through the smoke, the lettering high on the hood of the black truck came into view:

POLICE

The wail of the siren and revolving red light atop the patrol wagon gave me a start. Nervous, I pulled over and stopped in the block beyond the bridge, forgetting to engage the clutch. The car bucked and died.

"License and registration," demanded the dour white police officer. I rummaged about in the glove compartment and retrieved the three-day-old temporary registration card. I fumbled in my wallet and pulled out a temporary driver's license issued by the Division of Motor Vehicles exactly nineteen minutes before I was stopped.

"You didn't waste any time, did you?" the officer said, reading the date of issue. "You were doing forty in a twenty-five-mile zone. Because you are a minor, you will have to appear in court *with one of your parents.*"

I was now a dead minor.

"Mama, I can explain. I wasn't really speeding. Well, maybe I was a little bit but not because I wanted to."

Mama looked at me.

"Mama, we can't tell Daddy. Please. You can go to court with me. But please don't tell Daddy."

We heard his key in the front door.

"Maxie Senior, would you step here, please." And, of course, she told him.

"Jesus Christ. Jesus Christ. Jesus Christ." Daddy whispered it over and over, sibilantly, slowly, quietly, and from a strange register of his deep voice. I remained absolutely still. Dear twelve-hour-day Daddy. Dear rectitudinous, proud, principled, duty-bound Daddy.

In a fiercely segregated South, I was dragging him into the domain of a white judge. And he had signed for this.

He looked at me more in puzzlement than anger. He was thinking about his other children. Jewell was doing well at Goucher, and Max was at Oberlin College. Daddy missed Max greatly. The two would sit before the seventeen-inch black-and-white Daddy had bought in 1951 and watch *Meet the Press* with Lawrence Spivak on Sundays. Twelve-year-old Jeanie was his favorite. She had found the way inside. She had softened him.

Daddy looked at me again wonderingly, then wearily shook his head and walked out of the room. The whipping I had expected never came.

■

In the 1950s Richmond was a city of 200,000 people, more than half of whom were white. With the exception of the Jewish corner grocers for whom I worked from age thirteen, I was twenty-two years old before I actually *met* a white person. We saw whites all the time. They drove the buses and clerked the downtown stores. Mama even knew one through state Baptist circles. Polly somebody-or-other. We knew when Mama was talking to Polly on the phone that we got when I was fifteen. Mama's voice would have that talking-to-white-folks inflection. But so impenetrable were the spatial and social strictures of segregation that I never met a gentile white soul in Richmond, Virginia. That occurred only after I had left Richmond for U.S. Army basic training at Fort Jackson, South Carolina. It was 1963, just before the U.S. force buildup in Vietnam. I had dropped out of college and gotten drafted.

Mama had written to me at college more than once admonishing, "Do not waste your time and our money." But after a year on the dean's list I began to do both. I had no clear idea of what I wanted to be or do. I was years away from developing the faculty for performing academic tasks that were unpleasant or boring. My grades plummeted. I was a star basketball player. Girls had begun to turn my head. The distraction was more than a man-child could manage. I needed a respite. I needed to grow up.

PART TWO

Bridges to Seriousness

I have come to know race as a sealed dwelling with windows but no doors. One can look out but never leave. Perhaps it is this way for all people. Perhaps all feel keenly, ever consciously indexed—racially, ethnically, or culturally. I can make no thoughtful guess. I have difficulty seeing beyond the burden of my own particular American minority-ness. It is always there. I suspect this is the case for all African-Americans. Some will vehemently deny it. Others will luxuriate in it. Still others have driven the whole business down and away from mindful measure.

■ Winter 1963: Fort Jackson, South Carolina

Dropping out of college during the Vietnam War was not seen around the family as a wise course setting.

"How do you want it?" The poker-faced army barber made it sound like a sincere question.

"Just a touch off the sides, thank you." I made it sound like a serious answer.

Within thirty seconds I was a twenty-two-year-old bald-headed college dropout army private.

I'm sure that I must have gotten back in a line. I'm sure because we were always in line. Lined up for breakfast. Lined up for training. Lined up for lunch. Lined up for more training. Lined up for dinner. Lined up for hours more of deadtime moonlit tarmac assembly, the purpose of which, I must have divined, was to drill into the sorry frozen lot of us the equality of our unimportance. I had some advantage here. I had withstood twenty-two years of Ole Virginny's divination of my unimportance. I looked down the straight line of December red noses to see how my white platoonmates were coping, not so much with the implication of their unimportance but rather with the new equality of it that for the first time in my life placed us all, at least for a short time on a frigid army tarmac, in the proverbial same boat.

An important element of military training philosophy is the

intent (backed by the well-demonstrated wherewithal) to all but flatten out the social, economic, religious, ethnic, and racial differences that fence Americans off from each other in civilian life. The differences don't disappear in the army. They are disguised behind an olive drab sameness and a new language of deference to rank.

I am inveterately suspicious of authority. But the sheer weight of it levels. Remember, Yugoslavia's death followed closely upon Tito's. Too many people in a heterogeneous society shouting and acting on too many combustibly conflicting narrow-minded beliefs can produce chaos and disintegration. Such is not allowed in the military. Virtually everything one needs to know, think, or do is in the manual. Free spirits need not apply.

Of course I hated the army. It was a numbingly automatonic and partitionless experience. Blacks, whites, Asians, Latinos, Native Americans showered, shaved, ate, slept, marched, barked, crawled, ran, urinated, and defecated together, literally cheek by jowl. It was a picture of no small irony—a free-speech but racist American democratic society being protected by a less racist military enterprise that was, and necessarily remains, totalitarian in its operational aspect.

President Lyndon Johnson began the buildup of American forces in Vietnam during my two-year tour of duty. We feared that our terms would be extended and that our infantry unit would be sent to war. In the late spring of 1965, the President went on national television to pronounce our fates. At American military bases around the world, American soldiers were glued to television screens. Johnson announced that we would not be extended in service but that the buildup of American forces would be accelerated dramatically.

The antiwar movement on college campuses was only just germinating. I had no understanding of why American soldiers were fighting in an obscure country's civil war, eight thousand miles away in an Asian jungle. No one around me understood either. We didn't want to go but we would go if ordered to go. I have no memory of anyone in my unit questioning orders. We didn't want to die. But the truth is, at that time, dying seemed preferable to defying the U.S. government.

And so we waited. We trained and we waited.

◼ Summer 1965: Fort Benning, Georgia

Nothing is more essential to the successful completion of a military tour of duty than a well-trained reflex of obedience. Do what you are told. Don't think. Follow orders. Get an honorable discharge and rejoin the ranks of independent, reasoning people. Though I hated the army, I concede that the experience was developmentally beneficial to me. Having never really met any whites before the age of twenty-three, I had never competed against them and frankly had believed that I couldn't. If the South had taught me anything, it was that.

With no idea that Harvard Law School was in my future, I approached my first mainstream competition with some trepidation. Fortunately, in those early rounds I was thrown against the scrubs. At first I was elated. Later I was angry. These guys, to whom I had been taught all my life I couldn't hold a candle, were with some exceptions, well, not very bright. Segregation had done its job. I had been the victim of a cruel ruse.

In the Fort Benning evenings I would escape the olive drab regimented hell by burrowing into the post library. I read ceaselessly and with little selectivity. That it transported me, however briefly, away from Fort Benning was reason enough to treasure that library.

One evening I happened upon a small book entitled *A Kind of Homecoming* written by E. R. Braithwaite, an author from Guyana who had gained some measure of fame with the publication of his largely autobiographical work *To Sir, With Love,* later made into a movie starring Sidney Poitier. Braithwaite, of the Caribbean, having gone to Africa for the first time, had been moved to write about his experience in *Homecoming*. His Africa resonated so memorably with me, I suspect, because his curiosity was virtually identical to mine. He was describing Africa's look and feel through the eyes of a descendant of African slaves. This extended victim of the middle passage, born and trapped in the diaspora, had gone home at last.

I read Braithwaite's account with a great hunger. He was a credible witness who, though Guyanese, had shared my own experience. When he actually went to Africa, through a little army library in Georgia I went with him. Were I to reread this book now, some thirty years later, I don't doubt that I would take issue with much of Braithwaite's characterization. I remember almost none of his detail. I do remember that this personal-watershed account was the first positive thing I had ever read about the continent that had produced everyone I loved and trusted. This reading experience also may have been the genesis of some new reckoning that the problems of the black world were not a phenomenon solely of the American South. The magnitude of our dilemma was much greater than I had any reason to suspect. In the first twenty-three years of my life I'd seen only a small mean piece of the puzzle. I had had no opportunity to travel, either intellectually back through time or physically beyond a five-state radius. It may have been that I was just beginning to become a global person.

▪

The two of us were on our way to Phenix City, Alabama, to look around and return to Fort Benning later that warm Saturday evening. Warren Jackson, black and from Atlanta, knew more about the Deep South than I, and advised that we wear our uniforms when we ventured off the base. As we were about to leave for the bus station, a white soldier offered us a ride. "I'm going in the direction of Phenix City. Let me give you guys a ride."

"Thanks a lot. We're ready when you are."

The white soldier, wearing civilian clothes, drove. Warren rode in front and I in back of the middle-aged Pontiac.

By the time we crossed into Alabama, it had grown dark. We were on a two-lane road in the middle of nowhere when we heard the wail of a siren. The police car pulled off on the narrow shoulder behind us, its headlights streaming through our rear window.

The headlights died.

The officer shined a big flashlight beam into the car. He moved the light slowly from the driver's face to Warren's and then back to mine. He said nothing for a while. I could see only a silhouette of a face behind the light.

"You git outta the car and step to the back," the officer ordered the driver. "You two boys stay where you are."

Warren and I said nothing. We did not move. The pitch darkness was eerily punctuated by the slowly turning light on the roof of the officer's car. No cars passed on either side of the remote road.

I looked straight ahead at Warren's neck as I listened to the exchange behind the car.

"Open the trunk."

The driver complied. Then, the thump of the closing trunk lid.

"Where you from, son?"

"I'm from New York."

"What you doin' wit these niggas in yo' car?"

"I was going to Phenix City and offered them a ride from the base."

"Whatsa matta wit you, son? I was in the service, too. But I nevva hauled no niggas round in my car."

The driver did not reply.

It was very still then for a time, the slowly turning light continuing to flash against two motionless black soldiers in the car and the two whites discussing them behind it.

"I'm gon gi ya a break this time, son. Now you git outta here wit these niggas and don't lemme catch you wit um in yo' car agin. You unnerstan?"

"Yes, sir."

We were quiet for the rest of the trip. I remember nothing of Phenix City, Alabama.

■

Memory of distant events, or memory of anything for that matter, is not a function of discretion. One remembers what one remembers. Why one remembers is a great deal more important than what one remembers.

I remember much of basic training because it was grueling and put me in the company of white people for the first time. I remember Private Robert Matlock because I rode with him on his Triumph motorcycle over a bluff at high speed and nearly broke my neck. I remember Sergeant Monroe of Snow Hill, North Carolina, because he was my platoon sergeant and a strong leader of men, and black. I remember my rifle (or my "weapon" according to Sergeant Monroe and all the other career zealots who took ordnance nomenclature seriously) because its piercing report claimed half the hearing in my right ear.

I kept the new dial tone in my ear a secret because I wanted to be eligible to apply for six weeks of special duty at Aberdeen Proving Grounds in Maryland. At Aberdeen, after the first year of my two-year commitment, I would sleep in a bed instead of a bunk, in a room instead of a bay. I would drink from glasses and eat from plates. After months of meals plopped on dented metal, this was worth pursuing.

The quid pro quo was my willingness to participate in, of all things, an experiment conducted by a civilian scientist studying the effects of gunfire noise on hearing. It is superfluous to say that the scientist was white. With the exception of a lone captain I met six months before my discharge, I never saw a black officer, either.

I can't recall the scientist's name. I recall only what he looked like, that he was sourly opaque, and that he seemed to regard his subjects, black and white, merely as auditory organ fodder for his cheerless work.

Let it suffice for the purpose of this telling to call him Dr. Sour. For reasons I cannot reconstruct, Dr. Sour selected me, among others, for his work because he thought I had perfect hearing.

The idea was to fire guns next to the ears of subjects with perfect hearing and immediately afterward conduct a hearing test to measure their diminished hearing capacity. I'm not sure how the army benefited from causing, or certainly risking, the loss of hearing of some twenty of its nation's finest sons. For Dr. Sour, however, there was a paper in it. A career credit. I know because he told me in an unguarded moment. As our hearing went down, his stock went up.

Each morning we would report to the hearing lab for testing before going to the rifle range. A second test would follow the rifle fire. The test results would then be compared. This went on for weeks for all of the subjects save one. Me.

As I have said, I could not hear well in my right ear. (I hear less well in it today.) Fortunately, Dr. Sour would run bursts of sound first in my left ear. Without varying the sound duration or frequency sequences, he would start with the lower sounds and climb. As instructed, I would press the plunger when the sound began and release it when the sound stopped. Left ear, right ear, low sounds, high sounds, hum, humm, hummmmm. I memorized Dr. Sour's sound program. As the days went by, Dr. Sour seemed puzzled by my consistently perfect hearing. Perfect before and after the rifles were exploded inches from my eardrum.

He mentioned to me his concern that my hearing "was not deteriorating as it should." I was young and from the South. I was black. Dr. Sour was white. My face must have betrayed something. Satisfaction. The tiniest celebration of a small triumph. A hint of it perhaps in my eyes. And then, something in his eyes never there before.

He started the next test on my right ear. Sometime after his sound bursts had become indistinguishably mingled with my right ear's dial tone, he stopped his sounds altogether. I continued to punch and release from memory.

"Private Robinson, you have completely fouled up my data."

Lordy. I fouled up his data. A cicada convention screeched relentlessly on in my half-dead right ear. But I fouled up his data.

Within twenty-four hours I was once again in Fort Benning, Georgia.

Then of course I remember Sergeant Smith back at Fort Jackson, South Carolina. He was the boot camp sergeant of the platoon barracked next to ours. He was always perfectly turned out. Boots glistening, brass insignia and buckle at high gleam, sky blue ascot puffed just so. He looked like a shorter version of Clint Eastwood, with weather-beaten skin, an aquiline nose, and flint gray eyes that closed down in a let's-take-that-hill-men squint. He was an infantryman's infantryman.

One clear cold January afternoon, Sergeant Smith asked Sergeant Monroe if he could spare him three men to go on a cleanup detail five miles across the post.

"Nicoletta, Brunofsky, Robinson. Go with Sergeant Smith for policing detail."

We rumbled down our barracks steps to find Sergeant Smith on the company road sitting behind the wheel of an Army version of a pickup truck. "Nicoletta, Brunofsky, hop in here with me. Robinson, jump in the back."

Without wasting an army second I leapt into the back of the truck, bringing my bottom to rest on the icy corrugated truck bed. The truck moved out onto the main post road. I doubled over and hugged myself against the wind.

I was more embarrassed than angry at the realization. How far, how long had I ridden before knowing why I was where I was?

Come now, some might say. How can such an ordinary experience produce such a memorable muddle of humiliation and rage? The cab could only accommodate three. Somebody had to ride in back, in the cold.

Why then not three somebodies?

In retrospect, when reduced to writing, the incident sounds almost trivial. My voice may even have taken on a carping timbre to some ears. So I hasten to point out that this is not a complaint but merely a report of what I felt that day. I felt what all black people feel some of the time and what some black people feel all of the time. I am not usually given to flat pronouncements. But of this I am certain. Ask any black person whose job security or falsified self-image does not depend on the answer. Such small and ordinary experiences are so bitterly memorable precisely because of their cumulatively calcifying ordinariness. While I have no clear idea of what white people feel about anything, I suspect this preoccupation among blacks with race and racism would surprise even the most benignly oblivious of whites. <u>One cannot <u>know of pain</u> one has not felt.</u> Can one even care?

I began to shiver. I looked through the window into the heated cab. Sergeant Smith and Privates Nicoletta and Brunofsky were laughing about something. I couldn't make out what the joke was about.

■

An infantry major from Virginia with a Teddy Roosevelt strenuosity encouraged me to return to college.

"Robinson, this whole army division is going to Vietnam in August. You are eligible for the early-out program. The army will let you out up to ninety days before your scheduled discharge date if your college registration falls within the ninety days. I will support your application if you choose to go back to college in September."

The major had a ruddy complexion and a bluff manner. He looked to be in his mid-forties and his voice held a detectable trace of Old South money. I had no notion of why he volunteered his assistance. He obviously loved the army and knew well enough that I detested it. And yet he took from this no rebuke. I measured him to be a secure and decent man who asked no price or appreciation for his help.

The Southern white army major expedited the approval of my application for early discharge. In August the major and his army division went to Vietnam. In September I returned to Virginia Union University. In October more than half of my former army battalion died in the battle of the Ia Drung Valley. A disproportionate number of those who died in that far-off Asian thicket—in that battle and over the term of the war—were African-Americans.

■ Fall 1967–Spring 1970: Cambridge, Massachusetts

I put a soda and two oddly shiny doughnuts on my tray, paid, and looked around for an empty table in the Harkness Commons cafeteria of Harvard Law School. This was the first day of classes.

The day before, on Sunday, Dean Erwin Griswold had convened the first-year class of some five hundred students in the old moot courtroom of Austin Hall. He had held forth on the timeless beauty of the law, on the grandeur of the hallowed place to which the learning god of ivy had delivered our fortunate chosen souls, and on the surpassing intellectual caliber of the company in which we found ourselves. "Look around. One of every five here is Phi Beta Kappa." The room had old wood wainscot and eight-foot oil paintings. Dean Griswold, venerably ensconced in the overlap of late life and early legend, had intended to impress and indeed he had.

I bit into a doughnut. The doughnut fought back. With the mouthful I was claiming still very stubbornly a part of the doughnut, I looked around to see if there were observers. No one appeared to be watching. The doughnut had a tough chewy consistency. The sugar had been left out as well. I wrenched free the mouthful and chewed for an eternity. Jesus. My adjustment to Harvard, to living in the North, was to be more of a challenge than I had anticipated. I hadn't expected culture shock to be triggered by a goddamn doughnut.

I looked across at two male students eating and talking at the next table. One of them had sliced through his doughnut and slathered the open faces with a thick white cream.

■

I had arrived at Harvard Law School from Virginia Union University. It would seem, I suppose, quite a leap from a small poor black liberal arts college in Richmond, Virginia, to Harvard Law, the school that gave the term "self-absorption" institutional meaning. The students, current and former, even refer to the place, and not jokingly, as *the* law school.

There were dramatic differences, of course, but not so dramatic in ways that you might expect. Harvard was academically more rigorous than Virginia Union, but this was graduate level work and, in any case, Harvard was more rigorous than all but a few institutions. I had done well at Virginia Union. I did well at Harvard. A difference between the two schools, yes, but hardly unbridgeable.

Harvard had a surfeit of brilliant professors. A few of them could even teach. I was impressed to find almost all of my law professors' names on the spines of the textbooks from which they taught. There was, however, common ground between the two faculties, common ground obscured in large part by an enormous resource gap. Virginia Union had some exceptional teachers. Pearl Mankins, who taught me humanities, and Henry Jared McGuinn, who taught me sociology, I suspect were like many who labor by election in small poor schools, black and white, across America. They were no more unique than I. They would fare well anywhere just as I had fared well at *the* law school.

Beyond the obvious, the most compelling difference was in how the two school families saw themselves, which was little different from how they were generally perceived by the larger society. Harvard University is the oldest and wealthiest institution in America (from 1636 with an eight-billion-dollar endowment), attended by the children of families that own and run much of our nation's affairs. Needless to say, Virginia Union's students, many of whom were as talented as many of Harvard's, were neither wealthy nor influential. More important, they were black.

I am quite aware of the dangers of generalization; however, I'll brave them to illustrate my point. Owing to a flattering self-perception born, more often than not, of consciousness of their lineage, race, and class, all but an infinitesimally few white Harvard Law students would find it very difficult to undervalue their potential for general influence and efficacy in the American scheme of things. For students at Virginia Union, the opposite obtained.

As a result, students at Harvard Law School had a stunningly dialogistic relationship with teachers unlike the more vertical arrangement I had experienced in college and before. Students at Harvard, Yale, Columbia, and Berkeley protested against the Vietnam War because they believed, with reason, that they could influence its outcome—because they believed, with reason, that they mattered. Though the black community paid a disproportionately higher casualty price, black students on black college campuses did not protest the war because those students believed, with reason, that they could not influence national foreign policy and therefore the war's outcome. Black people have always known, often too well for our own good, in our collectively delimiting racial subconscious, who owns the country and just how closely those owners listen to us.

■

All of my courses were year-long in the first year of law school. There were no periodic exams. Classroom participation counted for nothing. Our grades would be determined solely by four four-hour examinations given in May. I began preparation months before the examinations were to be held. Routinely I would spend up to ten hours a day buried in the stacks of the law library in Langdell Hall.

There I sat, behind a desk overrun with books, on a late afternoon in April reviewing the contracts cases we had Socratically plumbed over the course of the year with the courtly Professor John Dawson. I was wearing a dark suit, a blue oxford button-down shirt, and a striped tie. I had been highlighting passages with a Magic Marker and making notes in a book's wide margins.

It was very quiet. The three other study cubicles in the cluster were empty. From where I sat in the stacks, I could see down three long corridors of books, a mere fraction of the seemingly endless collection that comprised the largest law school library in the United States.

I heard footfalls on the metal staircase.

A white student I did not recognize approached me. "Are you the janitor?"

I looked at him.

All he thought I could possibly be was implicit in his question. My rhetorical question in reply was quite unimaginative. "Let me ask you something. Do I look like the goddamn janitor?"

He reddened and hurried away.

■

The late sixties were very difficult years for Boston. I lived there, across the Charles River from Cambridge, in the black community of Roxbury. The Boston school system, one of the most backward in the country, was under a federal court order to bus children from one substandard school to another. South Boston was an Irish Catholic stronghold through which blacks could not safely travel, much less transport their children. Buses bearing black elementary school children were stoned. The life of the federal judge who had ordered the busing was under constant threat. Hate-stoker Louise Day Hicks, a South Boston member of the Boston School Committee and ethnic demagogue nonpareil, was rapidly becoming the George Wallace of New England. The whole city had about it the flavor of mean sectarianism.

I was not prepared for this. I had somehow expected to see a liberal, racially integrated, quaintly pretty city rife with historic landmarks, gilded domes, and well-groomed old churchyard grave sites of Revolutionary War heroes like Paul Revere. What I was met with instead was a city of rundown three-family-house ethnic neighborhoods arrayed suspiciously one against another.

I had been put off the trail by Edward Brooke's election from Massachusetts to the U.S. Senate as that body's first post-Reconstruction black member. Now that I was living in Boston, it became clear that while Mr. Brooke could win a statewide election, he could never hope to become mayor of Boston.

In more than a few ways the Firsts Era (first black this and first black that), of which Senator Brooke was a major First figure, was a deceptively mixed blessing for African-Americans. We succumbed, understandably, to the belief that we were making more progress than we were. *Jet* magazine might easily have been named *First* magazine. From its inception, virtually every week *Jet* brought us word of a new First. We even had two in our own family: Jewell at Goucher and Max at ABC.

For contemporary African-Americans the Firsts Era began in 1947 when Jackie Robinson with the Brooklyn Dodgers became the first black to play major league baseball. The news made loyal Dodger fans of most African-Americans, those who followed baseball and those who didn't. The New York Yankees and the Boston Red Sox were the last teams to field black players and we hated them. During my childhood, I knew of only two black Yankee fans. We believed them both to be mentally unbalanced.

It is difficult to know when the Firsts Era will reach its apex. As the complex structure of the American economic system continues to evolve from one technological innovation to the next, so too are created and expanded the executive level jobs and managerial positions from which blacks remain broadly excluded.

In any case, Firsts Era news was always bittersweet. For news by its nature remarks the exceptional.

■

Riots in inner-city black communities swept the nation in the sixties. The civil rights movement pricked the conscience of the country's liberal quarter. President Lyndon Johnson signed the Civil Rights Act of 1964. Harvard Law School, which until the mid-sixties never counted more than five blacks in an entering class of five hundred, was beginning to feel some pressure to burnish its bellwether credentials. *The* law school graduated fourteen blacks in 1968 and twenty-four in the class of 1970, my class. The Harvard family was plainly proud of its contributions to the Firsts Era.

After centuries of bloodshed and assaulted personhood, uncompensated toil and disdained talent, brave marches and protracted court cases, the American curtain in the 1960s was finally falling on de jure racial discrimination. But while this benchmark stride was seen as an important first step by many African-Americans, it was seen as an epoch-ending step by many whites, white liberals included. Lifting the starting gate for blacks long after virtually every other make and mixture of American had charged off over the horizon was all that the national white political establishment was prepared with any resolve to do. With de facto discrimination still to be contended with, and following so long a stretch of psychic, social, and economic injury, no reasonable person could have expected the achievement gap between the races to do anything but widen. A testament to this fairly axiomatic assumption was the tepid, guilt-driven support rendered by white liberals for palliatives like affirmative action programs and contract set-asides. The term "quota," kryptonite for white liberals and anathema to white conservatives, was banished from political colloquy and legislative language. Henceforth the objectives would be goals and opportunity as opposed to quotas and measured progress. The consequence of this concession was lost in a national self-congratulatory celebration crafted by the mainstream establishment and generally, if reluctantly, acceded to by black leadership.

Where we had been two Americas, whites and blacks, we were soon to become three, the whites, the blacks who would now rise, and finally the millions of bottom-mired blacks who could not. There would be no serious and sustained national compensatory assistance for that last group. For the first time African-Americans, class-riven and disunited, were no longer all in the same boat. It was a scantly noticed watershed leap backward for African-Americans.

The period was rich with irony. Beyond a new access to public facilities, the civil rights movement produced fresh career possibilities for only a well-defined sector of the black community. For them there was a guarded optimism, for the balance of the black community the old familiar desperation. It was the hurled anger of the poorest, the most desperate and chanceless of blacks that sparked opportunity for those who were poised to rise. The very blacks whom schools like Harvard would never have considered for admission had bought my ticket to *the* law school. Riots, if they accomplished little else, won national attention.

Most of the African-Americans in law school with me keenly acknowledged the debt. No one foresaw twenty years thence the fissures that would debilitate a postsegregation black America. No one could know that black leaders and organizations would become either so enfeebled by a lack of resources or so hamstrung by the strings attached to resources that their call to arms, if heard at all by the rank and file, would sound perfunctory or, worse, incomprehensible. No one contemplated the coming estrangement of an ascendant class of African-Americans from a much larger section of our community. Who could have foreseen this in the heady verbose flux of the activist sixties, a time that saw Douglass studied, Du Bois read, Fanon revered, King followed, Garvey remembered, Booker T. decried, Tubman lauded, Malcolm respected? Who could have known then that the black community would plummet to themelessness, its leadership blunted by the opiate of White House invitations—that there would come a time when the broader African-American community would have no well-crystallized idea of what its detailed social and economic objectives should be and how those objectives were tactically to be achieved?

We—I—too many of us—have become, I fear, too comfortable. Our public advocacy whittles safely around the edges of what those outside our community have told us is possible. In many ways the black community's current crisis is more vexing, if less painful, than that presented by segregation forty years ago. We were united then, if only in what we were against. Now with legal segregation abolished, we are without benefit of even that loathsome but unifying condition.

I am tempted to strike some or all of what I have said here. It is not that I don't believe it. I simply fear that I will be misunderstood by dedicated friends with whom I have worked for so many years. To include myself among the criticized should help.

This is not to disparage but to provoke. Our challenge now is infinitely more formidable than it once was. Problems are less tractable to outmoded messianic leadership models. Leadership, by definition, is not a collective activity. Many who are, largely for mainstream convenience, called leaders are not leaders. Many whom most have never heard of *are*. Leaders are those who chance the unconventional, who step forward of the line, doing bold new things with energy, innovation, creativity and, always, with sheer courage.

How can the attention of African-Americans once again be riveted on a common set of social objectives with definable tactics and quantifiable results? How can we mount a national campaign to make our schools effective, our neighborhoods safe, our children's values constructive, our airwaves (and cyberspace) wholesome, our hunger for learning insatiable, our confidence in ourselves abundant, our ambitions monumental, and our well-informed demands upon government for equitable domestic and foreign policies implacable? How can we elevate Seyi Fayanju, the twelve-year-old black child from Verona, New Jersey, who won the *National Geographic* Geography Bee in a competition of thousands, into a more compelling role model for our children than gangsta rap artists and NBA players?

How can we have these ideas catch fire with a resonance that ultimately will constrain government and the private sector to do their share? The leadership of which I sermonize fits no particular organization or famous face. It must come from all places, disciplines, classes—bottom, top, middle. And with a new urgency and relentlessness.

Many of my former black classmates at law school would appreciate this digression. Some few would not. People are people.

■

Those of my black classmates who had gone to preparatory school were more inclined than the rest of us to mysteriously forget who they were. They weren't bad people. They'd simply misplaced themselves.

One would not speak to his fellow black classmates, even to those who greeted him first. Once, when two of us spotted him sitting alone in Harkness Commons, we approached him, ready to offer him a deprogramming plan. He moved to another table the moment we sat down. Thereafter, whenever we saw him, either near or far, we'd yell out all too loudly, "Hello there, brother!" His face would flush, leaving us modestly pleased that he hadn't misplaced himself altogether.

Another such fellow was a great deal more likable. From time to time he would abandon his white friends and drop in when we were congregating for lunch in Harkness. He was very fair-skinned and had straight hair. We all thought he was a white liberal until we discovered after two years that his father was president of South Carolina State College, a black school in Orangeburg.

"Are you black?" one of us asked point-blank.

"Yes." It sounded like a confession.

"Why didn't you tell anybody?"

"No one ever asked."

Then there was the black preppie from Columbia University who wedged his way into a meeting that members of the Harvard Black Law Students Association were holding with the dean of admissions, Russell Simpson. We had requested the meeting to press for the admission of more black students. The black preppie had shown up to oppose the idea. He wanted a cap on the overall number of black admissions and exclusion en bloc of those who applied from historically black institutions. If the preppie had not already been nauseating enough, he'd now made it personal. Dean Simpson, a white centrist law academic, rebuffed the preppie. Sitting there, I had no easy time puzzling out the nuances of my embarrassment.

By and large, however, the black lawyers-to-be around me had large-scale career plans that would in one way or another benefit the black community. Some, like Reginald Lewis, had business careers in mind (and indeed Lewis's work habits and serious countenance presaged a corporate career of signal success). William Jefferson would be elected to Congress as a Democrat from Louisiana. Others like Richard White built influential law firms in cities like Detroit, Atlanta, and Washington, D.C.

Henry and Rosemary Sanders and I wanted to go to Africa on research fellowships upon graduation. It wouldn't be easy for us. The few foundations that made such grants were cool to our inquiries. One foundation official told me bluntly that "black Americans do not adjust well to Africa." The implication was that white Americans did. Harvard Law School's young white fellowship counselor advised: "If you're going to Africa you'd better be married or you'll find yourself very lonely." When I asked him, "Do you give the same advice to single whites going to Sweden or France or England?" he appeared flummoxed.

Traditional grantors were more than indifferent to our plans to work and study in Africa. Their resistance was only thinly disguised. The Sanderses and I took our dilemma to Walter Leonard, the black dean.

Perhaps I should pause here to explain the difference between "a" black dean and "the" black dean. "A" black dean is a dean who handles all of the responsibilities that deans customarily handle. "A" black dean is a dean who only happens to be black. Twenty-five years ago, almost all major institution black deans were "the" and not "a." Being a "the" meant that you had been brought to an institution to "interpret": that is, to interpret the attitude of the school administration to black students and their attitudes to the administration. For instance, when the administration set up, without consultation or the feeblest demonstration of need, a tutorial program for entering black students, we told Walter Leonard, "the" black dean, to tell the administration, "Thanks, but no thanks."

Now, told of our balked desire to go to Africa, Dean Leonard on our behalf complained vigorously to the law school administration, the Department of State, and the general foundation community. Within weeks the Ford Foundation created the Middle East and Africa Field Research Program for Afro-Americans. After graduating, the Sanderses would be off to Nigeria and I, for six months, to Tanzania.

■

"Are you political?" The acid-test question was put to me by a third-year activist black student only weeks after I had discovered the bagel.

"Yes." I had not the faintest idea what he was talking about.

There are not many fears greater than the fear of appearing stupid. One must at the very least look thoughtful at the brow. And so I said, "Yes. I'm political. What's up?"

In the sixties, one could be fairly described as "political" if one had, with a modicum of comprehension, fathomed complex political writings like Frantz Fanon's *The Wretched of the Earth* and developed from such readings a "view." I was clearly not "political." I had never heard of Frantz Fanon and had a view on little beyond the feral meanness of racism, which, before arriving in Massachusetts, I thought naively was largely a disease of the American South. Oh, I had done some reading. But more about Kant than Kush. Much about Copernicus. Nothing about Cabral. Braithwaite's *A Kind of Homecoming* was poignant and informational but hardly analytical.

Now I began to read beyond my law course assignments. Fanon, the black psychiatrist from Martinique who trenchantly described the tragic psychic consequences of European colonialism for Africans, I plowed through with more determination than comprehension. C. L. R. James's *The Black Jacobins* told of an epic Haitian slave revolt about which I'd never even heard. W. E. B. Du Bois's *The Souls of Black Folk* had not been assigned reading for me at any level in segregated Richmond, not even at Virginia Union, a black liberal arts college. Why? An impressive English literature professor had told our class of forty blacks in college that "the mark of a well-educated person is a mastery of Shakespeare and the Bible." This went unchallenged. He had blithely overlooked the literary output of three-fourths of the world's people, including that of his own fourth. What had he been thinking? What had *I* been thinking? (A white professor at Virginia Union, one Dr. Anderson, told our class that it was a documented fact that Africans had longer arms than Europeans. He despised us. He despised himself and our school as well for providing him academic refuge.)

I wrote to a newly discovered organization in New York, the American Committee on Africa, for information on the anticolonial wars flaring in Guinea-Bissau, Mozambique, and Angola against Portugal and its five-hundred-year-old African colonial empire. They sent reams. Black people in Africa had been for eight years contesting Portugal militarily for independence and freedom. The United States was supporting Portugal. Gulf Oil, pumping thousands of barrels per day out of Angola, was providing Portugal, Europe's poorest country, with forty-eight percent of its war budget. Harvard University held the largest block of Gulf Oil stock of any American university.

I was incredulous. Could I have been, for twenty-six years, that incurious? Could all these things actually be going on in the world (long have gone on, for that matter) without my knowing a thing about them? Could there be a connection between my South and Africa's anguish? Why was this news to me? I had been an avid news consumer. Why hadn't any of this been in newspapers or on television?

I was beginning to develop a mistrust of information about all things I could not see or feel. I was beginning to develop a thirst for other sources of information as well.

What do we really *know* about anything, anyway? Who deploys the information products that we get to select for consumption? Could there be some centuries-old Sons of Europe secret society of wizened and powerful grandees who decide what we can know and not know? Naaaah. But . . . ?

Please indulge me. The point here warrants some belaboring. How do we get to *know* things? Or more accurately, how do we get to *believe* we know things? From newspapers, magazines, books, television, movies, teachers. Who decides what to include or exclude? Which countries, cultures, religions, and peoples do we focus on or ignore, exalt or vilify? Just how and by whom are the thousands of such daily decisions made?

Dr. Albert Schweitzer was lionized throughout Europe and North America as a selfless humanitarian because of his half century of medical service to the people of Gabon. Groping for common ground with a Gabonese classmate at Virginia Union, I asked one day before Dr. McGuinn began his lecture, "Tell me, now that the great man Albert Schweitzer has been dead for some years, has he been well remembered?"

The classmate laughed. "In all the years Schweitzer spent running his hospital in my country, he always felt innately superior to the Africans he treated, as did the other French who were there to colonize us."

To my embarrassment, he continued, "Not one African was ever employed in a position of responsibility in that hospital. The place was so filthy with goats and dogs walking the halls dropping excrement that the villagers used to discipline their children by telling them they'd be sent to Schweitzer's hospital if they didn't mind their parents. He worked in our country for decades and did not form a close relationship with a single African."

Where does the truth lie? I suppose truth has many faces. Which do we get to see, if any at all?

Phillis Wheatley arrived in Boston from West Africa on a slave ship at the age of seven in 1761. She was bought by the merchant John Wheatley and his wife Susanna. Schooled in English and Latin, she became a gifted writer whose work won praise from George Washington and Voltaire. Was the slave-holding Washington's praise, I asked myself, prompted by Wheatley's gift alone or by the exculpatory gist of her verse as well?

'Twas not long since I left my native shore,
The land of errors and Egyptian gloom:
Father of mercy, 'twas thy gracious hand
Brought me in safety from those dark abodes.

Years later I stood on Goree Island off Senegal, in the slave house doorway through which the African child destined to be a poet had been shoved onto the slave ship *Phillis* bound for Boston. A plaque on a wall of the fortlike structure still bears her name. Of all the despoiled dark genius shoved to oblivion through that doorway, I wondered why Phillis Wheatley alone had been commended through the centuries to my attention.

In Boston's black community of Roxbury the name Trotter pops up now and again on schools and community centers. Who was Trotter? No one I asked seemed to know much about the person who bore the ubiquitous name. It may have been Muriel Snowden or her husband, Otto, directors of Freedom House, a Roxbury civic center, who told me. Muriel and Otto were faithful keepers of black community lore.

William Monroe Trotter was born in Ohio in 1872. He grew up in Boston, attended Harvard, and graduated magna cum laude in 1895, becoming in the process the first black student ever elected to Phi Beta Kappa. In 1901 he launched a Boston newspaper, the *Guardian,* whose motto was "For every right, with all they might." A relentless foe of the accommodationist Booker T. Washington, Trotter once spent a month in jail for disrupting a Booker T. speech. Trotter also got into a White House shouting match with President Woodrow Wilson, who had on one occasion described African-Americans as "sick of work, covetous of pleasure—a host of dusky children untimely put out of school." In 1915 the indefatigable Trotter was arrested, tried, and acquitted for leading a demonstration against the local screening of *Birth of a Nation.*

Until arriving in Boston, I'd never heard of William Monroe Trotter. Shouldn't I have? Shouldn't African-Americans generally have had a glimmer? I knew about Bill "Bojangles" Robinson, didn't I? Trotter might have fared better by history had the Harvard Phi Beta Kappa done a little soft-shoe with Shirley Temple.

Mama's father, Granddaddy Nathan, was past eighty when American astronaut Neil Armstrong stepped on the moon on July 20, 1969. Granddaddy and Grandma with sixth-grade educations had put five daughters through college during the Great Depression and seeded a flock of grandchildren that would include three doctors, two lawyers, three teachers, one network news anchor, and one psychologist. A worldly clan from special, smart, but very unworldly progenitors.

I watched the landing with Granddaddy that summer in the living room of the old comfortable house on Palmer Street. As Armstrong bounced down onto the lunar surface, mild amusement played across Granddaddy's weathered features. "You really believe that guy is standing on the moon?"

"Of course he's on the moon, Granddaddy."

"How do you know that's not New Jersey?"

I smiled and said nothing. A fair question, though. In a world of large-scale deceit, a fair question.

■

After my first year of law school, I all but knew that I would never practice law. I would stay in school and finish, if for no other reason than to prove an ever nagging point. Also to embellish my résumé. But I knew early that I simply couldn't endure the tedium of practice.

It had come down to a matter of personality. I couldn't make myself enjoy the numbing task of drafting coma-inducing legal briefs and then plodding through the even more deadly labyrinthine and dreary passageways of legal procedure to a who-gives-a-damn judgment. I knew I would someday need a lawyer. But, God, that would be a happier fate than being one.

"Now comes the plaintiff . . ." was the archaic language with which millions of boilerplate American lawyers began writing the simplest or the most complex of legal motions. By 1968 I was relieved to have decided that the plaintiff would not be coming with me. I would later take the bar exam, pass, and be admitted to the Massachusetts bar. I would even have a brief stint as a Boston poverty lawyer representing indigent clients. But I could only feign interest in the actual practice of law, and even that for less than a year.

I had been faced with the problem of career selection before. I started college without understanding the distinction between what one wants to *be* and what one wants to *do*. I had wanted to *be* a physician, and so I became a pre-med major and, in my sophomore year, enrolled in Dr. Wells's comparative anatomy course. But then one clear morning in the fall of 1960 Dr. Wells, dressed in a knee-length white lab coat, put a large dead cat on the lab table and directed me to cut it open. I had dissected frogs with callous disregard. Cats were different. I changed my major to sociology.

There are ways, however, to know early on whether or not you could be thrilled by the practice of law. In high school, if terms like valence, cosine, isotope, and algorithm lift your spirits aloft as if on the poet's verse, then law school could be for you. Law is the technocrat's heaven and more lucrative than science.

I have always envied, a little, those who could vigorously undertake tasks in which they had no real interest. In high school I could manage such for a semester. In law school, I knew early on. Not for life.

One of the graver consequences of the romantic personality is that its host has little natural inclination to craft a detailed career plan. I had come to law school to stave off for three years such decisions. Now, in April of 1970, I was at a crossroads.

At the age of twenty-nine, I knew only that I wanted to apply my career energies to the "empowerment and liberation of the African world." I protectively *quote* myself from the late sixties because such language over the years has been stripped of its old underpinning meaning and consigned to camp cliché. The language conveyed something then that it no longer does. Something well beyond bombast. Something, after a long and troubled estrangement, of a common black world striving, rekindled by a brilliant and proud new literature, with a rediscovered racial affinity, and nourished on three continents in the blood of a common and all too related suffering. The more I read, the more excited and angry I had become. I could see no real substantive distinction between my American experience and the painful lot of the Haitians, South Africans, Mozambicans, Angolans, Zairians, Afro-Brazilians, and other blacks in other places about whom I was reading. The American official hand was everywhere and invariably on the wrong side. Apartheid hadn't been the creature only of racist white Boers but of kindred-spirit American investors, lenders, diplomats, and presidents as well. The ruthless Haitian dictator François "Papa Doc" Duvalier had had his army equipped by the United States and trained in the methods of repression at the U.S. School of the Americas. The Central Intelligence Agency made little secret of its imposition on Zaire of Joseph Mobutu, who would block his country's path to democracy for the next thirty years. Our country talked of democracy, but in the black world there was little evidence of any concrete American support for it. In the United Nations, the United States consistently joined with Western Europe in blocking any punitive measures contemplated against the oppressive colonial power Portugal and the white minority regime in South Africa.

Before departing Boston for Tanzania, I organized the Southern Africa Relief Fund with headquarters on its letterhead. We raised four thousand dollars including a contribution from Derek Bok, who had become dean of the law school after my first year. I would deliver the money in person to the chairman of the Organization of African Unity's liberation committee based in Dar es Salaam, Tanzania, upon my arrival there late in the summer of 1970. The liberation committee raised and distributed relief funds and military support to Africans fighting against Portugal for independence in Mozambique, Angola, and Guinea-Bissau. The committee provided similar support for resistance efforts in South Africa, Namibia, and Rhodesia.

I had taken my first measurable step. Africans were actually fighting for their freedom and I was, at last, in my own largely symbolic and infinitesimal way, helping them.

■

My marriage of five years was dying, and had been for a time—before the eldest two of my three children were born, before we left together for Tanzania, even before we said the vows, I suspect. It would go on in law and living arrangement for seventeen years, but it was dying before either of us acknowledged the signs, long before voice was given to two privately held bitter despairs.

I was twenty-four and she twenty-one when we married. Nice decent people from nice decent families. We simply had each married the wrong person.

Men appear to mature from the outside in. We are seldom secure enough inside ourselves to talk about much of anything revealing before our mid-forties. Things never got said. In any case it would hardly have altered the outcome. Truth be told, marriage depends for its survival upon the most irrational and inexplicable of chemistries between people. Try as two might, it cannot be constructed of will alone. Moreover, how can one know another before one is old enough to know oneself?

■ Fall 1970: Dar es Salaam, Tanzania

It was a brilliant day. The white-crested breakers of the aqua Indian Ocean waters lapped soothingly onto the beach along Oyster Bay Road. Dar es Salaam, Arabic for "haven of peace," enveloped the quiet harbor with quaint Moorish-inspired buildings of pastel-colored masonry. The street was shaded by lavender blooms of jacarandas and lattice bark palms that swayed in breezes wafting in off the water.

People had begun to gather along the sidewalks on both sides of the street, looking expectantly in the direction of the Kilimanjaro Hotel, the direction from which President Julius Nyerere's motorcade would come. The mood was light with the lyrical sounds of Swahili rising and falling around me.

I knew on one level what I still found hard to believe on another. I was in Africa. I was leisurely standing on African soil. On my first venture outside the United States, I had flown, via Paris and Nairobi, nearly halfway around the world to this city of 200,000 on the East African coast.

I soaked in the sounds and smells. The spoken words were musical because they were spoken happily and I could not understand them. They melded with birdsong and the high-pitched din of small cars and motorbikes moving along the left side of the street.

The men wore sandals and colorful summery jacket shirts. Some had on collarless tunics of the style made popular by their president. Many of the women were in traditional dress, some in

Western clothes, and a few draped from head to foot in a flow-ing black lightweight fabric. The school day had just ended; chil-dren were all about in their neat uniforms, the colors of which denoted grade level and school attended.

Under the influences of weather and culture, the streets and sidewalks of African cities like Dar es Salaam belong more to pedestrians than cars. Everything is open—windows, doors, storefronts. The city does not hide its people. This was unlike anything I'd seen before. It was quietly exotic. Something heart-eningly incongruous about it. A languid bustle.

At six foot five I could look with an unobstructed view across the thickening crowd. I'd never been in an almost completely black city before. There were a smattering of ethnic East Indians in the crowd and a few Europeans, most of whom were British expatriates.

"Mwalimu! Mwalimu!" someone shouted. Everyone craned their necks looking down the street.

"What did he say?" I asked the Tanzanian teenager beside me.

"Teacher," he answered. "Mwalimu means teacher. It is what we affectionately call our president."

Tanzania had been a German colony from 1885 until Germany's defeat in World War I. From the end of the war until its independence in 1961 it had been under British rule. Julius Nyerere had led his country to independence and served since as its first president.

I could now see the first car of the motorcade with its head-lights on. Behind the lead car in an open black convertible stood President Nyerere and the Eastern European head of state he was hosting in an official visit. As the car moved to within a half block of where I was standing, the crowd began to clap and cheer loudly.

The car pulled abreast of my section of the crowd. Nyerere and his guest waved in our direction. He was a trimly built man, cocoa-colored, with gray hair and a neatly clipped mustache. He had an engaging smile, and kind, wise eyes. His record on human rights and openness in government was globally respected. He was widely thought to be brilliant, and although he led one of the world's poorest countries, he hadn't flinched from taking the United States and Western Europe sternly and formidably to task for their de facto support of white minority rule in southern Africa.

The response of the crowd seemed genuine and unalloyed, a pride of ownership bright on their faces. I became caught up in the moment but conflicted. The people who surrounded me, suffused with an affection I could only envy, had a national leader with whom they could identify without restraint or qualification. African-Americans had cut an uneven but sometimes enviable swath to opportunity in America, but when we looked at our president, what we would always see first would be a white man.

Although material opportunities had been denied to the vast majority of African-Americans, Tanzanians had been given quite a different impression. This was my thought as the motorcade turned right, moving past the New Africa Hotel and toward the Askari Monument (*askari* is "soldier" in Swahili) which commemorates the Tanzanian lives lost in the Allied cause during World War II. The motorcade was now within two blocks of the United States Information Service Reading Room where books, magazines, and large posters could be found illustrating the conspicuous and broadspread success of America's people of African descent. I had visited the reading room to learn what Tanzanians were learning about me and was stunned to discover in Tanzania how well I was doing. At the drive-in movie theater, before Burt Lancaster shot up the night in *The Professionals,* Tanzanians were shown a USIS short subject featuring Hayes Jones, the African-American former Olympic track star. Jones, looking very Savile Row, was seen striding through New York's Central Park with briefcase, arbitrage likely on his mind and, no doubt, heading toward his well-appointed business office.

The USIS information products weren't lies as such. They were merely tiny, woefully unrepresentative, slices of a much larger and unflattering American truth. Sadly it was all the "truth" that most Tanzanians had any opportunity to see.

Some, like a precocious seventeen-year-old restaurant waiter, surprised me. "Thomas Jefferson wrote a great deal about democratic ideals but obviously with a blind spot for slavery," or "I feel I must apologize to you for any role Africans may have played in the enslavement of your people." He obviously did his daytime reading at the Dar es Salaam Public Library and not the USIS Reading Room. Inasmuch as he worked nights at the Skyline Hotel restaurant he likely hadn't time for the drive-in.

The young man had cited Jefferson and beyond that was generally conversant with American history. Consider that. He was a Tanzanian high school student and part-time waiter. How many American high school students would know that Tanzania was formed from the union of Tanganyika and the storied Indian Ocean island of Zanzibar? How many American high school students would even have heard of Tanzania? Or could thoughtfully discuss Jefferson, for that matter.

Then there was my fourteen-year-old Tanzanian friend Godffrey Ngogoma who, shortly after we met, asked, "Are you rich?"

I laughed. "No, I'm not even close to rich, Godffrey."

"Well, then, how did you get here?" The unprepossessing Godffrey was a USIS Reading Room victim. I quickly disabused him by explaining the Ford Foundation's gift.

The motorcade now moved around the Askari Monument and along Independence Avenue, a winding downtown street of shops all owned and operated by Indians brought to East Africa from India decades before by the British to tend much of the commercial machinery of colonialism in Kenya, Uganda, and Tanzania.

After colonialism, and in position by British installation, Indians stayed on to control most of East Africa's private sector. Tanzanian rental housing, hotels, retail shops, car rental agencies, grocery stores, and all other conceivable businesses were virtually under Indian control. If that were not enough to exacerbate preexisting tensions, many Indians showed higher loyalty to India than to Tanzania (as evidenced by capital outflows), stayed socially to themselves, and harbored undisguised prejudice toward the indigenous people of a country that had made them rich or near rich.

When I needed to rent a car, I went to Riddock Motors, the Ford dealership on Upanga Road. "My name is Randall Robinson. I'd like to rent a Cortina. How much is the deposit and do you have any available?"

"The deposit is seven hundred shillings and we don't have any Cortinas at the moment," the Indian woman politely informed me. "It may be some time before any become available."

I returned to my room at the Skyline Hotel and called Riddock Motors within thirty minutes of my discussion with the desk agent.

"Good afternoon. This is Riddock Motors." It was a man's voice.

"Hello. I'd like to rent a small Ford. I understand that you have Cortinas. Do you have any available? And what is the deposit?"

"Sir, yes, we have many Cortinas available for rental immediately. The deposit is three hundred shillings. You are an American, yes?"

"Yes, I'm an American."

"Well, come right in and fill out the forms. The car will be ready. You said your name, sir, was . . ." He left his voice up.

"I didn't say. My name is Randall Robinson."

"Randall Robinson?" He said aloud after me.

"Yes, I was just in your office a half hour ago and I was told that you had no Cortinas and that the deposit in any case would be seven hundred shillings."

He did not respond. Then, a voice in the background. The woman's voice. "Oh, that's that Negro."

I heard a hand cover the telephone. Seconds passed.

Throat clearing. "Yes . . . er . . . Mr. Robinson." Trapped. "It appears that we can make a car available to you after all. I apologize for the, uh . . . confusion. Come back around at your convenience."

As with the abolition of American slavery, the effects of colonialism lingered long after the British had departed. Indian privilege, now sturdy at the root, had been meticulously and self-servingly cultivated by the British and was not to wither with independence.

Idling one afternoon, I counted twenty cars moving along Old Bagamoyo Road. Indians, constituting a tiny minority of Tanzania's population, were in nineteen of them. Africans lived largely in national housing, reserved for citizens and built by the government. The private apartment market was completely controlled by Indians. I was the first person of African descent to live in a hundred-unit Indian-owned apartment complex, located, as it turned out, directly across Upanga Road from Riddock Motors.

Tension between Africans and Indians had been increasing throughout East Africa. Although economic privilege as a residue of colonialism was not peculiar to East Africa, a certain malignancy of relations may have been. Throughout the Caribbean and much of West Africa, Lebanese and Syrians held on after independence to remain disproportionate private sector owners. But never were postindependence Caribbean societies, with the exception of Haiti, so riven with the baldly expressed racism that East Africans had been constrained to endure at the hands of Indians.

Cuban race relations may be a useful reference point. Under the dictator Fulgencio Batista, Cuba was a racially segregated country. After the 1959 revolution of Fidel Castro, segregation was outlawed and Cuban officials have vigorously contended that racism has been banished from a Cuban society that is significantly black. While the government's efforts may well be sincere, racism, as opposed to its measurable practice, is not a disease amenable to a speedy legislative cure. A few years ago I visited the Havana home of a black woman who proudly displayed a picture of her daughter's nineteenth birthday party. Twenty-four friends were pictured. All except one were black. Race remains very much a factor in social selection in Cuba. That much is apparent from any street scene. This is neither surprising nor alarming. It does tend to illustrate, however, that race continues to make a difference in a society that remains dominated at the top politically and economically by whites. This notwithstanding, blacks (and women) are demonstrably better off under Castro than they were under the Batista dictatorship, and there is no gainsaying the fact that the Cuban government has made a concerted effort to reverse an age-old legacy of racial discrimination in Cuba. Cuba's challenge is to liberalize politically while preserving and building on the gains of blacks, women, and the poor generally.

I sat with Fidel Castro in his Havana office on a Saturday past midnight more than a decade ago.

"Cuba has no racism," he said. "African blood flows in all Cubans and we are proud of it." True or not, Jorge Mas Canosa, right-wing leader of Miami's anti-Castro Cuban community, would never have said such a thing. Hardly either would a single Indian living in Tanzania in 1970.

On Sunday mornings I would drive along the ocean to Oyster Bay, a neighborhood of lovely homes of well-to-do Tanzanians and expatriates. It was a short walk from the houses across Oyster Bay Road onto the gleaming flat white sand beaches of the Indian Ocean. At the water's edge, I waited one such Sunday with a group of Tanzanian men for the fishing dhows to return with the predawn catch.

Four Indian men in their twenties drove up in a red late-model convertible. They parked on the road and walked toward the water. They were dressed casually but expensively. Two of the young men had single-lens reflex cameras hanging from their necks. The Tanzanians watched closely as the Indians waded out toward the luxury powerboat moored some seventy-five feet from where we were standing. The Indians boarded, fired the engine, and turned the sleek craft in the water with a flourish, carving a curling wake behind them. One of the Tanzanians yelled out to the departing Indians in Swahili. The Tanzanians roared with laughter. The Indians did not look back.

"What was he yelling?" I asked a Tanzanian standing near me whom I recognized as a cab driver.

"He told them that he hoped they would all drown."

In the early 1970s, shortly after Idi Amin came to power in Tanzania's neighbor Uganda (and before he began willy-nilly killing his own people), he undertook a campaign to expel fifty thousand Indians from his country. The expulsion order included Indians with British passports and those who were Ugandan citizens. It is estimated that the Indians were stripped of property worth a billion dollars—and everything else they owned, including luggage the Ugandan military promised to ship but never did. The move was well received throughout East Africa. This entirely natural if wrongheaded reaction could not be understood in the West and particularly in Britain, the country to which most of the Indians fled. Demonstrating a considerable degree of political courage, the steadfastly nonracialist Julius Nyerere would countenance no such course for Tanzania. He strongly believed revenge to be a fool's foundation for national social policy: in fact, he encouraged Indians to choose citizenship and full participation in Tanzania's development. By his own admission, Nyerere's communalist economic development policies did not work for Tanzania. But his commitment to public education and literacy afforded Tanzania a chance for long-term economic growth. Furthermore, the high ethical road of Nyerere's pre- and postindependence brand of leadership gave Tanzanian political society a stability unexcelled in all of Africa.

By the late 1960s, Nyerere had earned a reputation not only as a great Tanzanian but as a great African. No African leader enjoyed larger stature in global councils. The feat was accomplished without compromise of principle. While dependent upon the industrialized West for foreign assistance, Nyerere strongly criticized Western countries for their support of Portuguese colonialism and the white minority regimes of South Africa, Namibia, and Rhodesia. He also invited African-Americans to come and work in Tanzania, just as Kwame Nkrumah had invited us to come to Ghana after it became sub-Saharan Africa's first country to win independence, in 1957. Eager to rediscover the land of our ancestors, we came. Culturally stateless and emotionally binational, we came. Back across the gulf of the mean centuries, we came. Back from abduction. Back from the ocean's depths. Back from Charleston slave auctions. Mama gone. Papa sold. Back from Birmingham and Memphis. Back from Richmond. We came by the hundreds, armed with a rich and wonderful new hybrid culture of the terrifying night's shelter. We came in search of ancient kin. We came looking for remnants of our stolen selves.

Or course nothing is ever as simple as that. There were disappointments, to be sure. If we expected every Tanzanian to turn out at the airport to welcome us home, we'd have done well to run our expectations through a critical mind before surrendering to such hopes. The welcome was as warm as it could have been from people who had not en masse been taught to know of us cousins as in need of repair. They had been as damaged as we. I had no foreknowledge of the toll colonialism had taken. Then, too, no people have a totally uniform view. Tanzanians, led by a rare man, were as varied of trait as African-Americans—or any other group of two or more people, for that matter. They were liberal and conservative, friendly and unfriendly, globalist and provincial, self-loving and self-loathing. The symptoms of the last condition were not unfamiliar to me.

I might as well have been sitting in the Globe Theater on Second Street twenty years before with Max and Uncle Jim the projectionist. But I wasn't in the Globe. I was in the Indian-owned Dar es Salaam downtown movie theater for a rare screening of a non-Indian-language film. (That the vast majority of Tanzanians could not understand Hindi and other Indian dialects appeared not to affect film selection by the Indian owners who, like all other Indians in Tanzania, spoke and understood English.) The English-language feature was preceded by an English-language commercial with Tanzanian actors. The young Tanzanian male executive in the commercial needed every edge in an effort to win professional success and the heart of a beautiful African woman. The executive's male colleague advised his troubled friend to use Ambi lotion. "It will make your skin lighter and make you brighter."

Such experiences gave me a broadened common ground with Tanzanians, drew me closer to Africa's sufferings and it to mine, sufferings that I would come to see over time as indistinguishable, one and the same. I might have stayed comfortably in Tanzania for years. It had been an enriching and life-changing time. But I would always be a guest at an ancestral family table: a long-gone son involuntarily reacculturated in a far-off land. I could never be Tanzanian for the simple reason that I had not been born there, socialized in its mores and inconspicuously woven, throughout my formative years, into the rich mosaic of its culture. While I would always be African, linked indissolubly in soul and spirit to these people and this precious land I had been blessed to touch, my working and living place would be in a land that had become mine centuries ago through Goree's door.

I could best serve Africa by going home to America, for America had become a substantial contributor to Africa's problems. I had decided to spend my life in an effort to bring the general American black public to the obscure and clubby table of U.S. foreign-policy decision making vis-à-vis the black world. The United States was doing Africa a terrible disservice and African-Americans, in general, were none the wiser.

PART THREE

Toward Washington

Only from the study of America in its foreign relations can African-Americans hope to appreciate the full measure of America's insult to them.

■ Winter 1971: Boston, Massachusetts

I needed a job and thought one could be found in Boston. I returned there to a snowstorm and subfreezing temperatures in January of 1971. Although I was all but certain of the outcome, I had decided to give law practice a short trial.

Looking for the least unpalatable work, I eliminated private law firms from consideration. Newly hired associates could not choose the cases on which they would work, and too often private firms represented interests that I opposed. In 1971 there were fewer than thirty-five black lawyers in the entire state of Massachusetts, a third of them sprinkled across the Boston private-firm world like peppercorns against a snowbank.

As it turned out, the universe of black lawyers was minuscule because it was meant to be. I would take the state bar examination in the summer of 1971 along with several hundred hopefuls, including thirty-seven blacks. The examination was a blind test of twenty essay questions, with identifying numbers but no names or pictures on the test booklets. On the application form were blanks for the applicant's name and law school attended. Inasmuch as all of the black applicants had attended predominantly white law schools, there seemed no way to know the race of an examination taker.

The test results were disclosed in the early fall. While more than half of those who took the examination passed, only three of the thirty-seven blacks did. I was fortunate to be one of the three. Immediately, more than a few of the unsuccessful blacks charged discrimination and threatened a class action lawsuit against the Massachusetts Bar Association. I was asked to sign a petition of support. I signed, but not without lingering doubts about how discrimination could have occurred in the administration of an apparently blind examination.

Months after the lawsuit had been filed, the blind examination was given again to a field of several hundred aspirants. Included were the previously unsuccessful blacks, some of whose names may have been identified with the lawsuit, but most not. This time all of the blacks who had failed the "blind" test before passed, as did all the blacks taking the test for the first time. The stark contrast in test results had obviously been provoked by the filing of the lawsuit. Only then did it dawn on me that the test couldn't have been blind to begin with.

My job search, however, had ended with success six months before I took the bar examination. The Boston Legal Assistance Project (BLAP) was the federally funded program that provided free legal representation in civil and juvenile court matters to those too poor to afford it. It was, in essence, a Boston outpost of the federal war on poverty, a far-flung empire of good-doing, well-meaning young lawyers with offices in poor neighborhoods across Boston including the black community of Roxbury. While there were a few black lawyers working in neighborhood field offices, there were no black faces to be seen at headquarters.

Within weeks of my return from Tanzania I appeared for an interview at the downtown Boston offices of BLAP's director Robert Spangenberg, a bearded self-assured middle-aged man who took pains to put me at ease. We were soon joined in an "informal" discussion by Spangenberg's chief project administrator.

For twenty minutes or more the discussion moved cordially and unmemorably between Spangenberg and me. The chief project administrator, seated like me in a chair angled toward Spangenberg's cluttered desk, then made a "hhrrmph" sound.

"Mr. Robinson, can you define for me the constitutional phrase 'due process of law' and how a court might apply it? Also can you tell me what the equal protection clause of the constitution means?"

I learned later that mine was not a typical BLAP job interview.

My Harvard Law School *juris doctor* degree, which ordinarily would carry considerably more weight than the diploma hanging on the chief administrator's office wall, created in his mind no presumption of my competency or grasp of legal concepts. He proceeded with the inquisition. I answered his questions and accepted a job at $9,750 per year.

I was assigned to the Grove Hall office on Blue Hill Avenue in the heart of Roxbury. There were some ten lawyers in the office, headed by Brian Olmstead, a brilliant but off-puttingly unkempt man with dirty fingernails, a ruddy complexion, and oily red hair. Brian and all but three of the lawyers were white. The three black lawyers were new, not just to the staff but to the practice of law itself. All of the Grove Hall office's clients were black. It was trial by fire—a phrase that would soon assume for me an embarrassing new meaning.

At the better law schools, one learns little about how to actually *practice* law. At Harvard, the law of no particular jurisdiction is taught. Motions and where to file them are never mentioned. And few graduates of that school would ever find themselves representing an indigent.

I carried a caseload of more than a hundred clients, with case files greatly outnumbering the faces I could readily recall. One face I recall to this day was that of a fourteen-year-old girl who was charged in juvenile court with a forgettable infraction. Before appearing in court, I had met with the girl and her worried mother, reassuring them and demonstrating more confidence than I felt. "Everything will work out," I told the mother. "We will straighten this out in court tomorrow. Your daughter has never been in any trouble before and any record of this problem will be expunged later."

"Okay, Attorney Robinson, if you say so. I guess I feel a lot better. I just wanna get this mess behind me. She's really a good girl."

Robert Spangenberg and the headquarters staff of BLAP had negotiated an understanding with the Boston judges before whom BLAP attorneys might find themselves appearing. Under the agreement, once the bar examination had been taken, a BLAP bar applicant would be allowed to make court appearances pending the October disclosure of exam results. It was

September. I had taken the exam in midsummer. I was approved to make court appearances. I would fly solo for the first time representing my fourteen-year-old client the next morning.

I sat in juvenile court on one side of my client with her mother on the other. The girl was small for her age and seemed to grow smaller as the clerk boomed, "All rise! Juvenile Court is now in session, Judge Poitrast presiding."

Judge Poitrast swept into the courtroom, climbed three steps, and assumed his elevated place. He was a big man whose jowls appeared to pull his head down. He peered balefully over his half glasses at those assembled with business before his court. I could not know whether the scowl derived from disappointed ambition, gout, or some other disorder, but Judge Poitrast did not seem a happy man.

"Call the first case," Judge Poitrast said. I heard my client's name. The two of us stood before the judge as the clerk read the charges. The judge did not look at my client. He looked straight at me. Before I could open my mouth he asked, "Are you a lawyer, Mr. Robinson?"

"I don't understand, Your Honor."

"Are you a member of the Massachusetts bar?"

The child's eyes were wide and riveted on me. "Your Honor, I'm with the Boston Legal Assistance Project, and this young woman is my client."

"You did not answer my question, Mr. Robinson. I will repeat it for you. Are you a member of the Massachusetts bar?"

I felt the mother's eyes on my back. "Your Honor, I have taken the bar examination and I am waiting for the results. I was told that my appearances here had been approved by you."

Judge Poitrast looked sardonically at the court clerk, his willing foil in some game of court sport that they appeared to play with regularity.

"Mr. Robinson, would you walk to the back of the courtroom and turn around."

"But, Your Honor—"

"Please, Mr. Robinson."

I turned and walked down the aisle alongside which my client's mother was sitting.

"You're not a real lawyer?" she asked, pleading and hurt mingling in her eyes.

I reached the rear of the courtroom and turned around.

For the first time, Judge Poitrast smiled. "Now, get out!"

The balance of my short legal career was a great deal more prosaic. I drew up simple contracts and wills. I handled a divorce settlement or two. I sought and received countless continuances. I wrote long and aridly unreadable memoranda of law. In the ceaseless quest for common-law precedents, I researched the chains of case law back through time to within hailing distance of the Magna Carta obtained from England's King John in the year 1215. I even won a judgment for a defrauded client against a dishonest auto mechanic in Superior Court before an avuncular Judge Rubin who was kind enough to translate his decision into plain English so that the neophyte lawyer appearing before him could know he had indeed won.

I became modestly proficient. I was bored to death. More significant, I was disturbed by the white BLAP lawyers' paternalism toward their poorly paid and poorly educated black clients further burdened with an ambivalent and damnable gratefulness. And then, there was the issue of the way they dressed.

I hated suits and neckties, but I wore them for my clients, believing that lawyers should look like lawyers, particularly to clients inclined to interpret tennis shoes and unshorn hair as marks of no respect. The idiosyncratic and brilliant Brian Olmstead looked homeless. While it is no disgrace to look homeless when one *is,* looking gratuitously tattered and unclean serves only to mock the poverty of those painfully trapped in it. Brian couldn't have gotten past the lobby of a State Street law firm clothed in his badge. I knew that and so did our clients, who were offended.

In any case, I believed strongly that an experienced black person should be found to head the Grove Hall office. The other two black attorneys agreed. One of them, Geraldine Hines, a talented young lawyer from Mississippi and the University of Wisconsin Law School, was quite insistent about the matter. The other black, whose weak hold on his job matched his talent, supported the call, but nervously and with significantly more at stake. And so we three formally requested of Spangenberg and Olmstead not only that the office be headed full-time by an experienced black attorney but also that more black lawyers be recruited for the Grove Hall office. We broadened our pressure by seeking and receiving support for our efforts from Roxbury's most prominent organizations, including the Roxbury Multi-Service Center, the community's largest social service agency, headed by Hubie Jones, a highly respected black leader.

Spangenberg and the downtown BLAP braintrust became uncomfortable with the new pressure and responded with a hoary ploy gift-wrapped as compromise. Spangenberg's stratagem: They want a black; well, we will give (or lend) them one.

He was borrowed on temporary assignment from a major Boston private law firm and dispatched to our impoverished backwater with the charge of defusing the crisis and restoring, if possible, the status quo. The black damper's name was Harrison Fitch, and no man ever looked more like his name. Barely thirty years old, he smoked a curved-stem pipe, wore Ben Franklin spectacles, and spoke as if afflicted with chronic constipation. Where heredity and socialization had left off, affectation had taken over. There was no evidence of humor or irreverence. I seem to remember a pocket watch and chain, but I can't be certain. In repose, he might have been contemplating a return to the gold standard (off which Richard Nixon had only just taken the United States) or a proposal for an attractively regressive new tax system.

"Harrison," I said, "we need a full-time black lawyer who wants to work in this community. Can't you see why they asked you to come here?"

I saw no evidence that he could.

We three malcontents were offered an ultimatum. Desist in demanding black leadership for a legal services office that served an all-black clientele or be fired. One of us buckled. Geraldine Hines and I refused to back down. We were fired. Geraldine Hines survived to become a successful Boston attorney. My legal career, after less than a year, had mercifully come to its end.

◼ 1972–1975: Roxbury and Cambridge, Massachusetts

I stayed in Boston for three more years before leaving for Washington in 1975. During those years I worked at the Roxbury Multi-Service Center as a community organizer. Percy Wilson, the new director, believed in political activism and gave me leeway to pursue a range of activities. I targeted the Gulf Oil Company's support of Portuguese colonialism in Africa. By the early seventies, the wars against Portugal's army were a decade old in Angola, Mozambique, and Guinea-Bissau. Portugal, financially strapped and dependent upon Gulf for Angolan oil revenues, was prosecuting a particularly brutal military campaign on all three African fronts. I had seen authenticated press photographs of smiling Portuguese soldiers hoisting by the ears the severed heads of African civilians. We made the pictures into three-by-five-foot posters bearing the orange Gulf Oil logo and the legend BOYCOTT GULF. Fifty thousand posters were put up in twenty-five major cities. The posters shocked many Americans with their depiction of the gruesomeness of a war about which few had even heard. We took our campaign to churches, schools, labor unions, political leaders, journalists. Money for our efforts flowed in from the Protestant church agencies housed in the Interchurch Center in New York.

Henry Kissinger oracularly declaimed that Portugal would remain a colonial master in Africa into the foreseeable future.

He would be proven wrong. By now I had organized (with James Winston, a former law school classmate, and Christopher Nteta, a South African graduate of Harvard Divinity School) the Pan African Liberation Committee, a group of some hundred local activists.

We pressed our campaign with Harvard after the university declined to divest its portfolio of Gulf Oil stock then valued at more than $300 million.

We ordered enough lumber, nails, and paint to start a furniture manufacturing company. Black students for weeks gave of their spare time to hammer into the night and paint until morning. We waited for snow and got two feet of it a week later. By the snow-reflected light of a full moon, we went to work at two o'clock in the morning. By dawn we had turned Harvard's campus into a symbolic graveyard of more than a thousand black crosses planted in a blanket of white snow. We had memorialized Africa's war dead and called Harvard's role in the carnage to public attention. The *Boston Globe* carried a picture of the crosses on its front page above the fold.

National figures started to take note. Congressman Charles C. Diggs Jr., chairman of the U.S. House of Representatives Subcommittee on Africa, along with Congressmen Louis Stokes and William Clay met with us in Cambridge. Once back in Washington, Chairman Diggs issued a strong statement of support for the Pan African Liberation Committee, its Gulf Oil boycott, and its campaign at Harvard University. Still there was no indication of Harvard giving any thought to divesting the Gulf stock. The Harvard treasurer, George Frederick Bennett, the principal manager of an endowment portfolio then valued at roughly a billion dollars, was adamantly opposed to even gesturing in our direction. Derek Bok, my former law dean and now president of the university, was gracious but little more.

We were not discouraged. We could achieve our overall objective without a Harvard capitulation. We were conducting a national public education campaign with no money, no national membership network, and no marquee leaders. All we had was a surfeit of committed young minds, bottomless energy, and a near religious certainty of the rightness of our cause. And we had the perfect media target in Harvard University, the most famous institution of higher learning in the world.

Massachusetts Hall, Harvard's oldest building and the office of the president, is built of age-pitted red brick and stands inside Harvard Yard directly across the green from University Hall and a bronze statue of a seated John Harvard, the school's English-born namesake and early benefactor. On April 21, 1972, at 6:30 A.M. in the predawn mist, James Winston, Chris Nteta, and I joined with thirty-six black undergraduates in taking over Massachusetts Hall.

We had gone over the rules countless times. We wanted public attention focused not on ourselves but on the little-known wars in Africa that were claiming thousands of civilian lives. We agreed that we would leave the building exactly as we found it. Nothing was to be damaged or even moved. Those few who were in the building when we arrived were allowed to leave. Displaced President Bok took up office residence a block away across Harvard Square in Holyoke Center.

We hunkered down to wait for the university's response while continuing to hand out information through the windows about the role of Gulf Oil and Harvard in Africa's colonial wars. By the end of the first day university officials had reconsidered their decision to have us arrested by Cambridge police officers. Such a move might have provoked a riot. All during the day people from throughout the Boston area—whites, blacks, young, old, white-collar, blue-collar—made their way to Harvard Yard. By nightfall there were thousands with candles ringing Massachusetts Hall and jamming the yard from end to end. Food was donated by a Boston soul food restaurant and delivered three times a day. The crowd stayed, its numbers constant around the clock. Two, three, four o'clock in the morning, thousands standing with candles. For long stretches of time, an eloquent silence. No fulminating harangues to mar a mass communion of joined spirits.

And then from time to time, voices would swell across the night in the stirring protest anthem:

We are soldiers in the army.
We fight although we have to die.
Hold up the blood-stained banner,
Hold it up until we die.

On the evening of the second day Harvard's only black law professor, Derrick Bell, came to Massachusetts Hall to visit. "Randall, I would be happy to join you all in the building if you think it would help."

I considered. Derrick Bell was self-effacing, bright, principled. "No, Derrick, we couldn't ask you to do that. It would be very helpful, however, if you would strongly support our position to the university administration."

All during the days and late into the nights, the occupying students found quiet corners in which to study for the final examinations just weeks away. They were all hardworking, disciplined young people. Steven Pitts would become a college professor in Houston. Mary Bassett would become a physician. Harvard Stephens would settle as a Roman Catholic priest in the Virgin Islands.

By the fourth day rumor had it that the university's patience had been exhausted and arrests were in the offing. Hearing this, supporters linked arms and cordoned the building three deep. Behind them remained more than a thousand vigil keepers.

The mother of a student inside the building was allowed through the cordon to speak to her son, an eighteen-year-old freshman. "Please, son, come out of the building. We've worked so hard to get you here. Don't throw it all away by getting thrown out of school when you're just starting. Your father and I are worried sick."

The young man was torn. He turned away from his mother to his friends. They encouraged him to leave and he did. His mother slumped in relief. Although all of the occupying students feared expulsion from school more than arrest, that freshman was the only one to leave.

The fifth day brought a carrot-and-stick proposal from the university. The stick was a court order for our expulsion and arrest to be served by marshals within the ensuing twenty-four hours. The carrot was Harvard's commitment to send a high-ranking university official to the war zone in Africa to do a ground-level evaluation of our assertions and then prepare recommendations for Harvard's decision makers.

Our protest had produced a partial victory. On day six, to a tumultuous reception, we walked out of Massachusetts Hall.

In August of 1972 Stephen Farber, special assistant to President Bok, traveled to Angola for two weeks, looked around, talked to Portuguese colonial officials, returned to Harvard, and reported that beyond a few sporadic skirmishes he had found no war to speak of. Harvard did not divest itself of its Gulf Oil stock. Between 1961 and 1975, more than a hundred thousand Mozambicans, Angolans, and Guinea-Bissauans died in a war Harvard University claimed did not exist.

◼ Summer 1976: Washington, D.C.

Many would feel that attempting to balance the public scales for a politician convicted of graft is a fool's undertaking. The scales cannot be balanced. They can only be accurately calibrated and fairly observed—both sides.

I had worked for Congressman Charles C. Diggs Jr. for two years before he was forced to resign from Congress and sent to prison. His downfall, from payroll-related crimes committed in the years before I was invited to reorganize and run his staff, came as a major blow to the interests of African-Americans and the peoples of Africa as well. In the mid-1970s Diggs was chairman of the House Committee on the District of Columbia and of the House Subcommittee on Africa. His seniority of more than twenty years in Congress put him in line to become the first African-American chairman of the full House Committee on Foreign Affairs. By the time I joined his staff in 1976, he was on the verge of becoming a very powerful man.

His father had been a Michigan state senator and successful Detroit funeral home owner. Charles Diggs Jr. had marched into Mississippi following the lynching of Emmett Till, founded the Congressional Black Caucus, and kindled, virtually alone, what little congressional interest there was in Africa.

Privately he was an inscrutable figure I had not expected to like. But beneath a gruff and misleading exterior lived a somewhat shy man who seemed to me the unlikeliest of politicians. He cared about people—too much and too many. Ex-wives. Exin-laws. Hangers-on. Never an administrator, he landed himself in deep financial trouble and used his congressional payroll to keep himself afloat. He paid for it and paid dearly. So did much of the black world, and to degrees that cannot be easily calculated. His wrongdoing was inexcusable. For a time I was angry: he had betrayed a trust larger by far than any one person's private burdens, and thus not his alone to sully and mismanage.

In the 1970s, African-Americans who wanted to do policy work on Africa hitched their wagons to Congressman Diggs's star. When the charismatic African-American activist Owusu Sadauki brought thirty thousand marchers to Washington in 1972 to protest U.S. policy toward southern Africa, Diggs was a featured speaker at the Mall demonstration. Before Goler Teal Butcher became the Peace Corps director for Africa in the Carter administration, she was counsel to the Diggs-chaired Subcommittee on Africa. When *National Geographic* writer Charles Cobb Jr. returned from Tanzania just after me, he worked on the Africa Subcommittee under Diggs. Whether tied to official Washington or burrowed in some remote university study carrel, all who were interested in Africa and foreign affairs recognized the near-solitary and indispensable leadership of Charles Diggs Jr.

He gave his young and idealistic staff members opportunity and space for growth. He encouraged initiative by simply allowing it. The apparent curmudgeon who answered his phone with a terse four-digit recital—"2261"—and looked at the floor as he spoke in one-on-one meetings proved easy to work for, supportive of our development, and fatherlike in his pride for his young charges' successes. As tenaciously as he fought for new and constructive American policies, he saw himself also as something of a steward for young African-American policy professionals. I was newly hired and with him in meetings with Alex Haley and Secretaries of State Henry Kissinger and Cyrus Vance. More with a grunt than with ceremony, he opened doors to countless careers and shoved us through.

By late fall of 1976 Portugal had retreated from Africa, making way for a troubled independence in its former colonies. In the breakaway British colony of Rhodesia the tiny white minority was fighting a losing war against Robert Mugabe's Zimbabwe African National Union (ZANU) and Joshua Nkomo's Zimbabwe African People's Union (ZAPU). White-ruled South Africa, along with Namibia, the territory South Africa illegally occupied, was at a low boil.

Throughout the summer of 1976 Secretary of State Kissinger had practiced a shuttle diplomacy that threatened to leave effective control of Rhodesia in the hands of a white minority that comprised less than three percent of the population. As he had with Portuguese colonialism, Kissinger forecasted no imminent demise for white rule in Rhodesia. He would be proven wrong again.

In September, during the Congressional Black Caucus weekend, amid the annual swarm of black glitterati, Diggs and Congressman Andrew Young convened a meeting of thirty leaders of national black organizations to discuss and respond to Kissinger's diplomacy in Rhodesia. Among those represented were the NAACP, black church groups, labor unions, Greek-letter organizations, the National Council of Negro Women, and the black business community. The meeting lasted two days. After the first day Herschelle Challenor, counsel to the Africa Subcommittee, Charles Cobb, and I worked through the night with the meeting rapporteur, producing from discussion notes a policy paper to be formally taken up the following morning. Entitled *The Afro-American Manifesto on Southern Africa,* it called for nothing short of one-person-one-*equal*-vote democracy for Rhodesia, South Africa, and Namibia. It further harshly criticized Kissinger for his all too apparent willingness to retard momentum toward black majority rule in Rhodesia if not to block it altogether. The paper was unanimously adopted.

During the afternoon of the second day, the conferees called for the establishment of an African-American foreign policy advocacy organization. I was asked to chair a working group that would plan for this new institution's founding. It would be incorporated in Washington, D.C., on July 1, 1977, and open its offices the following spring on Dupont Circle. It would be called TransAfrica and I would become its executive director.

The idea for TransAfrica grew out of the broadly recognized

need for an institutional mechanism through which African-Americans could be informed, galvanized, and moved to a focused, thoughtful participation in the formulation of U.S. foreign policy toward Africa and the Caribbean. It would prove to be a difficult challenge. Americans (unfortunately including African-Americans) knew little about Africa and the Caribbean. They knew even less about their nation's tradition of shameful attitudes and actions in these areas, a tradition often belied by the much ballyhooed image of America as a beneficent, compassionate, and freedom-loving superpower. By the mid-1970s the mortar in American Cold War policies toward Africa had hardened into an impregnable barrier to anything but minor revision. The African beneficiaries of exceptional U.S. largesse were, to a man, corrupt and undemocratic tyrants who, prompted by Washington, conveniently described themselves as anti-communist. They ruled in the handful of African countries deemed strategically useful to the U.S. Routinely, and with American blessing, they quashed any hint of dissent. To the rest of Africa's new nations emerging unsteadily from colonialism, the United States showed relative penuriousness if not total indifference. At the Department of State, Africa was a policy afterthought—and has largely remained so through Republican and Democratic administrations alike.

To be sure, the Republican Party had never systematically sought African-American support. The Democratic Party had done so successfully, but had never been constrained to give, in exchange for the black community's consistently rendered support, anything in the area of foreign policy concessions toward Africa. While Congress provided upwards of a thousand dollars per Israeli in foreign assistance, it gave less than two dollars per capita to the people of the developing countries of sub-Saharan Africa (including the tyrannies under U.S. sponsorship).

African-Americans, overburdened with problems born of domestic discrimination, could not proclaim en masse an opposition to unfair policies about which they and the American people in general knew little. And no one in official Washington saw anything to gain by disturbing the general quiescence.

A virus of racism had mutated its way through the larger foreign policy community as well. Difficult to see and even more difficult to fight, the virus is with us still, asymptomatic and deadly. It can't be seen because it has been seen too long. It can't be eradicated because it has been forever elemental in our policy environment. And every pernicious manifestation of the virus can be explained evenly in rational policy terms:

- Why there are so pitifully few black foreign service officers
- Why we have paid so little policy attention to Africa
- Why Europe merited a Marshall Plan and Africa a pittance
- Why we had to blockade Cuba but not South Africa
- Why we trained killer soldiers to let loose on Central America
- Why we chose to demonize Haiti's beloved Aristide but not its demon Duvalier
- Why we could give an Oval Office welcome to Romania's Ceausescu and none to Angola's dos Santos
- Why we cast the democratic Caribbean islands defenselessly adrift on a tide of drugs flowing from Colombia to markets in America
- Why our nation must be as insidiously racist in its relations with the outside black world as it has been historically with its own black citizens

Somewhere Americans acquired the reflex of a pitiless bully. This is illustrated in the near comical extreme in a September 1996 Center for Strategic and International Studies paper on Caribbean leadership in which author Douglas Payne criticizes Denzil Douglas, the newly elected prime minister of Saint Kitts–Nevis, one of the world's smallest nations (population 45,000), for renaming the international airport to honor Robert Bradshaw, the father of his island country's nationhood, who in the 1950s and 1960s stood up to the British colonialists and sugarcane field owners. If the democratic leaders of independent black countries the size of my residential neighborhood can't be allowed to name their own airports, what discretion, in God's name, would our smug colossus be prepared to cede them?

December 1976: Cape Town, South Africa

"Down there just ahead is the mouth of the Congo River." The air force pilot raised his voice so that it could be heard over the roar of the Boeing 707's engines.

I was looking over his shoulder through the cockpit window from an altitude of 39,000 feet. The river snaked inland from the shimmering Atlantic Ocean. We were approaching landfall, flying perpendicular to the southwest African coastline.

"On this side is Zaire. You can even see the country of Congo. Over there to the right of the river is Angola."

The early morning sky was clear. The slanting rays of the sun made the waters of the river and ocean appear luminous, outlining sharply the looming green landmass ahead.

I was traveling with a congressional delegation chaired by Charles Diggs. En route to Bloemfontein, South Africa, we had flown from Andrews Air Force Base, Maryland, in a windowless air force jet that had been retrofitted for passenger use and bore the legend *United States of America*. From Bloemfontein we would travel overland by bus to the small enclave country of Lesotho. Its capital, Maseru, was the venue for a conference convened by the African-American Institute, a New York–based organization that facilitated dialogue between African and American leaders. The conference would last for the better part of a week. Diggs had traveled separately and ahead of the delegation by a few days. Congressman Andrew Young would leave the group later so that he could visit with an old South African friend, Robert Sobukwe, the dying leader of the Pan Africanist Congress, a prominent black South African political organization. In all, the delegation comprised nine members of Congress. From the House came, in addition to Diggs and Young, Charles Rangel, Walter Fauntroy, William Clay, Yvonne Braithwaite Burke, and Cardiss Collins, making it the largest number of black representatives ever to visit Africa together. The lone Republican and white House member was John Anderson of Illinois, and the lone senator Joseph Biden of Delaware.

The plane rolled to a stop in front of the Bloemfontein terminal building. We had arrived in the Orange Free State, the ideological nerve center of the South African white redoubt. The mood on the plane was somber. Unable to see out, we had to wait what seemed an interminably long time before the door opened.

We drew more than perfunctory notice as we deplaned. To the eyes of whites locked on us we must have been a disquieting sight. From this official American aircraft stepped an overwhelmingly black congressional delegation, followed by U.S. Air Force Colonel John Farr, commander of the aircraft and black, followed by the State Department medical officer, a black physician, and fifteen or so congressional staffers the majority of whom were, again, black.

We were received on the tarmac by a small retinue of jittery white American consular officials whose body language conveyed unmistakably that we had arrived in a very tense place at a very bad time. Just days before, South African security operatives had used deadly force to quell riots in Cape Town's black township of Gugulethu. We had been fully briefed on the township uprisings that appeared to be spreading from city to city. Although we all had read a great deal about South Africa, only one or two in the delegation had ever visited before.

No one knew quite how to behave or what might happen, least of all the consular officials who, with a forced friendliness, seemed bent on distracting us from an atmosphere charged with unpleasant potential. They grew even more nervous as many of us spoke greetings to black ground workers in coveralls who, though silent, looked at us without the hostility plainly legible on the faces of the white airport officials.

"I need to use a rest room," I said to a consular official. We were in an airport lounge waiting to board the bus hired to take us to Maseru.

The official started to speak, then stopped, his diplomatic skills deserting him. He was embarrassed and I thought I knew why.

"I'm not going to a segregated rest room."

"I think I should warn you how things are here now. This is not the United States. They are shooting people here without warning. If you are going to use the main airport rest room, I think I had better go with you."

The young white American consular official stood lookout by the rest room door as three African-American men urinated into white porcelain urinals hanging from the wall of the whites-only Bloemfontein airport bathroom.

■

Lesotho is a poor, hilly country completely surrounded by, and dependent upon, South Africa. We stayed at the Maseru Holiday Inn, a stone's throw from the South African border. The hotel was fully booked. Besides conferees from the United States and much of Africa, there were also white South African men on holiday who could be found in the company of black women, at poolside by day and at the hotel's casino tables by night, in pursuit of pleasures that were criminally *verbode* across the border in South Africa.

The conference itself was unremarkable. Much of the talk was about South Africa's racial policies and their effects on Namibia and on Rhodesia, where white prime minister Ian Smith clung to power by his fingernails. There was no talk, however, from American Assistant Secretary of State for African Affairs Richard Moose about U.S. economic sanctions—or any other measures, for that matter, that could possibly faze South Africa's white rulers. These had come to know the United States as a kith-and-kin relation unwilling to do anything more than issue image-maintenance admonitions. Accustomed to their pariah status, South Africa's whites had long since learned to disregard criticism from countries whose corporations and banks underpinned their economy. President Jimmy Carter had made it clear that he opposed the imposition of economic sanctions. Charles Diggs had been unable to get a moderate sanctions bill out of his own Africa subcommittee.

When the conference ended, we flew to Cape Town, a picturesque city on the South Atlantic coast at the bottom of Africa. I found something very American about the city but could not immediately identify what. The grid of major thoroughfares and streets was very like any American city. The architecture as well bore greater similarity to Anglo-American styles than to those of other major African cities like Nairobi, Abidjan, or Cairo. At first blush, the people hurrying across Cape Town's traffic-heavy downtown streets might easily have been mistaken for Americans. Certainly the whites looked indistinguishable from American whites, and while black South Africans do have a distinctive cast to their facial features, they were as varied of skin color as African-Americans. The cars *were* American cars, and the billboards further evidenced the sordid partnership: General Motors, Colgate-Palmolive, Ford Motor Company, B. F. Goodrich. Cape Town not only looked like America, in many ways it was America.

We were in a large bus of European manufacture on our way to meetings at the U.S. consulate. The white driver, to my mind forgetting his place but to his very much remembering it, began feverishly defending his country's racial policies to a black congressman sitting in the right front seat by the door.

"You Americans just can't understand how what we're doing here is best for everybody, blacks and whites. This is not America. We have to work this out in our own way."

"Oh, we understand, all right. We understand better than you know. . . ."

The exchange churned on between the driver and the congressman. I stopped listening, blocked it out. In this beautiful city I felt like a child again, hurt and hate-filled. A deep, dormant injury, long scarred over, was freshly abraded. I was not the new me in Cape Town but the old eviscerated little-boy me in segregated Richmond, Virginia. I sat toward the back next to a window looking out, closed up in myself.

We were meeting with five English-speaking white South African businessmen. English-speaking whites, who dominated the business sector, were generally more liberal than the more numerous Afrikanns-speaking whites who ran the country's politics. The businessmen were well mannered and spoke evenly of South Africa's problems. There was nothing pejorative, or even mildly patronizing, in the words they chose. They appeared earnest about finding solutions to South Africa's vexing racial problems. All of us understood that the stakes for South Africa were higher than they had been for America during its racial turmoil. In America, the struggle had been for inclusion, for civil rights. In South Africa, because blacks comprised a majority, what was at stake was state power.

We had been talking for a half hour when Congressman Diggs raised the issue at the center of South Africa's racial crisis.

"We've been talking around the real issue here and that is the franchise. When will black South Africans get the right to vote?"

It was as if the question had come unscrambled from another galaxy. The businessmen appeared stunned. Nearly a minute passed before anything was said. The businessmen looked at each other before one of them said, with no apparent malice, "But, Congressman Diggs, giving blacks the vote would be like putting a gun in the hand of a five-year-old."

Time slowed. The room was still. We listened again in our heads to what we'd just heard. *He couldn't have said that, could he?*

Senator Joseph Biden exploded. "Do you all know how the world sees you? Do you know that this country could burn to the ground and the United States would not lift a finger to help you? You don't have a clue about what you're doing here, do you?"

I sat in the same seat on the bus ride to the Cape Town airport. I was struggling to identify and throttle feelings I had not experienced for many years. Senator Biden took the seat next to me.

"You must be very angry," he said.

"Yes, I am." We rode for a while. "Are you sure the U.S. wouldn't lift a finger to help white South Africans?"

"No. But I thought it needed to be said."

Ready to depart South Africa, our group was cleared through the airport terminal to find Colonel Farr talking through a padlocked eight-foot chainlink gate to a white South African ground official. The normally unflappable Colonel Farr was gesticulating and appeared upset.

"I am Colonel John Farr of the United States Air Force and commander of this aircraft. I will ask you once more, has the aircraft been serviced and fueled? I will ask you once more to open this gate."

Behind Colonel Farr stood a young white enlisted man who had served as cabin steward during the trip. The South African official seemed to have difficulty interpreting what was to him a new and strange social structure. He looked behind Colonel Farr and addressed himself to the young enlisted man. "Are you in charge here?"

The cabin steward, struck dumb, looked like he had been shot for being in the wrong face at the wrong time.

Congressman Diggs had a meeting not on the full delegation schedule and thus was not with us. It was Congressman Charles Rangel who moved to Colonel Farr's side.

"I am Charles Rangel, a member of the United States Congress. *This* is the commander of *that* aircraft—Colonel Farr. You will open this gate now or have an international incident on your hands. Do you understand?"

Uncertain and visibly bollixed, the South African airport official unlocked the gate and allowed us to board the plane.

■ September 1977: Washington, D.C.

"I am trying to think of ways I can help you put together the resources you will need to launch TransAfrica," said Max.

We were sitting in the basement of his Northwest Washington home watching a tape of an award-winning documentary he had produced and narrated for local broadcast about the social culture of Anacostia, a neighborhood of the city where Frederick Douglass once lived.

I said nothing as he pondered. I looked at the television and thought back ten years.

I had been lying in bed in Richmond on a Sunday morning in the mid-1960s waiting for Julian Bond's appearance on NBC's *Meet the Press*. Bond had burned his draft card in protest against the growing American role in the Vietnam War and had become, as a result, a national figure. During the thirty-second teaser in which Bond was introduced, only the backs of the four still-to-be-introduced interviewers could be seen. Intending to read through the commercial break that preceded the discussion, I focused again on the newspaper. A moment elapsed and then a dawning. I dropped the paper and looked at the back of the second panelist's head. The ears. The ears. "Oh my God! Oh my God!"

Mama answered on the first ring. "Mama! Get Daddy and turn on *Meet the Press*. Max is on national television!"

Mama and I called everyone we could in the space of a minute—Jeanie, Jewell, grandparents, aunts, uncles, cousins. It had come as a thunderbolt even to Max, who had been invited to appear less than an hour before airtime.

I tried very hard but couldn't listen. I heard words but could not arrange them for comprehension. My heart banged against my eardrums like a mad timpanist. At the end of the discussion I had little idea of what Max had said except that he had appeared confident and masterful. Other than Arthur Ashe, it was the first time I had seen anyone I knew on national television and he was my brother.

Max had started his broadcast career in radio in the late 1950s as a part-time disk jockey at Richmond's black music station, WANT, under the tutelage of Tom Mitchell, a family friend. By 1962 he had his own show in Petersburg, called the Mark Cabot Show. Max was Mark Cabot, and occasionally I would appear as the host's brother, Vance Cabot. Later Max worked briefly as an off-camera voice at a Portsmouth television station. The viewing audience was given to believe that the polished deep baritone they were hearing in voice-overs was that of a white man. When Max conspired with a station cameraman to have his face shown, he was fired.

During the early 1970s, when I was in Massachusetts campaigning against Harvard University's investment decisions, Max was becoming a highly regarded television news anchorman in Washington, D.C., working first on NBC's WRC and then at CBS's WTOP. By the time I arrived in Washington in 1975, his face was known to everyone living in the Washington area. For the first time in twenty years, the four Robinson children were all living in the same city. Jeanie was teaching elementary school in the public system. Jewell was working for the Washington Urban League.

Daddy had died the year before at sixty-eight, after forty years of teaching followed by three years of illness-laden retirement and the only vacation trip he and Mama were ever to take, a seven-day package cruise to Bermuda. Other than making church-related public speeches, Mama hadn't worked since leaving teaching in her early twenties. Still living in Richmond on East Thirty-ninth Street, Mama, at sixty, went to work as the executive director of the local YWCA, learned to drive, got a license, and bought a Chevy Nova.

■

"Why don't we get TransAfrica off the ground with a fund-raiser here at the house?" Max was now saying to me in the summer of 1977. "We can do a reception around the pool for a hundred or so people and see how much we can raise."

He had always been supportive, even before it became relatively painless. The father he idolized had been a sports legend in Richmond. Alas, the firstborn son who so wanted to please Maxie Sr. had been gifted with little to no athletic aptitude. In high school Max had toiled excruciatingly hard to make Daddy's basketball team but with no success. Yet he was there for my games in high school and college whenever he could be, shouting encouragement with a selflessness I can never forget.

The September Saturday afternoon benefit reception at Max's house exceeded our expectations. About a hundred people attended and we raised in excess of ten thousand dollars. Among the turnout were Arthur Ashe and U.S. Treasurer Azie Morton, who had worked for Charles Diggs and owed her position to him. Benjamin Hooks, leader of the NAACP, was there with his board chairperson Margaret Bush Wilson, from whom he would later acrimoniously split. The writer John Killens dropped by, as did Botswana's ambassador Bias Mokoodi, the Urban League's Vernon Jordan, and labor leader William Lucy. Thelma Daly, president of Delta Sigma Theta sorority, attended along with academicians James Turner of Cornell and Ronald Walters of Howard.

Months earlier Walters had met with Herschelle Challenor, the Africa Subcommittee counsel, and me at the Washington home of C. Payne Lucas, president of Africare, to lay plans for the new organization. It was Challenor who suggested that we name the organization TransAfrica. All of us thought that Richard Gordon Hatcher, the young black mayor of Gary, Indiana, would be a good choice to chair the board of directors.

"Who knows him?" I asked.

"I know him," said Walters. "I'll call him now." He did and

Hatcher agreed to fill the position he would hold for fifteen years.

Robert C. S. Powell was a large man, in girth and style. A black Episcopal priest, he chaired the Africa Committee of the National Council of Churches at the New York building known to all who did business with the Interchurch Center as the God Box. Equipped with an instinctive understanding of ecclesiastical politics, an intimidating intellect, and a velvet-cloaked arrogance, Father Powell, a founding TransAfrica board member, thought the idea of TransAfrica was seminally important and won for it from his church colleagues a funding stream that would flow unbroken for several years until his untimely death at the age of forty-two. He had only just returned home from Kenya the evening before he died of a heart attack while sitting beside his wife, Bernice, at the Sunday morning worship service at New York's Cathedral of St. John the Divine.

Early in 1978 I resigned my position as administrative assistant to Charles Diggs. Shortly thereafter, in a made-over second-floor one-bedroom apartment on Eighteenth Street in Northwest Washington, TransAfrica began its work with a two-person staff—myself as executive director and Dolores Clemons as my assistant.

High on our agenda was the creation of a fundamentally different U.S. foreign policy toward the white minority regimes of southern Africa. Since 1948 and the codification of apartheid, the Republic of South Africa had successfully buffered its racialist tyranny with Western corporate investment and the sympathetic company of neighboring white minority regimes that Pretoria either ran or influenced in Namibia, Rhodesia, and the Portuguese colonies of Angola and Mozambique. When Portugal pulled out of Africa in the mid-1970s and its colonies became independent, South Africa's rulers began sponsoring armed insurgencies aimed at destabilizing the new black-run nations. Public declarations notwithstanding, the United States during the Nixon and Reagan presidencies supported South Africa's policies unreservedly.

The Carter administration, falling between the Republican presidencies, had a mixed record, demonstrating resolve to Rhodesia's obdurate whites, political cowardice to Angola's beleaguered government, and, for all quantifiable intents and purposes, neutrality to South Africa's white rulers.

TransAfrica's task was to effect a 180-degree turn in American policy toward South Africa and the general region. How could this be done? We had no money and no reliable place to find it in large amounts. Virtually none could be expected from the corporate community. Some three hundred American corporations had invested upwards of two billion dollars in an apartheid system whose labor inequities produced extraordinary returns on investment.

What constituency could we count on to give money or rally to a call? While in Cape Town, I had gone to Table Mountain and looked westward across the South Atlantic toward Robben Island where Nelson Mandela had been imprisoned for life. But almost no one in the United States knew who Nelson Mandela was, or anything else about South Africa, much less American policy toward it.

What could we reasonably expect from approaches to the conventional establishment forces? The prospects there seemed dim indeed. After all, the chairman of the House Africa Subcommittee, Charles Diggs, could not coax the subcommittee to approve even modest sanctions against South Africa. Many thoughtful African-Americans saw possible value in surmounting the de facto barriers to black membership in virtually all white old-line foreign policy ballast organizations like the Council on Foreign Relations. But what had Council members ever done, save bury human suffering abroad in esoteric writings and pedantic talks? After all, the Council was and remains a citadel of motionless hand-wringing where the parameters for suggested foreign policy adjustment are so close as to touch each other. What could prospective African-American members hope for, in any case, sharing membership in the Council with the likes of foreign policy's P. T. Barnum and every tyrant's presumptive sponsor, Henry Kissinger, who seemed to think that a human right was a punch landed by a prizefighter?

We could not hope to win by wiggling the conventional levers, testifying before change-deaf committees, writing futile letters to habit-guided policymakers, or depending alone on the cogency and decency of our views. It was not nearly enough to be *right*. No group in America was listened to less in Washington than the amiable but fangless liberal church establishment. We could not allow ourselves to be sapped of energy and buried in circular debate with the defenders of the status quo.

We had to find a way to set our own terms and break the long-standing control of the anonymous graybeard policy bullies. With an even firmer conviction, we had to assume that they had not the faintest idea of what they were doing or talking about. Foreign policymaking, as near to a science as phrenology, had to be demystified. Americans had to be made aware of all the needless hurt that had been caused in their name. African-Americans had to be made to understand that this American policy affront to Africa was an insult to them as well.

I arrived at this rudimentary wisdom through painful experience. For the first two years of TransAfrica's existence, I testified before congressmen who talked to their staff members throughout my increasingly spiritless readings. I organized letters from black leaders to the congressmen who hadn't listened to my testimony—or, from what I could see, to anyone else's on the subject. I debated on television, with Senator George McGovern, against Senator James McClure of Idaho and Senator S. I. Hayakawa of California, the former president of San Francisco State who had won his Senate seat on the heels of quelling a much publicized student uprising at his school. Senator Hayakawa, a conservative crusader for continued white minority rule in Rhodesia, regularly slept through hearings and was known to feel that the Panama Canal Zone should forever be a possession of the United States inasmuch as we had "stolen it fair and square." Senator Jesse Helms asked me, in the middle of a hearing on South Africa, how much my suit had cost me and how I could afford it. During another Senate hearing, being questioned by Jacob Javits, of New York, I responded on one occasion with a question of my own. "I ask the questions here," he said in reproof. Why, I thought but didn't say, must that be? Mark Siljander, a Republican on the House Subcommittee on Africa, once argued strongly in a public session that Congress should appropriate millions of dollars in arms to support the destabilizing insurgency in "Angolia." That no such country existed appeared to matter little to the foreign policy "expert" Siljander.

In order to prevail, we had to find a way to focus public pressure on the White House, State Department, and Congress. We had, somehow, to provoke media coverage. The news industry had never evinced much interest in Africa and the Caribbean. When these areas were covered at all, they were usually covered negatively, and without context or linear comprehensiveness. It further appeared that what little interest the American media had in the black world was disproportionately paid to areas with significant concentrations of whites. This gave us a chance to win media, and thus public, attention for proposed and existing policies affecting South Africa, Rhodesia, and Namibia, where whites were tenaciously swimming against the tide of history. From this new attention, we thought, would follow accountability for policymakers, and thus better and more humane American policies. But for the rest of Africa and the Caribbean, where no whites to speak of lived, our chances of building media interest, and our own influence, were significantly smaller.

Fall 1980: The Western Sahara

During the Cold War, in corners of the black world unseen by American public eyes, American policies were often implemented with insupportably cruel results. Haiti, Zaire, and Liberia are but a few examples. The Western Sahara, however, might be an even better example because scarcely a handful of Americans had heard of the northwest African territory, rich in phosphates and petroleum, scrambled over by Morocco and Mauritania after Spain abandoned its former colony in 1975.

I visited the Western Sahara in the fall of 1980 at the invitation of the indigenous Polisario movement which had since 1976 pressed its claim for independence by doing battle against Mauritania and Morocco. By 1979 Mauritania had relinquished its claim. But Morocco, at odds with the United Nations and the Organization of African Unity, persisted in its effort to forcibly annex the Western Sahara. The United States had come to Morocco's aid with a $235-million arms package, pitting Washington against Africa and the better part of the world while alienating a war-weary desert people whose right to independence was morally and legally unassailable.

As one could not fly directly to the barren battleground of the Western Sahara, I flew first to Algiers, capital of the North African Arab nation of Algeria, a thousand miles to the northeast. Algeria, which shared a brief border with the Western Sahara, supported its quest for independence and quartered 140,000 of its Saharawi refugees in olive canvas tents dotted across the desert floor near Tindouf, a small west Algerian city of sand-colored dwellings. Sent from New York by publisher Earl Graves to cover my trip was Lynda Hill, a writer for *Black Enterprise* magazine.

Algiers is a romantic place of hilly, winding, narrow streets overlooking the Mediterranean. The daytime city is kinetic with the sounds of Arab shop commerce, French-made cars, and singing one-cylinder motorbikes. The warm, quiet nights are made exotic by the strangely calming cadences of the muezzih's wafting chants that slide over without bruising the night air.

The air terminal was large and quite old, but meticulously clean. Flight departures and arrivals were chalk-listed in Arabic on a large blackboard. I had not visited an Arab country before and was at once fascinated and unnerved by the depth of my foreignness. The only familiar symbols to be seen, the Arabic numerals (a Hindu and Arab invention, remember, not ours) on the flight schedule blackboard, jumped out like old friends. The majority of the terminal patrons were men, some attired familiarly, some wearing long white robes. There were few women, most of whom covered their faces with the chador. I heard in the din of voices not a word of English. Algeria had been a colony of France. Pitiably, I remembered nothing useful of my high school French. Needless to say, I neither understood spoken Arabic nor recognized its written characters, which I would in any case have read, wrongly, left to right. No doubt I felt more conspicuous than I looked. Indeed, as I glanced about the terminal for my hosts, no one paid me the least attention.

"Mr. Robinson, allow me to welcome you to Algeria." The speaker was short and slight with a sandy complexion. He spoke in a light, slightly raspy voice. "My name is . . ." He gave his name but my Western ear lost it. He was accompanied by another man of similar build to whom he spoke briefly in Hassanya, a dialect spoken informally by the Saharawi.

They extended their hands. I shook them. The speaker then made to Lynda Hill a suggestion of a bow that appeared all the more courtly for its subtlety.

"Tomorrow morning you will be flown to Tindouf and from there taken by Land Rover into the Western Sahara. We will keep your passports and return them to you here in Algiers upon your departure for the United States."

At Tindouf I was assigned a translator, Ahmed, who took me around the tent camp describing schools, artifact production sites, an infirmary, dining halls, living quarters, and enclosures for Moroccan prisoners of war.

I drank sweet steaming tea from tiny glasses and listened to Saharawi elders talk with fervor of their quest for independence. I inspected American weapons that had been captured by Polisario guerrillas from Moroccan soldiers. Some of the weapons were M16s, the rifle I had trained with during my time in the army.

In the evening a rally was held with thousands of people gathered under an open sky around a raised platform. The women were dressed festively in red, orange, blue, and black. Men sat cross-legged on the ground around the plank stage. A man exhorted the crowd in Arabic over the public address system. The crowd chanted back. Ululant calls pierced the night.

The tall bespectacled speaker on the stage appeared to be captivating his audience in Hassanya when suddenly in the midst of an unfathomable stream of Eastern word-sounds I heard clearly "Randall Robinson."

"What did he say?" I asked Ahmed.

"He said that you will now speak." No notice. No warning.

Ahmed mounted the platform to translate. I followed slowly, desperately trying to compose a single lucid thought. There was something almost literally otherworldly about the occasion. Here I was, passportless at midnight in the featureless vastness of the North African desert, about to attempt an open-air extemporaneous speech to an Hassanya- and Arabic-speaking rally of berobed Saharawi thousands.

My brief speech combined deeply held beliefs with a dash of hyperbole. "I am honored and pleased I have been invited to visit. We have shown and will continue to show our support for the Polisario and for the independence of the Western Sahara. Black Americans, in particular, are sympathetic to your cause because in many ways our struggles are similar. I will go back to the U. S. and try to change the policy toward those who have committed aggression against you."

The audience erupted. Hope made them generous. Had my remarks been misleading? I felt a twinge of something akin to guilt.

After the rally I met with a group of ten elders in a large tent. One of them strongly resembled my mother's younger brother, Maurice, who lived in Atlanta.

"I must tell you that you look uncannily like my uncle."

He laughed. "I could be your uncle."

We all laughed in the lamplit tent in the Saharan desert.

We talked quietly for a long time. There were spaces in the discussion but they were not awkward. The spaces accepted our moods and feelings which were, on the whole, warm and sanguine. Memorably, toward the end, a wiry sun-leathered man with rheumy eyes and looking to be in his late seventies spoke for the first time. "How can a great nation of free people like the United States help Morocco deny us our freedom?"

I cannot recall my response. It probably amounted to little.

At 4:00 A.M. we crossed the border from Tindouf into the "liberated" zone of the Western Sahara. We traveled in a convoy of four battle-equipped heavy-duty Land Rovers with twenty-one men and one woman, Lynda Hill. I was told by Ahmed that besides ourselves, the convoy contingent included sixteen Polisario soldiers and three visitors from Western Europe. I recall that one of the three was a Portuguese journalist who became ill during our seven-hundred-mile race across the desert, shortly after we had dined on rabbits skewered and roasted over an open fire. Animal life in the desert was scarce. The soldiers killed the game and we ate it. I experienced no squeamishness, surprisingly, not even upon learning that my half-eaten pasta curls were rabbit entrails. A Polisario physician appeared out of the desert's endless black nothingness and ministered to the Portuguese journalist.

I had never experienced such thick darkness. The world seemed reduced to the arc of the Land Rovers' bouncing headlights. Since seeing the last wind-tossed lightbulb disappear behind us at Tindouf, we had traveled for two hours at alarming speeds across rocky and rutted terrain.

I rode in front beside the driver. Lynda and Ahmed sat in back.

An armed guerrilla was wedged behind them peering into the pitch. The windshield of the Land Rover had been locked down fast against the hood. The roar of the onrushing unimpeded air made communication impossible. We were wearing army camouflage uniforms with goggles. Our heads, faces, and necks were wrapped in a burlap-like cloth, giving us the appearance of Bedouin guerrillas in a sandstorm. The driver, who spoke no English, searched the darkness ahead for lethal obstacles which our excessive speed gave us little chance of avoiding.

I could make out nothing of human manufacture. No road. No building. No guidepost or marker of any kind. Nothing. Hard earth. Scrub plants. Stunted, gnarled trees. I could no more guess at our direction than understand the driver's method of navigation. For stretches of time I could discern in the distance the lights of the other three Land Rovers. They seemed to have no assigned place or route, appearing variously on the left and right of us, to the front and then the rear, before vanishing altogether for long periods.

At dawn the convoy trucks converged upon the gutted remnants of Lebuirat, a tiny village from which the inhabitants had fled on foot and camel across the desert to safety at Tindouf. Refugees had been known to walk more than five hundred miles to the tents across the border in Algeria. We stopped in Lebuirat to rest. The rear-guard soldier with our vehicle ventured thirty yards away to fill at a waterhole the animal-hide bags from which we all drank. I wandered off. The sun was only just nudging above the flat earth line. It had been cool during the night. In eight hours the temperature would rise to 120 degrees Fahrenheit. I turned around. I had never before seen from land a 360-degree unbroken circle of horizon. Aside from the detritus of war, struggling flora, and the sand-colored masonry ruins of a tiny ghost village, there was absolutely nothing to see. Anywhere. In any direction.

"Look over there." Ahmed had come up beside me and pointed to the rusting husk of a burned-out Moroccan tank. Beside it were parts of a human skeleton.

We reboarded the Land Rovers and pressed northward. The desert was a litter-field of abandoned weapons. A soldier shot a gazelle and hoisted it into the back of Land Rover #2. A few miles on we rumbled through the towns of Haouza and Mahbés, which had suffered much the same fate as Lebuirat.

As we bore on, our driver, without sleep for twenty-four hours, misjudged a sharply banked curve over large jagged rocks and nearly flipped the topless vehicle into a deep ravine. Had the sure-footed vehicle fallen to the ravine side from its two-wheeled cant, we'd all have died anonymously there in the vast uncharted battleground litter-field of the Western Sahara.

As it was, no sooner had I regained my composure than the convoy ground to a halt on a plateau overlooking a seemingly endless red plain.

"We are in Morocco," Ahmed said to me over my shoulder. Only then did I understand why I had been asked to sign a statement in Algiers clearing the Algerian government of responsibility for me pending my return to the capital. In the desert, I had no passport and thus no identity. I was a nonperson, illegally in Morocco in the company of enemy soldiers.

Ahmed pointed again, ahead and below, toward a fortified encampment situated the equivalent of four city blocks directly in front of us. "That is Zag. It is a Moroccan military base."

I had been misled.

Well, that's not quite fair. I *had* badly underestimated the danger I had been in since leaving Algiers. Although I had studied Saharawi culture academically, I knew nothing of how to interpret overt Saharawi personality traits. It occurred to me on that undefendable, unobscured plateau in Morocco within range of Moroccan guns that not only had I underestimated the danger we all were in, I had also underestimated the very young, cherubic-faced soldiers around me to whom danger seemed no more remarkable than the featureless desert itself.

I looked at Ahmed, another whose very physiognomy had been for me so deceptive. His was not the kind of visage I had been socialized to expect in a fearless guerrilla soldier. He had a boyish, mild, almost angelic face. He was small, as were all of the Saharawi I had seen. And, like the others, he had a light voice. I had detected not a trace of swagger in any of these heavily armed men with their distinctly un-Western mien. During our rest stop at Lebuirat, one of the guerrillas, with a shy smile and no further meaning, had even presented Lynda with a wild yellow bloom he had plucked from the desert.

I have often since thought how very silly these obscure brave desert men would make American popular culture heroes look by contrast. Charlton Heston was never El Cid or Moses. He was an actor, tall and posturing, on a safe movie set aided by stuntmen and surrounded by cameras, lights, and directors asking for yet another take before calling it a day. Ahmed and his compatriots, however, were the real article: courageous, implacable, steady, hard men who flourished in an unforgiving environment that I could not have survived alone for a quarter of the journey.

We began the long run back to Tindouf. The air beating against us could almost be tasted. Never in my life had I endured anything close to the scorching standstill heat of midday Western Sahara. At nightfall we stopped to sleep for an hour or two on the cooling desert floor before beginning the final push for camp. I lay on my back with my head and outstretched arms flat against the hard ground. The black sky held more stars than I knew could burn there.

I thought about the women and children in the Tindouf tents who had fled on foot across the burning earth. I thought about the strip of baked plain for which its gentle/fierce legatees were so apparently willing to die. I thought about my government whose captured weapons I had handled hours before. I thought about the American people who, with the rarest exception, had never heard of the Western Sahara, its people, their plight, or America's lamentable role in it. I thought about the Saharawi elder's question for which I had no adequate answer: *How can a great nation of free people like the United States help Morocco deny us our freedom?*

I had no illusions about the difficulty of altering U. S. policy. Morocco's King Hassan had been for the U. S. a reliable anti-communist ally who had earlier deployed his troops at Washington's behest to help put down a rebellion in Zaire's Shaba province aimed at toppling Zaire's CIA-installed dictator Mobutu Sese Seko. The Shah of Iran had been deposed not long before. Washington would be hard put to risk a similar fate befalling Hassan's monarchy.

Given the Polisario's political invisibility in the United States, the Washington foreign policy establishment would never give a single damn about the Saharawi people's suffering and yearning for self-determination. To make our policy more humane, and indeed more in keeping with our own well-touted public support for principles of self-determination, would have constrained Washington in this case to "sentimentalize" foreign policy. Heaven forbid. Particularly when the sentiment is simple decency.

In the early 1950s the United Fruit Company (now Chiquita Brands) was operating in Guatemala as a near-sovereign entity when it ran afoul of the newly elected democratic government of President Jacobo Arbenz. At the urging of United Fruit, the CIA organized the overthrow of Arbenz, then instigated and sustained a civil war that would last thirty-six years. The Eisenhower administration's lever pullers for the policies that ultimately resulted in the deaths of hundreds of thousands of Guatemalans were Secretary of State John Foster Dulles and CIA director Allen Dulles, brothers who were both on the payroll of the law firm that represented United Fruit.

When insider avarice is the sentiment, sentiment can be made an allowable policy ingredient.

It was 3:00 A.M. when we arrived back at Tindouf. Out of the inky darkness of hundreds of miles, the convoy drivers had hit the single wind-tossed lightbulb dead on.

The following morning I promised my hosts that I would do all I could upon my return home to win attention for their little-known struggle in the United States. But my efforts were to prove inadequate. Over the ensuing years the black community in the United States would play little to no role in the development of American policy toward Morocco, and the Western Sahara's quest for self-determination remains to this day unfulfilled.

The crisis of the Western Sahara is an obscure but illustrative failure for TransAfrica and African-Americans in general. For in this failure can be discovered the limits of African-American foreign policy influence, limits imposed by a powerful and traditional white foreign policy establishment and, nearly as vigorously and as frequently, by African-American opinion makers and leaders who remain trammeled by an unconscious belief that foreign policy causes warrant their attention and support only when they derive legitimacy and prominence from the very white mainstream institutions traditionally arrayed against them. The Western Sahara is not important to mainstream white America. Thus it does not merit significant attention from influential African-Americans disinclined by reflex to impose upon the American public landscape issues that should be of independent and inherent consequence to the black world.

The month following my return *Black Enterprise* magazine published a major article on the Western Sahara based on my findings. It was the only media interest in the Western Sahara I could stimulate.

The Caribbean gives us an example of the black Self-Defeat Syndrome seen closer to home. In 1996 the Clinton administration, acting at the behest of Chiquita Brands, asked the World Trade Organization to invalidate a trade agreement that guaranteed Caribbean banana-producing countries access to the banana market in countries of the European Union. A pro-Chiquita ruling by the WTO would mean: for Chiquita, marginally higher banana sales; for the U.S. economy, nothing; and for the Caribbean, incalculable economic upheaval and increased drug trafficking. For stable democratic Caribbean countries like Saint Lucia and Dominica that depend on banana sales for survival, the loss of European market access would likely be followed by the collapse of their economies and, in turn, their democracies. The threat to the stability of the black English-speaking Caribbean cannot be overstated. "If we lose our banana industry, it will be very difficult for any Caribbean government to tell young people not to go into drugs," said Eugenia Charles, former prime minister of Dominica.

Some prominent African-Americans expressed concern. (*New York Times* columnist Bob Herbert excoriated Chiquita and the Clinton administration). Most were either indifferent or unaware. And a few like *Chicago Tribune* columnist Clarence

Page and *Emerge* magazine editor George Curry appeared curiously perturbed that Congressional Black Caucus chairperson Maxine Waters and I would even raise the issue at all. At the invitation of Caribbean heads of state, Representative Waters and I had organized a delegation of prominent Americans to undertake a four-day fact-finding visit to three of the threatened countries, Jamaica, Saint Lucia, and Dominica. The delegation included Jason Hill, the Black Entertainment Television news anchor and panelist on the black network's public policy show, *Lead Story*. During a *Lead Story* discussion following the trip, George Curry said dismissively that neither the banana issue nor the trip was a story worthy of coverage inasmuch as, in his view, I had attempted months before to stir interest in the issue and failed. Clarence Page wondered why the new chairperson of the Congressional Black Caucus would be "running around" the Caribbean, given all the more important things she needed to be doing at home.

No public policy issue in memory exceeded the banana trade issue in importance to the democratic English-speaking Caribbean. At risk were black regional democracies whose basic political and economic stability was being seriously undermined by the United States egged on by a single powerful, rapacious multinational corporation. White American mainstream political leaders and opinion shapers, however, thought the matter of little significance (as they thought the nations of the Caribbean in general to be). So, all too malleably, did many of their black counterparts.

Black social progress, both domestic and global, has historically been impeded by those among us of position and capacity who have been unwilling or, owing to conditioning, unable to explore and decode the evolving, complex global assaults against our peoples and nations, and hence unavailable to offer penetrating, original, and relentless advocacy.

This has likely always been so. I suspect this quiet undertow has been more particularly evident in the early stages of any new black-led foreign policy initiative, when there is cause but no cachet, when the chances of success are small, when few follow and some ridicule.

I am not without critical self-understanding. Blacks are, wherever on the planet we live, a battered and damaged people, estranged from one another in our long and calculated victimization. It is not easy to see through the keloid blinders of centuries-old scar tissue that isolate African-American from African, African from Caribbean, Caribbean from Afro-Latin— branches of a black world cast asunder by mean experience, time, and oceans; common-source victims hemmed into separate and narrow alleys of stereotypical distortion.

The daughter of Archbishop Desmond Tutu commented of African-American leadership of the U.S. antiapartheid movement that African-American interest in apartheid often appeared to exceed that of black South Africans because African-Americans, and not black South Africans, had been slaves. Mamphela Ramphele, widow of the martyred Steven Biko and one of South Africa's leading black academics, criticized the role of African-Americans in the Agency for International Development's new postapartheid $50-million ten-year higher education project: "You sometimes get the impression that blacks in America are trying to win political battles in South Africa they felt they never won at home."

After the virtual entirety of the African-American leadership had petitioned President Clinton to impose sanctions on Nigeria's military dictatorship, after countless protest demonstrations and civil disobedience arrests at the Nigerian embassy, Wole Soyinka, the Nigerian Nobel prize–winning playwright, wrote to me: "The role of the African-American community in the United States has been frankly disheartening. Even if the rest of the world feigns indifference, our kinfolk in the United States cannot fold their arms in complacency at the looming disaster that threatens to overtake Africa's most populous nation."

Damned when we do, damned when we seem not to.

Without the imposition of American economic sanctions, there would be no post-apartheid South Africa, no Mandela presidency, no democracy, no $50-million AID grant. Just as certainly, without the impassioned and irrepressible coaxing of African-Americans, there would have been no American economic sanctions imposed against the old South Africa to begin with.

As one can see, I am overly sensitive in these larger black family matters. Such is the consequence for us all of estrangement and, the downtrodden's albatross, the insidious tug of horizontal hostility.

Black South Africans may simply be little aware of the African-American contributions to their freedom. But clearly Mr. Soyinka, a thoughtful man, sees the problem of compassing in a phrase like "the role of the African-American community" a group one-third as large and just as diverse of view and activist inclination as Nigeria's populace.

As I have said, there are some African-Americans who would have our community ignore the Caribbean's plight. In the beginning, twenty years ago, there were African-Americans who thought it was unwise of me and others like me to apply our whole energies against apartheid, given the intractable problems of blacks in America. And so it is with Nigeria. There is no consensus that it should be a top priority for African-Americans. We are forever deluged at home. Catching rain with our hands. The bulletins arrive daily. Black neighborhoods redlined by banks. Black farmers denied U.S. Department of Agriculture loans. Black foresters discriminated against by the National Forest Service. Blacks denied service at Denny's. Black unemployment up. Black wages down. Continuing black victimization in all aspects of American life resulting in, according to one study published in the *American Journal of Public Health,* a higher incidence among African-Americans of high blood pressure, a potentially life-threatening disease. It is thus not hard to understand why those in immediate distress see un-immediate problems like Nigeria's crisis as remote.

In constructive counterbalance, however, to this compelling gravitational pull of domestic crisis are a growing number of African-Americans who believe that their work on domestic and foreign policy issues need not be mutually exclusive. The United States is now far and away the most powerful country in the world. Acting virtually alone and against the expressed will of the world, the United States effectively dismissed one United Nations secretary-general and imposed another. For American policymakers it is no longer a stretch to suggest that few places on the planet are beyond American influence and power. Black world citizenries cannot coordinate themselves with, explain themselves to, avail themselves of, or defend themselves against the might of the United States without the vigorous and salutary involvement of African-Americans in the development of American foreign policy.

It is a responsibility African-Americans have begun to take seriously. The antiapartheid movement is but one illustration of this increased interest and the success that it can bear.

PART FOUR

Moving Against Apartheid

American decision makers, who walk the power corridors of media, government, industry, and academia, are characterized by a blissful and self-serving forgetfulness. When the great global and domestic social problems that beset our society are divorced from their derivation or history, public policymakers do not feel constrained to attend to such problems before or beyond the predictable intermittent flare-up. Like impressive dreams that cannot be recalled moments after waking, Americans quickly forget about the crises whose evolution they never studied to begin with. The Somalias, the South Central L.A.'s, the Three Mile Islands—with the loss of media interest these dissolve quickly from all public memory. Policymakers then without solving much of anything, move on to the next lighted stage. And so it has been in the main with the problems of the black world: problems rooted in slavery, colonialism, de jure segregation, and persistent racism. The roots are all but forgotten, conveniently by whites, ill-advisedly by blacks. No slavery memorial stands on the Capitol Mall. It would only remind whites and to some unfortunate extent embarrass blacks. Thus the world's problems and pathologies are viewed by Americans only in their present dimension, without sight of instructive past or perilous future.

■ May 1981: Silver Spring, Maryland, and Washington, D.C.

The call was made in the early evening to my home on Park Valley Road in Silver Spring, Maryland.

"Mr. Robinson? Is this Randall Robinson of TransAfrica?" The caller's voice was nervous and uncertain.

"Yes." I had left my voice up in response to the mysterious hush in the caller's. There was a long pause. I thought the line had gone dead. "Yes," I said again, this time a little impatiently.

"Mr. Robinson, I am with the United States Department of State." The voice, deciding something, collecting resolve, had gotten louder and then modulated itself. "I have possession of classified State Department documents that describe the framework for a new alliance between the United States and the Republic of South Africa. This is awful. But there is nothing I can do to stop it."

The caller did not sound like a flake. I decided that it was best to say little and listen.

"How can I help you?"

"I am prepared to turn copies of the documents over to you, but my name cannot come into it."

"I don't think we should discuss this further on the phone. Would you be prepared to meet?"

"Yes. As long as you assure me that my name will not be disclosed. You don't know me but I have followed your work and I have decided that what's in these papers must be made public."

"Can you come to my home tomorrow evening?"

"Yes. What time?"

"Is seven all right?"

"Yes."

I gave the caller my address.

"I'll be there tomorrow at seven."

Introductions were made at the door. Looking out, I noticed no car in the driveway behind my beige 1976 Chevrolet. At my bidding, the caller edged into the living room and took the chair nearest the door. "I can't stay long."

"I understand. Please, may I get you something to drink?"

"No, thank you." The caller drew from a leather briefcase a sheaf of papers and placed them on the coffee table between us. After contemplating them for a moment, the caller took a breath.

"These papers were drafted for Secretary Haig by high-level State Department officials in preparation for the recent meetings held here with South African foreign minister Roelof Botha. Also, here is the paper prepared by Botha for Haig, which outlines South Africa's strategic commitments to the United States in this proposed new alliance."

I looked at the CLASSIFIED on each document. I then stacked them neatly and looked up.

"Use them as you see fit. This is a terrible and indefensible thing the administration is doing here. And please remember—"

"Yes. You have nothing to worry about."

I never saw the caller again.

■

The long and hellish ordeal of South Africa's black inhabitants dates back to 1652 when the Dutch East India Company founded a settlement at the Cape of Good Hope. By 1795 the whites known as Afrikaners or Boers had, through superior weaponry, conquered the indigenous blacks, the Khoisan people, and begun importing slaves from Indonesia, India, Ceylon, Madagascar, and Mozambique. In the late 1800s mining formed the basis for a South African industrial expansion fueled by wondrously rich gold deposits, the availability of cheap and controlled black labor, and the technical skills of American engineers and managers. As early as 1896 half of South Africa's mines were run by American engineers, one of whom, John Hays Hammond, had become the dominant force in South African mining two years before. American engineers brought with them to South Africa American equipment and American capital, which combined to establish an American foothold in South Africa's nascent industrial economy. It was also in the rapidly expanding mining sector that South Africa pioneered its unique system of labor control, along the way inextricably tying American companies and their burgeoning profits to the emerging institutions of South African white-minority rule.

In 1913 Parliament passed the Natives Land Act, which drove rural Africans from their farms and relegated them—seventy-two percent of South Africa's total population—to thirteen percent of the country's land, and indeed the least arable part. The new law virtually compelled Africans to work in the cramped, hazardous gold mines for meager wages that would remain stagnant for most of the twentieth century. When seventy thousand or more mine workers struck in 1946 for higher pay, South African troops drove them back into the mines.

Well before the layered corpus of racially discriminatory legislation was codified by Parliament in 1948 into full-blown apartheid, American corporations had become vital and enthusiastic partners in South Africa's growing machinery of racial tyranny. Many had arrived early and measurably enhanced the white minority's wherewithal to suppress the country's black majority. South Africa had none of what was strategically indispensable to its military: petroleum. By 1897 Mobil Oil had arrived to play a critical role in keeping the army supplied with oil, gas, and chemicals. General Electric came in 1899 and, with Honeywell and Allis-Chalmers, would later assist South Africa in building its nuclear industry.

By 1940 American general corporate investments in South Africa had mushroomed to $50 million. By 1981 it exceeded $2.6 billion. Parallel to this development ran a dramatic and systematic expansion of draconian racial strictures. To the Natives Land Act were added scores of restrictive laws, including the

Population Registration Act requiring the classification of people by race, and the Group Areas Act restricting the residence of blacks to remote areas zoned for them.

Black rebellion, always an undercurrent, boiled over in 1976 and 1977 with riots that spread from Johannesburg's black township of Soweto to black urban centers throughout the country. The police shot down more than 575 protesters, many of whom were children.

The South African economy was shaken by the resultant plummet in investor confidence. The International Monetary Fund, supported by the Ford and Carter administrations, responded with an eventual infusion of $464 million, exceeding the IMF total for all other African countries over the same period.

In May 1981, as Secretary of State Alexander Haig sat with South African foreign minister Roelof Botha on the seventh floor of the State Department to discuss a new era of friendship between the United States and South Africa, twenty-eight million black South Africans were completely without rights. They were required to carry racial identity passbooks. They had no right to vote, assemble, or express themselves freely. They had long before been stripped of their land, and they worked for a fraction of what whites received for comparable labor. They had no right to trial or counsel. Unlike African-Americans a generation before, they had no recourse to law or constitution. For them, no writ of habeas corpus could issue, no due process of law could obtain. The state and its laws and instruments of authority were all arrayed against them. Nelson Mandela was in his twentieth year of imprisonment.

Up until the inauguration of President Ronald Reagan in January 1981, the United States had responded to South Africa much as one would to a wayward blood relation—"he ain't much but he's ours"—with criticism heavily alloyed by acceptance and material indulgence. Breaking new ground, the incoming Reagan administration laid plans to make American acceptance of the white supremacist regime virtually unconditional.

It was this decision, taken quite cavalierly by Reagan administration officials, that would ultimately catalyze the American antiapartheid movement and lead to the eventual dismantlement of the apartheid system.

■

I read the classified documents three times that evening before going to bed. The administration in clear terms had offered to "open a new chapter" in U.S. relations with South Africa in exchange for two things: Pretoria's assistance in combating Soviet influence in southern Africa and cooperation in finding a solution to the problem of Namibia, the adjoining territory illegally occupied by South Africa.

The administration had in effect asked for virtually nothing. Pretoria had historically been rabidly anti-Soviet, and a promise on Namibia would be just a promise.

In exchange, Secretary of State Haig would pledge to South Africa that the United States would "work to end South Africa's polecat status in the world and seek to restore its place as a legitimate and important regional actor with whom we can cooperate." Crafted by the assistant secretary of state for African affairs, Chester Crocker, the new approach to South Africa would draw the U.S. away from "confrontation" and into a watershed relationship of "constructive engagement."

Upon returning to South Africa, Botha, foreign minister of the world's only constitutionally enshrined racial dictatorship, hailed the new American overture to his globally maligned government: "All round I found a much greater grasp and understanding, the ability to look at South Africa in a different light, to see the importance of the Cape [of Good Hope] route in a clear way, our strategic minerals and other things."

■

I trudged up the stairs and looked in on my six-year-old son, Jabari, who was soundly sleeping. I moved a few steps along the hall and poked my head into my ten-year-old daughter's darkened room.

"Goodnight, Daddy," whispered Anike.

"Goodnight, sweetheart."

I took a deep breath and entered the morgue of my bedroom.

The room was illuminated dimly by a streetlight across the sloping tree-lined lane. My wife was turned on her side toward the wall. I thought she might have been feigning sleep but I couldn't know.

We seldom talked, and when we did, we did so tightly, often arguing but never about what we were arguing about. I did not understand these discussions. They had about them a combustible illogic. We used vengeful voices that were not really ours. We appeared unable to talk to each other more than briefly in any other way. We stopped talking. And then there was nothing.

I tried to sleep but couldn't. I had all but decided what I would do with the classified documents. That was not what occupied my thoughts. The document language running through my head left an unshakable impression of a Haig foreign policy team that was indistinguishable in tenor from Roelof Botha's. I closed my eyes and saw them all sitting on the same side of the table laughing and proposing toasts to the new coming-out-together policy.

Botha, his florid face full with the relief of a mass murderer's absolution, is saying to Haig, "I knew you would understand us, I just knew you would, Al."

Haig smiles a beneficent smile at Botha, who Haig suspects may be slightly drunk. According to intelligence reports this is frequently the case. Haig, as he is reported to have actually done on occasion in White House meetings about Africa, starts to beat out tom-tom rhythms on the dark wood conference table.

The members of the South African delegation are silly with glee. The Reagan administration is too good to be true: these people don't care what we do to the blacks.

Form has broken down. Now the men in the room, all fiftyish and self-satisfied, begin to embrace and slap backs as if they are attending an affirmation rite of a secret society. Chester Crocker, scholar and architect of the new policy, wears a pinched smile as if he has exceeded his anal allowance for that day.

I woke up. It was 3:00 A.M.

The next morning I turned all of the documents over to Joe Ritchie, a writer for the *Washington Post.* Within two days the papers were authenticated by the State Department. The story ran a day later, on May 29, 1981, on the front page of the *Post.* Within a week the story was around the world.

I was informed by an acquaintance in the Department of Justice that the Reagan administration had begun exploring the possibility of bringing criminal charges against me.

Mayor Richard Hatcher of Gary, Indiana, was asked by members of TransAfrica's board of directors to convene a special meeting to discuss my failure to consult with the board before passing along classified materials. The discussion ended almost as sharply as it had begun with a question from a savvy labor leader: "If Randall is given top secret classified material again, how many here want to know about it, discuss it in an open meeting, and decide in a recorded discussion how to dispose of such documents? I, for one, would just as soon Randall not consult with me on a matter like that."

Later in the spring I went to Nairobi to address the Organization of African Unity. I was only the second American, after Malcolm X, to be so honored. I took with me copies of the classified documents and distributed them to every African foreign minister attending the conference. Ronald Reagan, Alexander Haig, and Chester Crocker had made plain how little they cared about the deepening misery of black South Africans, and I thought the world ought to know it, in great detail.

There is a tendency in public discourse to depersonalize the products and policies of government. U.S. DETAILS TERMS FOR CLOSER SOUTH AFRICAN TIES read the headline for the *Washington Post* story, which began, "The United States has indicated to South Africa in clear terms that it is willing to open a new chapter in bilateral ties . . ." Of course the United States hadn't indicated anything. Only shadowy government appointees who clawed their way to power had: men who may have been loved or unloved by their mothers, secure or insecure, misogynist or uxorious, racially bigoted or racially tolerant. From mammoth government bureaucracies, far-reaching policies are handed down daily by saints, wife batterers, philanthropists, drug addicts, Christians, race baiters, and xenophobes.

I do not know the motivations of the gray Reagan men who decided to accommodate apartheid. But anyone who could read on a sixth-grade level would easily have known that *accommodate apartheid* was exactly what they had done. Was it that they really wanted black South Africans to languish forever rightless? Or was it that they were genetically deficient in some natural ability to care? Were the black victims of apartheid invisible to them? Because they were black? Because they were victims? Because they were remote, faraway, expendable? Was much of this about money?

Years later I met with Chester Crocker and Jeff Davidow, a high-ranking Africa Bureau assistant to Crocker. The subject was Namibia and a recent meeting the two had had at the State Department with a black Namibian leader. During that meeting, the Namibian had taken exception to a point made by Davidow. "The next time he comes, we won't feed him," Davidow said. He smiled. I winced. Crocker remained impassive.

Then there was Haig.

By nature my brother was a more charitable man than I in the measure he took of people. There weren't many of whom Max spoke ill. The favorable assessments far outstripped the unfavorable. In his industry, among others, he liked Channel 9's Gordon Peterson and thought highly of Peter Jennings, his co-anchor on ABC's *World News Tonight.* (The other co-anchor, Frank Reynolds, he detested.) There was only one man in public life that I knew Max believed with conviction to be racist: Alexander Haig.

Not long after my return from Kenya, African-American leaders requested a meeting with Haig, very much in keeping with a tradition of regular meetings we had held with Secretaries of State Cyrus Vance and Edmund Muskie. Haig agreed, set a date, and submitted a list of the names of blacks he would receive at the State Department. My name was not on the list. Coordinated by TransAfrica's staff, the black leaders submitted the names of those we would choose to represent us in a foreign policy discussion, including mine and others not on Haig's list.

Responding, Haig indicated he would meet with no group of black leaders that included me. The black leaders made it clear to Haig that we would have to reserve the prerogative of selecting those blacks who would speak for blacks.

No meeting was ever held.

Spring 1981: Washington, D.C.

American official tolerance for apartheid amounted to a great deal more than an inadvertent policy jag for the Reagan administration. Six weeks after his inauguration, on March 3, 1981, President Reagan had made a nationally televised speech in which he described South Africa as a friendly nation, a country of strategic consequence to the free world, and a wartime ally. (The President should have known that during World War II South Africa's Afrikaners had been sympathetic to Germany and that many members of the Pretoria government had been interned by the British because of their collaboration with the Nazis.)

On March 9, five senior South African military intelligence officers arrived in Washington for meetings with officials of the National Security Council and the Defense Intelligence Agency. The meetings, a violation of an existing ban on meetings with South African military personnel, had been arranged by John Sears, a registered agent for South Africa and Reagan's former campaign manager.

More emboldened than ever, the Pretoria regime moved to expand its efforts to preserve apartheid at home and hegemony over the region. The whole of southern Africa had become a war zone. Since Portugal's withdrawal, Pretoria had militarily undermined Mozambique, supported with arms the white minority's faltering effort to hold on in Rhodesia, menaced Angola, and invested heavily in its war efforts in Namibia against the independence-seeking soldiers of the South-West African People's Organization (SWAPO).

A week after the five South African intelligence officers arrived in Washington, South African Air Force jets decimated a SWAPO base in Lubango, Angola, two hundred kilometers north of the Angolan-Namibian border, marking South Africa's deepest incursion into Angola in six years. On April 30, 1981, the Reagan administration joined with Great Britain and France to veto four United Nations resolutions calling for sanctions against Pretoria.

Over the next three years, the administration would continue on its course of attempting to remove South Africa's "polecat status in the world." Sales to the South African military were renewed. Nonbinding UN Security Council resolutions condemning South Africa were routinely vetoed by Washington. The Commerce Department granted a license to export a Sherry Univac 1100 series computer to South Africa's arms-producing corporation, ARMSCOR, which was owned in major part by the South African government.

In September 1982, CIA director William Casey would meet in South Africa with military and government leaders to propose, according to press reports, a U.S.-backed cordon sanitaire that would secure South Africa's borders.

Two months before Casey's visit, I would make available to the Washington press a leaked classified State Department cable that described South Africa's intention to seek a new loan from the International Monetary Fund. In the wake of this disclosure, Secretary Haig would advise South Africa to delay its application until after the World Bank meetings scheduled in Washington for early fall. On November 4, with U.S. support, the IMF would approve a loan to South Africa in the amount of $1.1 billion.

It seemed the captains of white Western political society and technology still believed that they, alone among men, could reconstitute nature and reverse the mysterious and inexorable tides of global history. Vietnam, Cuba, Afghanistan, Guinea-Bissau had taught them little. They proceeded apace in arrogant blindness. They owned much of the world and ran it from small rooms.

Despite the white world's massive provision of arms, technology, resolutions, loans, markets, and investments, South Africa's grip on the region it had dominated for two centuries was slowly slipping away. After five hundred years, Portugal had withdrawn its armies and retreated home with everything it had brought that was not attached to African soil. Pressure on Pretoria to relinquish control over Namibia continued to grow. The buffer of sympathetic states had been breached. South Africa, now exposed from without, was vulnerable from within as well. In December 1982 the African National Congress would detonate several bombs at nuclear power plants near Cape Town, calling the attack a warning to foreign investors. By then such urban forays were becoming routine.

By 1980, after fifteen years of bloody guerrilla war, white resolve in Rhodesia had begun to crumble. Ian Smith, Rhodesia's prime minister who represented only a three-percent white minority, found himself hopelessly pincered between global economic sanctions and the African armies of the Zimbabwe African National Union and the Zimbabwe African People's Union. In April of that year Robert Mugabe, following his renamed country's first democratic election, became Zimbabwe's first African prime minister. The tide had now reached South Africa's northern and eastern borders.

I and other blacks, in and out of Congress, had worked tirelessly to support President Carter's resolve to sustain American compliance with the global economic sanctions imposed against Ian Smith's white minority regime. The work had borne fruit.

On April 18, 1980, I was seated in Rufaro Stadium in Harare as Zimbabwe's prime-minister-elect Mugabe, Britain's Prince Charles, and the two victorious African armies marched in. The African crowd overflowed into the surrounding streets. Bands played. Bob Marley, then near death, performed. The prince lowered the Union Jack, and the flag of the world's newest nation unfurled against the night sky. I was sitting beside a black South African woman named Louise Africa who cried unashamedly as the flag lurched upward on its pulley rope.

As if to importune the gods, she said over and over in the

tones of a mantra, "Please let me live to see this happen in my country."

Nearly overcome, I said, "You will live to see it, Louise. I know that you will live to see it."

■ August 1982: Washington, D.C.

I was sprawled across the couch in the basement reading the Sunday paper. My wife came halfway down the steps to tell me she was going out for a while with the children.

That was how our marriage ended.

We had been lonely together for a long time. I felt grief for Anike and Jabari. I would not see them every morning and night into their adulthood. Those who rationalize earnestly about the resilience of children understate the cost of a parent's absence. I have come to know this more keenly through the years and not without feelings of guilt.

Parents can never become known well to their children through discussion and self-description. Either by commission or omission, good parents lie persistently, and rightly so, to their children. About their extended disappointments and foibles. About the events of their adolescence. About their sexual behavior and use of coarse language. About their ambitions and failures. About happiness as expectation. In essence, about who they are. We rear our children from behind a facade of reasonable double standard. We rear them as we were reared. We have little choice in the matter. I never knew what Mama and Daddy wanted either from life or from each other. Parents don't talk of such. In our youth they mercifully decline to burden us with friendship.

Children can only know their parents from what they feel and observe. Love is to be felt—from presence. From day-to-day observation, children gather data often to be stored and formed into insights at a time later in life when the child reaches the age the parent was when misunderstood. As a child I thought Daddy with all his immense physical courage to be stronger than Mama. I grew up to know and understand them both quite differently.

It disturbed me that a constant view of me had been prematurely closed off to my two oldest children. It bothers me that they still may not know definitively who I am. Nor I them. It is not the sort of deficit one can easily talk away, even in a now warmly shared parent-child adulthood.

■

The family is also worried about Max. He has become rich and famous but he is not happy. He is a journalist but he reads the news and he is not pleased with himself. It was Jewell who always aspired to be an actor. Max, I fear, now despairs that he has become one. The network has given him far less opportunity to practice interpretive journalism than it has afforded many of his colleagues, some of whom are not anchors and, doubtless are less talented than he. It rankles him that he has not been assigned to cover a national political convention or other event of that magnitude. The work climate in which he now finds himself could be both cause and effect of a speech he made recently at Smith College in which he charged that American news organizations, including his own, are infected with racism. ABC executives were upset. Max had only told the truth. Ask black journalists, many of whom Max has gone well out of his way to assist in their apprenticeship. He is a gifted man, troubled by a racist work environment he has remarked on to his detriment. But there is more to what is tormenting him, with the false god Celebrity a new and needless exacerbation.

Life is not static. Happiness as a constant, unless one is simpleminded, cannot exist. The best one can hope for is a chance for happiness allotted to the fortunate in periods of contented existence. Most of us, I suspect, have little talent for exploiting the chance that, in any case, only blind fortune provides. Buried under modern life's here-and-now burdens upon our inner selves, we spend our short lives seeking relief looking for-ward—to the work day's end, to Fridays, to next year's vacation, to retirement, to the very day before the event we avoid only because we fear it. The only chance for happiness to my mind is little more than a newborn inner self unmarred by the psychic blight that arrives for the cursed like a birthmark and bedevils the length of life.

Never in his life has Max been happy. He has not been gifted with a chance. The demons he never talks about are always there. He has become erratic in his work, and women are more than lavish in their attentions to him. He drinks to excess. He is at the same time generous, principled, and decent of spirit. Bravely so, through unrelenting pain. I love him but I do not know how to help him. No one can.

December 1982: Washington, D.C.

I seemed to be spending more time with Jeanie and Jewell now that I was alone. Anike and Jabari lived with me a third of the time. For the balance, my sisters had taken seriously to sistering, accompanying me to concerts, stores, and movies. I had no thought of dating.

I was spending a great amount of energy on antiapartheid issues to no visible effect. There were many who must have felt this way. Edgar Lockwood and Chris Root of the Washington Office on Africa lobbied Congress tenaciously for sanctions but produced no result beyond valuable public education. The American Committee on Africa under the leadership of Jennifer Davis, a white South African, continued to disseminate research materials nationally that sharpened public advocacy but accomplished little else.

I had appeared on panels and keynoted conferences in London, Toronto, Geneva, and Amsterdam. The conferences were always well funded and taken seriously by globetrotting antiapartheid participants who debated ad nauseam resolution language that interested no one save the framers. The resolutions could not be implemented, in any case, because so little time separated one conference from the next and so many of the antiapartheid conferees attended all of the conferences. I was to learn that this was in fact what many of us *did*. The *talk* about the fight against apartheid *was* the fight against apartheid.

In early December I prepared to attend another such conference, in Harare. A statement had been drafted for me by a twenty-eight-year-old TransAfrica volunteer who had only days before migrated to Washington from Saint Kitts via Halifax, Nova Scotia, and Montreal. Her name was Hazel Ross. The statement was brilliantly written. Ross had heard about TransAfrica upon her arrival in Washington, liked our work, and wanted a full-time position. Her résumé was impressive. She had an MBA from Montreal's Concordia University, had been a senior financial analyst in the international division of the Royal Bank of Canada, and, perhaps most impressive to me, had made an A in calculus while in graduate school. She had a poetic command of language and a serious presence.

At the same time, though, I wasn't certain how to weigh any of the above—or very much else, for that matter.

She was also, I observed uncomfortably, very pretty.

■ July 1983: Washington, D.C.

Frank Reynolds just died. At the funeral service yesterday Max was slated to sit beside Nancy Reagan. He did not attend. Network officialdom is livid. Max is unrepentant.

■ September 1984: Washington, D.C.

Ronald Reagan was the leader of the Western world and the most powerful man on earth. P. W. Botha (no relation to Roelof "Pik" Botha) was the aging but tough prime minister of South Africa. He had scaled the ranks of his all-white National Party without benefit of a college education. Not a man for nagging nuance and philosophical complication, he remained, despite growing pressures for change from home and abroad, inflexibly committed to the idea of unadulterated white minority rule. In Ronald Reagan he could believe he had discovered a kindred spirit. The two men had much in common. They were both old. They were both doctrinaire. They were both, quite apparently, unmoved by the lots of their respective racially downtrodden. And they would soon unwittingly combine as incendiary dinosaurs to light the fire of a global movement that would erase apartheid from the face of the earth.

On September 3, Prime Minister Botha implemented a new South African constitution that provided for a tricameral parliament including a controlling body for whites and separate decorative bodies for South Africa's Indians and Coloreds (mixed race). Blacks were excluded altogether from representation. Riots broke out in black townships across the country. Twenty-nine blacks were killed near Johannesburg alone. The country was coming to a low boil.

Within weeks Botha arrested the virtual entirety of South Africa's complement of black trade union leaders. The UN

General Assembly deliberated on a nonbinding resolution that condemned the arrests. The resolution passed overwhelmingly. The United States abstained.

Abstained? The United States of America had *abstained*?

I was incredulous. It was a resolution of moderate criticism, and Ronald Reagan had declined for us all the merest gesture of sympathy, ignoring with a shrug hypocrisy's gentlest, most perfunctory demand.

An unthrottled old racist visigoth was killing, torturing, and cowing dark souls by the thousands. The bravest were dying hideous deaths in custody. Dangling in cells. Falling from windows. Imploding from blunt-force trauma. Mothers' headstrong adolescent children "disappearing." Fathers dying alone in unventilated mine shafts, a mile down, a thousand miles distant. Organizations banned. Leaders arrested. Leaders banished. Leaders shot. Thousands flooding into exile.

The United States had abstained. Reagan had absolved Botha with what summed up to a tacit endorsement. My country. This two-faced democracy. This peacock that would not see itself.

I was disordered with anger.

How long ago had the exiled ANC leader Thabo Mbeki come to see me? A month? Two months? No matter. In the depressing limbo of exile, he had come seeking my help in arranging meetings with American officials. To make them see, listen. His family had paid a dear price for their convictions: a brother, Moeletsi, also in exile; a father, Govan, an ANC leader, serving a life sentence on Robben Island with colleague Nelson Mandela; a mother who stayed behind to be near her husband, perhaps never again to see her exiled sons.

The visigoth had arrested everybody arrestable, and the United States had abstained.

I called my chairman, Richard Hatcher. "Dick, I can't recall being angrier about anything than I am about this."

"It's an outrage," he replied.

"We've got to do something and the something's got to be dramatic."

"I agree. We can't let this kind of thing slide by."

"I've got an idea, Dick, but I don't think it would be wise to talk about it on the phone. Let me flesh it out, see if it's workable and get back to you."

I had to meet with three people, quickly.

My plan required the participation of a member of Congress, and Walter Fauntroy was the only one who I thought would seriously consider my proposal. Fauntroy was the representative from the District of Columbia, a local pastor, and a trusted lieutenant to the Reverend Martin Luther King Jr. during the civil rights movement. We met in his office in the Rayburn House Office Building. The discussion was short.

"What do you think?" I asked.

"I'll do it," he said without ceremony.

I met next with Mary Frances Berry, a lawyer, college professor, and member of the U.S. Civil Rights Commission, over lunch at the Mayflower Hotel on Connecticut Avenue.

"Of course," Berry said with a steely smile. "I'm as upset as you and it's the right thing to do."

A day later I talked with Eleanor Holmes Norton at her home on Capitol Hill. Norton was a nationally prominent Georgetown University law professor, former chairwoman of the Equal Employment Opportunity Commission, and member of several Fortune 500 corporate boards. Years later she would succeed Fauntroy as the District's representative in Congress.

"If that's the role you think I should play, I'd be happy to do it," said Norton.

"I'll try to schedule the meeting and then get back to Walter and Mary and you. I'd like to get this done before Thanksgiving."

In the first week of November, Hazel Ross called the South African embassy on Massachusetts Avenue and requested an appointment for Fauntroy, Berry, Norton, and me with South Africa's ambassador to the United States, Bernardus G. Fourie. The woman on the phone, who spoke English with a decided Afrikaans accent, was polite. "May I tell the ambassador why they wish to meet with him?"

"They would like to discuss with him the current problems in South Africa and how the United States might be more helpful," Hazel answered smoothly.

"Very well. I will call you within a week with Ambassador Fourie's answer."

Three days later Hazel received a call from the embassy. It was the woman with whom she had spoken earlier. "Ambassador Fourie would be pleased to meet with the group on Tuesday next at two p.m. if that would be convenient for them."

"I am all but certain that they will be able to be there at two on Tuesday." Hazel was careful now to restrain the pace of her speech.

We were somewhat surprised. We had never quite believed a meeting would be granted. The four of us and our views were well known to the ambassador.

I began to lay plans with our staff members. Cecelie Counts, a Harvard Law graduate and a superb organizer, would go with us to the embassy at the appointed time. Someone else would visit the embassy beforehand on a pretext of general interest and provide us with a detailed report, including floor plans. During the Tuesday meeting, Hazel would remain at the TransAfrica office with David Scott, a Brown University intern, to handle inquiries and make phone calls to a long and laboriously constructed list.

The following day Hazel received a call from the woman at the embassy. "I am very sorry to inconvenience you, Ms. Ross, but we've run into a scheduling problem."

Hazel's breath caught.

"The ambassador has a conflict and will have to reschedule your meeting for a later date."

Hazel paused. "Can you suggest some days now when the ambassador will be available?"

"No. I'm afraid I'll have to get back to you."

Our hopes dimmed. "Do you think they know?" I asked Hazel.

"There was no way to tell from our conversation. She sounded sincere, but I don't know."

Five days passed before the woman from the embassy called again. "Ms. Ross, the meeting has been rescheduled for Wednesday, November twenty-first, at four p.m. Is that acceptable to you?"

"Yes, I'm sure it will be."

"Now just let me reconfirm that attending the meeting will be Congressman Fauntroy, Dr. Berry, Ms. Norton, and Mr. Robinson. Is that correct?"

"Yes, it is."

"Then we will see them on November twenty-first."

Wednesday, November 21, was the day before Thanksgiving, always a slow press day in the nation's capital. We couldn't have chosen a better date ourselves.

■ November 21, 1984: Washington, D.C.

Bernardus G. Fourie was a kindly-looking septuagenarian with bushy black eyebrows and a face of deeply lined planes and sharp angles. At a second glance, one noticed that the eyes were friendly. His white hair was parted slightly to the left of center and combed almost straight back. The face vaguely reminded one of the economist John Kenneth Galbraith; perhaps because of that, one felt that it ought to be on a taller body. Fourie was a small, frail-looking man who moved with a slight but detectable tremor. There was something incongruous about the whole of him. While he massaged his horn-rimmed glasses like a talisman, his eyes, though smiling, betrayed a spirit stronger by half than the failing flesh.

We were seated in his office on the second floor of the South African embassy. Through a large window you could see the statue of Winston Churchill outside the British embassy across the street.

Seated next to the ambassador, on a couch, was a tall thin man in his early forties introduced to us as Herbert Beukes. Another man, meaty, glowering, unexplained and unintroduced, sat at an angle that suggested he would not be a part of the discussion.

We likely knew as much about Fourie as he had been able to learn about us. He was a conservative Afrikaner and, inside the Boer laager, he was regarded as a venerable and tireless exponent of apartheid's merits.

I cannot recall how the discussion began, but from the look on the ambassador's face, after twenty minutes of it things appeared to him to be proceeding swimmingly. We were pleased as well, if for quite different reasons. Fourie wanted to explain his government's policies to us and we had reason to listen as long as he wanted to talk. After a time he almost audibly relaxed as if deciding that these black leaders were more reasonable than he could have hoped. At the forty-minute mark, he even seemed to be enjoying himself.

Eleanor Holmes Norton excused herself, as planned, and left the embassy. The discussion went ahead for another ten minutes until an aide to Fourie entered the room and asked if the ambassador would step outside for a moment. Smiling, Fourie excused himself and followed the aide through the door. He was gone for no more than seven minutes. He returned wearing a face we had not seen. Written there were embarrassment, rage, confusion, and a hint of fear.

Fourie took a few steps into the room but did not sit. Before he spoke, he cast a troubled glance at Congressman Fauntroy. "We're getting calls from the press. Mrs. Norton is outside telling the media that the three of you will not leave the embassy until your demands are met."

"That is true," I said simply.

There was a lengthy silence.

"Mr. Ambassador," I said quietly, "please convey for us to your government our basic demand, which is twofold. All of your government's political prisoners must be released immediately. These would include, among others, Nelson Mandela, Walter Sisulu, Govan Mbeki, the thirteen labor leaders arrested recently without charge, and the three black leaders who have taken refuge in the British consulate in Durban. We are further demanding that your government commit itself immediately and publicly to the speedy dismantlement of the apartheid system with a timetable for this task."

At the same time that I was addressing Ambassador Fourie, Eleanor Holmes Norton was speaking outside to a massive gathering of journalists representing all of the American television and radio networks, the wire services, and every important news publication in the country. As television cameramen jostled for position, Norton raised her voice above the Massachusetts Avenue rush-hour traffic. ". . . our own government is no recourse for us at this point. The Reagan policy of constructive engagement amounts to little more than letting the South African government go and do what it feels like doing. . . . We felt we had to do something. If there was a government in Washington that looked like it was going to use its pressure, even diplomatically, on the government in Pretoria, we wouldn't be here tonight."

Behind the press throng and jamming the sidewalks in front of the embassy were chanting demonstrators. We could barely hear them through the glass of the ambassador's second-floor window. "Freedom yes! Apartheid no! Freedom yes! Apartheid no!"

Ashen-faced and speechless, the ambassador appeared to be locked in some purgatory of indecision. Nothing in his upbringing, in his training, in seventy years of assumptions about us and himself, had prepared him for this. He looked again at the fifty-one-year-old Walter Fauntroy. "You are a member of the United States Congress." The statement had to it a beseeching quality.

"I am indeed a member of the United States Congress and I am there because I have devoted my life to civil rights and the pursuit of racial justice. I am here for the same reason."

The ambassador turned and left the room. We sat silently in the ambassador's office with Herbert Beukes and the meaty man who remained mute. We sat like this for twenty minutes, the quiet broken only by the chants wafting to and away from us on the shifting late fall breeze.

Beukes said, "Is there anything we can do to work this out?"

"You can comply with the demands," said Mary Frances Berry with her typical intimidating self-confidence.

"No," said Buekes. "I mean, is there anything we can do other than that?"

"No," said Berry simply, settling the matter.

In our planning meetings we had talked about the responses available to Ambassador Fourie and his government. Of course, we had no expectation that our substantive demands would be met. We saw Pretoria as having three options. (Undoubtedly it was Pretoria that would decide and Pretoria that Fourie had called the moment he left us in his office.) They could elect to unceremoniously pick us up and dump us onto the embassy lawn. They could allow us to stay in the embassy through the Thanksgiving weekend without food, water, heat, or light. They could have us arrested. We calculated that Pretoria, regarding us as little more than cheeky American "kaffirs," would lose all sense of judgment and have us arrested—a course, at that very moment, being aggressively opposed on the phone to Ambassador Fourie by Pretoria's registered lobbyist, who was also a former member of Congress. Arrest was the worst possible choice, Fourie was admonished.

"If you do not leave the embassy immediately," said Fourie, reentering his office, "I will have you arrested."

There is a God, I thought.

Six uniformed U.S. Secret Service officers entered the ambassador's office and read warnings to us three times at twenty-second intervals. We were then handcuffed, removed from the ambassador's office, and led through a thick crowd of press and cheering demonstrators. We were driven to a D.C. police substation in Northwest Washington and charged with unlawful entry of an embassy, a misdemeanor that could draw a sentence of up to six months in jail and a hundred-dollar fine. Pending a hearing in D.C. Superior Court on Thanksgiving morning, Congressman Fauntroy and I spent the night in a cell at the police department's central cellblock. Mary Frances Berry spent the night in the D.C. jail's facility for women.

The story made every network and the front pages of the *Washington Post,* the *New York Times,* and the *International Herald Tribune* published in Paris. It had become global news before we were released on Thanksgiving morning.

We had been visited in jail that evening by Congressman Charles Rangel and the Washington mayor Marion Barry, who had said to the *Washington Post,* "I am sympathetic with their protest against the apartheid system of South Africa. My heart and mind and soul are with them." Calls of support poured into

TransAfrica's office well into the night. Not everyone, however, from whom we might have expected support was happy. The call, made with a familiar hoarse voice, was given to Hazel to handle. The caller, clearly angry, had asked for me and, when told I was unavailable, spoke bluntly to Hazel. "This is Harry Belafonte and I am a member of the board of directors. I want to know who authorized Randall to go into the South Africa embassy. The board never discussed this . . ."

On Thanksgiving morning following our release from jail, I met at my home on Geranium Street in Northwest Washington with Hazel and Congressman Fauntroy. Berry and Norton could not make the meeting but agreed to join us in a press conference scheduled the next day at 11:00 A.M. in a Rayburn House Office Building full committee hearing room.

We talked that morning for two hours about steps we could take to harness and build on what was developing into a groundswell of support. We decided to set up a steering committee of national organizations and leaders with TransAfrica as the lead institution. The structure would exist, as first conceived, only for coordination of continuing demonstrations and arrests at the embassy. We would test the depth of public interest and discover how far it would take us.

As we talked on, we concluded that civil disobedience demonstrations, notwithstanding their publicity value, were of no real consequence unless we could push sanctions legislation through Congress on a parallel track. This was our chance to impose on South Africa meaningful punitive economic measures. The chance might never come again. We would have to quickly design a campaign with synergistic balance between demonstrations at the embassy and lobbying on Capitol Hill. We ended our discussion by agreeing on a name for the new national campaign.

The next morning, to a press gathering of more than one hundred journalists and a score of television cameras, Congressman Walter Fauntroy, Mary Frances Berry, Eleanor Holmes Norton, and I announced the founding of the Free South Africa Movement. Its principal objective would be the passage of comprehensive economic sanctions against South Africa. We could anticipate a Reagan veto but we would cross that bridge when we came to it.

On the Monday following Thanksgiving the daily demonstrations began at the embassy. They were scheduled to last for one week with Cecelie Counts of TransAfrica's staff as coordinator. They lasted without interruption for well over a year. Not a single weekday went by without an arrest. On some days the number of those arrested exceeded two hundred, with the number of demonstrators lining Massachusetts Avenue reaching five thousand. In snow, sleet, rain, frigid cold, and searing heat, they came from near and far to march. Bill Lucy led hundreds of trade unionists to the embassy for arrest; Gay McDougall brought a thousand lawyers to march; John Jacob brought the national Urban League convention. A clergyman drove a busload from a small town in the Midwest. Big-city mayors like Detroit's Coleman Young were handcuffed with the small-city mayors of Annapolis, Maryland, and Highland Park, Michigan. Coretta Scott King was carried away with her children Yolanda, Bernice, and Martin. Rory Kennedy and her older brother Douglas were arrested days before their uncle Senator Edward Kennedy came to address the crowd.

The mayor's wife, Effie, went to jail with hundreds of city workers. Led by senior congressmen Ronald Dellums, Charles Rangel, and Julian Dixon, every member of the Congressional Black Caucus save two went to jail. Jesse Jackson was arrested, as were all his children, and my son Jabari as well.

Stevie Wonder was mobbed by crowds outside my office before he would be handcuffed at the embassy an hour later. Lowell Weicker, a Republican from Connecticut, became the first and only United States senator ever arrested in an act of civil disobedience.

Over the course of 1985 Arthur Ashe, Gloria Steinem, Congressman Ben Cardin, United Mine Workers president Richard Trumka, *and* Harry Belafonte would count themselves among the more than three thousand people arrested in Washington at the South African embassy.

And the movement spread across the country. California state assemblywoman Maxine Waters camped with a group of protesters in the lobby of the South African consulate in Beverly Hills. The Reverend Herbert Daughtry, activist Elombe Brath, and others organized massive turnouts at South Africa's consulate in New York City. From Boston to Houston, Chicago to Pittsburgh, the demonstrations continued to grow, with more than five thousand arrested nationally by the end of 1985. Black and white. Young and old. From sea to shining sea.

There would be low moments. As the days stretched into the hundreds—two hundred, three hundred, and beyond—the turnout on the coldest, shortest late afternoons of winter would sometimes shrink beyond our ability to form a small circle of pickets. Cecelie Counts, who was there every day, would say that by month nine she had begun to experience symptoms of "picketitis," a disease that causes one to involuntarily walk in circles even when at home. Against reason, we persevered.

In the early months, many thought our efforts futile. Just before the arrests in Ambassador Fourie's office, a dear and brilliant friend tried vigorously to dissuade me from carrying out the plan. "You will look foolish and juvenile," he had said. He hadn't understood what made us feel that we had no choice. He likely thought us all hopelessly quixotic.

Years later, I would be arrested alone in the Ethiopian embassy as crowds and cameras rushed past our six pickets to get to a huge demonstration at the Chinese embassy a half block away. The crowds were protesting the Chinese government's suppression of prodemocracy demonstrators in Tienanmen Square. The seven of us were protesting the brutal policies of Ethiopia's dictator Mengistu Haile Mariam. I was arrested on that hot summer day and chained to a wall in an unventilated D.C. jail cell. The demonstration at the Chinese embassy won front-page coverage in the *Washington Post.* My arrest was noted in a two-inch box story sandwiched in the back of the paper between the obituaries and the classified ads. While a great deal more attention had been paid to the human rights dilemma in China than to the harsh conditions besetting Ethiopians, the crimes inflicted upon the citizens of the two countries were of equal moral, if not quantitative, dimension.

The prospect of success never factors large in the planning calculations of human rights advocates. Berry, Fauntroy, and I had no reason to believe at the outset that our visit to Fourie would result in anything more than our arrest and imprisonment. From the blind side of knowledge, absurdly to some, we did it anyway. We did it because our action carried with it a slightly better chance of success than doing nothing and, more important, we did it because it was, as Berry had said, the right thing to do.

It was this overriding consideration that sustained us all when quitting seemed a sensible choice. Those who marched month in and month out with stoic consistency appeared to intuitively understand that the most estimable behavior was that which was unwatched and practiced selflessly without promise of glory or success.

The white-haired Jake Wells, tall and regal in retirement, appeared at least twice a week throughout the campaign. Pulitzer Prize winner Roger Wilkins, a steering committee member, often brought his three-year-old daughter, Elizabeth, who traveled above the marchers on her father's shoulders. Mark Sharp, an NIH research chemist, would arrive every Tuesday and Thursday in his wheelchair with his mother and his wife, Cecilia. Another retiree, Conwell Jones, became the movement's unofficial photographer, while Baba Ngoma became its drummer.

Peggy Cooper Cafritz, a prominent figure in the Washington arts community, organized large demonstrations on Mother's Day to remember the travails of South African mothers and celebrate the blessing of her own baby's birth.

There were of course snafus, often comic and sometimes operatic in scope. Once, as President Reagan was to deliver to Congress his State of the Union address, we laid plans to circle the capital with demonstrators bearing Glo-Lites that would be filmed from a helicopter by a local television station. As darkness fell, more than two thousand demonstrators joined hands around the Capitol as the helicopter rose into the sky. When the cameraman radioed us to turn on the Glo-Lites, we regretfully informed him that the Glo-Lites had gone missing. Then there was the time when two hundred out-of-town demonstrators waited in Congressman Fauntroy's church basement as we searched fruitlessly for the keys to the church bus that was to shuttle the nervous arrestees to the embassy.

All in all, things went smoothly in a multifaceted operation run on a shoestring budget and by a very small staff. On one occasion at the embassy, we would present Archbishop Desmond Tutu with a Freedom Letter signed by one million Americans. On another, Sylvia Hill, Congressman Fauntroy, Mary Frances Berry, Roger Wilkins, Bill Lucy, and I would shut down for days the currency exchange dealer Deak-Perera, occupying their offices by day and sleeping nights on a cold slate floor, in protest of the coin marketer's sale of South African gold Krugerrands. Late in the campaign we would take our protest to the State Department with thousands of demonstrators joined by actors Tony Randall and Paul Newman. By the close of our efforts, I had been arrested seven times, the last occurring at Shell Oil's office on Connecticut Avenue in protest of that company's relationship with South Africa's white minority regime.

In South Africa, by July 1985, the township uprisings had lasted more than a year and claimed more than seven hundred lives, causing the government to declare in most parts of the country a state of emergency.

The American television networks now broadcasted stories on South Africa's crisis nearly nightly, combining coverage of the broadening uprising in South Africa with footage from the embassy demonstrations in Washington. The legislative wheels had begun to turn as well with a clutch of punitive measures filed in both houses of Congress. At least weekly, we would meet with members of Congress to discuss legislative strategy. Many of these sessions were held in Senator Edward Kennedy's office. Usually attending from the Senate would be, in addition to Kennedy, Democrats Alan Cranston, Paul Sarbanes, Christopher Dodd, and Carl Levin. Lowell Weicker attended as a bridge to the Senate's Republican majority leadership, notably Richard Lugar and Nancy Kassebaum. Attending from the House would be Congressmen Fauntroy, Mickey Leland, Steven Solarz,

Merv Dymally, George Crockett, William Gray, and Howard Wolpe.

Congressional support for sanctions of relative severity had become broad and bipartisan. Perhaps the first sign of a shift that would bode ill for the white regime in Pretoria came soon after the initial embassy arrests in a letter from House Republicans to Prime Minister Botha demanding an end to apartheid.

This was something of a sea change from the period before, when all too many influential center-right Americans had energetically afforded South Africa's rulers the comfort of innocuous criticism. The damage in the U.S. had never really been done by the fruitcake fringe who expressly supported apartheid, but rather by a much larger community of eminently respectable people who opposed apartheid and opposed in virtually the same breath any punitive measure that would have helped end it. This group of business and political leaders had for decades successfully interposed itself between the advocates of sanctions and the regime they, wittingly or unwittingly, protected. J. Wayne Fredericks, the executive director of the International Government Affairs Office of the Ford Motor Company, seemed to have been speaking for the class when he testified before a Senate subcommittee in July 1978: "Ford is unequivocally opposed to the policy of apartheid. . . . Nonetheless, we believe that a legislative prohibition at this time on new investment, in the absence of convincing evidence as to the impact of such an action, is unwise."

All that changed after November 21, 1984. No longer was the question whether the United States would impose sanctions, but rather how severe the sanctions would be. The ground had shifted. J. Wayne Fredericks and his corporate peers would now struggle to expunge an old greed-fed alliance from memory and find new footing with those who promised to be the leaders of a new black-led South Africa.

By early 1986 the successful legislative initiatives of William Gray, Ronald Dellums, Steven Solarz, Julian Dixon, Edward Kennedy, Richard Lugar, Nancy Kassebaum, Charles Rangel, and others had been folded into the Comprehensive Anti-Apartheid Act of 1986, which for the first time mandated serious American economic measures against South Africa. As expected, President Reagan vetoed the bill.

Not surprisingly, the House of Representatives, with a large Democratic majority, overrode the Reagan veto on September 29. All of our hopes rode on the Senate vote scheduled for October 2. I sat in the gallery of the Senate chamber that evening between Coretta Scott King and Jesse Jackson. Awaiting the decision of the Republican-dominated Senate were all of the members of the Congressional Black Caucus circulating down on the chamber floor. Vice President George Bush was in attendance, hoping for a tie vote that he could break in favor of sustaining the Reagan veto.

The veto was overridden by a margin of 78 to 21. The Comprehensive Anti-Apartheid Act of 1986 had become law and with its passage was sounded that evening the death knell of apartheid.

We had won. We had turned the course of the most powerful country on earth. Democracy in South Africa, something I had pursued for nearly twenty years but thought I would never live to see, was within sight.

American sanctions provoked similar measures from the British Commonwealth and the European Community. Credit windows were closing to Pretoria across the world. Foreign Minister Roelof Botha, sensing the tide, had said: "The sooner sanctions come, the better. We will show the world that we have not been made soft." In reality, though, the Pretoria government had come to view its increasing economic isolation with galloping alarm.

South Africa's antiapartheid leaders had through the years been concise and singleminded in telling black leaders here what they wanted from us. "Sanctions are what we need from the United States," Johnny Makatini, the longtime ANC representative to the United States, would tell me time and again. "If black Americans will lead the effort to deliver economic sanctions, it will make for us a big difference. If you can do the job here, we can do the job at home."

African-Americans had led the Free South Africa Movement. U.S. economic sanctions had been imposed on South Africa. We had delivered.

Senator Lugar, Republican chairman of the Senate Foreign Relations Committee, would later say of the sanctions that he only reluctantly supported, "Sanctions did have an impact through our political relationship. . . . The ground shifted. There was a sinking feeling that life would never be the same again."

■

I thought about Albert Green (not his real name) recently, and how he has done in his life. I have not seen him since we were twelve in Sunday school at Fifth Street Baptist Church. Albert, even then, was such a contrast to me and, well, all of the Robinson children. Because I liked him, I never told him that I thought of him as Dudley Do-right. He never cursed. He did his homework in ink the moment he hit the door from school and may have worn a suit to Disneyland. I would guess that he achieved stable success as an accountant, actuary, insurance adjuster, or something along those lines. I would guess further that Albert has been happy enough, but not intensely or even consciously so, because he and others with life-plan linear personalities tend to husband their highs by spreading them out like annuity payments for rainy decades. They would much prefer to drive across a flat treeless Kansas than to chance the scenic narrow mountain roads of southern Spain.

Well along in the game now, I have found myself in occasional moments envying people like Albert who only drive on straight flat roads and always smack down the middle. Oh, I know I would have suffocated of boredom. In the grip of convention there is that, all right, but there is shelter as well. I have been tilting at windmills for a time now. I've had to beg my salary and salary for my staff for too many years. We don't sell a product. The fundraising cycle has frightening dips and we are never more than two months from the till's bottom.

But we have won a great battle. We won because neither Mary Frances nor Walter, Eleanor nor I was Albert, or ever could have been. That we have won, however, does not mean that the eminently respectable people for so long arrayed against us have lost. The powerful pause. They never lose. Not even the victims-turned-victors in South Africa will resist their overtures for long. The newly reconstructed white American moneymen, in and out of government, are more important to black South Africa's future than we are now. This is a practical world.

PART FIVE

Of Triumph and Tragedy

The indefatigable amongst us never sally forth to policy war needing as sustenance victory or recognition. Neither outcome is ever likely. Those of us who do this work do it often to small reaction and are met more frequently with defeat than success. But we do it still, for no clearer reason than that we somehow viscerally know we must. For bound up therein, more with the fight than its improbable fruit, is the lifelong defense we make of our very souls.

June 26, 1987: Virginia Beach Boulevard, Norfolk, Virginia

Mama remarried in 1977. His name is James Griffin, and he is a retired chaplain and former pastor of Banks Street Baptist in Norfolk, Virginia. We children, each in our own small way, tried very hard to dislike him but failed. He is self-evidently a fine man and has made Mama very happy.

Jewell has been working for the Smithsonian's National Portrait Gallery for some time. Nights she pursues her real passion, acting, appearing in plays put on by local theater companies.

Jeanie is toying with leaving teaching to attend divinity school. Ultimately she wants not to church-preach but to form a neighborhood ministry with a service mission. I like the idea. This would be real Christianity and, no doubt, off-putting to more than a few Sunday orators. Jeanie would do this well. She is far and away Mama's kindest and least self-absorbed child.

Max is on his way here today, along with family members from both sides, for my wedding to Hazel. The ceremony will be in the living room of Mama and Father Griffin's home. He will perform the nuptials. Jabari, thirteen, will be my best man.

The house is a comfortable ranch style. Mama sold the house on Thirty-ninth Street in Richmond and moved here after her marriage. Over the years, Father Griffin has invested prudently. While they are not wealthy, they are far from poor.

Mama has taken some pains to prepare for us. In the foyer is a pleasant-sounding string ensemble. The wedding cake is already on the dining room table and cut flowers are all about. Hazel's mother is here from Saint Kitts, as are two of her sisters, one from Toronto, the other down with her husband from Washington.

Love is the least logical of emotions. I had not intended ever to attempt love or marriage again. I thought I might never heal. Then I met Hazel. Is it conceit to find affirmation in discovering in another the very things you've come to know or believe privately about yourself, those obscure and complicated qualities that exist in one's deepest soul, qualities theretofore unilluminated, unappreciated, unseen by an outside heart? I can now share easily, wholly, without fear of misunderstanding. . . .

I have no gift for this. Words fail. Hazel is strong, smart, independent, irreverent, decent, generous, compassionate. These qualities I saw early and liked. Beyond these and whatever she saw in me, we found something I'd held little hope for, an indefinably wonderful love.

Hazel and I have taken the vows, kissed, served the cake, hugged a homeful of family. In a short while we are leaving for Dulles International to make the evening flight to Paris. A little earlier Hazel's mother whispered in her ear, "Is anybody going to say anything?" The question was in the minds of all those present from the Caribbean. After the vows in Caribbean weddings, family members render brief testimonials. And so we have done just that.

It has been a joyous occasion of aunts, great-aunts, siblings, cousins, nieces, nephews, mothers, mothers-in-law we care for and who care for each other.

Hazel and I are about to leave. So is Max, on his way to Mexico. He does not look well. He has been ill recently and has lost a great deal of weight.

◼ Fall 1987: Chicago, Illinois

I talked to Max a week ago. He has been plagued all summer with flu-like symptoms. He has not taken a drink in more than a year and is deservedly proud of his progress. Now this. The doctors ran a series of tests including a test for HIV although Max does not fit the profile for the virus. All the tests came back negative.

Then Max called this morning. He sounded very low. The test results had been wrong. "Randall, it's AIDS. I've got it."

"Oh, God. I'm so sorry, Max. I'm so sorry." Just days before, we were all so relieved to learn that whatever it was, it wasn't AIDS. I started to cry quietly.

"Are they . . . are they sure?"

"They say so," very softly.

"Jesus. Jesus."

Silence.

"I don't know wh . . . " I started and stopped.

"I know. I know," he said, now comforting me. "I have not lived well. I only hope that I can find the courage to die well."

Things could not have gone more wretchedly for anyone than they have for Max over the past two years. He left ABC to anchor the local news for a station in Chicago. The new position did not work out. Now he is doing only infrequent work with Essence television. His illness has also caused him to cancel a number of scheduled lectures.

Money, however, is not a pressing concern. He loves art and

has built a large collection of museum-quality paintings valued in the hundreds of thousands.

"Why don't you leave Chicago and move back here to Washington?" I asked.

"I think I'd rather stay out here, at least for a while."

We were quiet.

"I think I know where I got it," he finally said, naming a woman on the East Coast he had known for years.

"Why stay out there?" He lived alone in a high-rise apartment. Three marriages had failed, one to Hazel O'Leary, who would later become a cabinet member in the first Clinton administration. She would deny that they had been married. This both puzzled and irritated our family. What kind of person would do such a thing?

"I'd just feel more comfortable in Chicago, at least for a while."

■

In December, Jewell got a call from a Chicago friend of Max's. He had been hospitalized earlier in the day with pneumonia and was in critical condition. Mama, Jewell, Jeanie, and Hazel and I flew to Chicago that afternoon. Three of Max's four children arrived around the same time. Max had been placed on a respirator in the intensive care unit of Saint Francis Hospital. The doctor, a hospital resident, told us it was unlikely that Max would survive the night. He was suffering unendurably with every thimble of air fought after with strenuous heaves.

We took turns in the intensive care unit throughout the night. We couldn't be certain Max knew we were there.

In the morning, the doctor told us that he was unimproved and remained alive only because of the tremendous fight he was waging.

We lived in the hospital lounge for three days and nights with no cause for hope. We could see that Max was completely worn out by his exhausting efforts to draw the smallest measure of air into his lungs. The respirator appeared only to be prolonging his agony.

We cried alone in hallways and together in the lounge. We

prayed and waited, not knowing what Max would have us do. His ordeal seemed beyond any human being's capacity to bear. But bear it he did and with a heroic tenacity of which I'd never have thought him or anyone else capable.

A hospital priest had administered last rites. A staff person had made arrangements to deliver Max's jewelry and other personal items to us.

Weeks later Max walked out of the hospital. He would live for another year. But we thought it nothing short of a miracle that he had been given more time to live and for us to love him.

The marked road to death is known only to those who tread it. Dying is done alone. Staring into the abyss, it would seem no simple task to find easy fellowship with loved ones in robust health with prospects and plans for the distant future. In his shoes, I might have withdrawn from society, near and far. Max did not. When asked if he had ever said to himself *Why me?* Max replied, "I didn't ask 'why me?' when I was a national celebrity and making hundreds of thousands of dollars and I won't ask 'why me?' now."

In that final year we drew closer as a family, saying to each other the important things, leaving aside the extraneous. We took our cues from Max. Never for an instant pitiable, he gathered us to him. He held forth. He laughed. He touched. He loved. Never did his courage falter. Never was his dignity compromised. He left to us a gift of precious memories from those last times, a period that must have been one of the most fulfilling of his and our lives.

Not long after Max died, I received a long, poignant handwritten letter from Congressman Charles Rangel, who had lost a brother years before. I was ironically comforted to read that beyond grief over the death of a sibling, the odd feeling of incompleteness wears on forever in grief's wake. We are all perennially children arranged in the unbroken small circle of our first families. Max, Jewell, Jeanie, and I had been inseparable, discovering each other before fully discovering ourselves. From childhood, we had defined ourselves either in relation to or as parts of each other. Now Max was gone and with him much of us. We would never be completely whole again.

■

Moments after the original Senate passage of the Comprehensive Anti-Apartheid Act of 1986, Senate majority leader Robert Dole stopped me just outside the Senate chamber to congratulate me. Following our exchange, the expected Reagan veto came swiftly. The battle in the Senate to sustain the veto of sanctions against South Africa ensued, quickly becoming hot and furious. The vigorous if unsuccessful effort to rally Republican opposition to sanctions was led by the man who had congratulated me days before, Senator Robert Dole.

Though we won an important victory with the override of Reagan's veto and final passage of the act on October 2, I had no illusion that President Reagan, Senator Dole, and others who had opposed sanctions would give way compliantly to the call for strong enforcement of the new law. Congress may make laws but it is left to the executive branch of government to enforce them. For this the Reagan administration had little appetite. The administration wrote porous regulations and only halfheartedly enforced those. The sanctions, far less punitive than they might have been, leaked like a sieve.

At the beginning of 1988 P. W. Botha remained in control in Pretoria and as implacable as ever in his government's brutal efforts to maintain white political supremacy. Dole, unreconstructed in his opposition to sanctions, began his own run for the White House. Botha seemed still hopeful that his government could escape the tightening grip of rising unrest at home and spreading sanctions abroad. Our task was to see to it that he found no enhanced cause for hope in the 1988 American primary and general elections.

When Dole campaigned in New Hampshire and Iowa, we showed up with hundreds of students in New Hampshire and farmers in Iowa placarding and chanting Dole's sympathy for white minority rule in South Africa. We produced a television advertisement documenting his voting record and opposition to sanctions. The advertisement ran in New England but no Iowa television station would sell us airtime.

When asked by reporters about my efforts, Dole described

me as a "big lip liberal." Later when told by reporters that "big lip" could be interpreted as a racial slur, Dole explained that he had meant to call me a "big lib liberal," an artless concoction of novelty and redundancy.

We had elected to focus on Dole because his record on apartheid-related issues was worse by far than any of the other Republican or Democratic presidential primary candidates. Our larger objective was to keep the American public concerned about the plight of black South Africans. Sanctions had been tepidly in force for little more than a year. Apartheid's demise could not be taken for granted.

Not until the election of F. W. de Klerk to power in South Africa in the summer of 1989 and the release from prison of Nelson Mandela in February 1990 did I allow myself to believe that momentum toward democracy in South Africa had become virtually unstemmable.

Our work of nearly twenty years was finally coming to fruition. I had marched, testified, written, orated, debated, petitioned, proselytized, and committed repeated acts of civil disobedience. One day I had cochaired with Senator Edward Kennedy a meeting in the Senate's ornate Russell Caucus Room of American leaders and South African clergymen Desmond Tutu, Allan Boesak, and Beyers Naude. Virtually the next day I had gone to jail.

We had done everything seemly and imaginable in our efforts to turn the United States onto a humane course and keep it there.

■ October 1989: Luanda, Angola

Luanda, a city in need only of paint to be beautiful again, bends gently around the surf waters of the South Atlantic. It is the capital of Angola, an oil-rich and war-weary southwest African country the size of Texas.

I stood with Ibrahim Gassama of my staff and our Angolan foreign ministry escort on a hill overlooking the city and the Atlantic Ocean. From the tall grass of the elevated empty lot we followed the escort's gaze as he pointed out the buildings around us. The escort was a short small-boned man with an earnest manner. English, which he spoke with facility, was his fourth or fifth language after Kimbundu, Portuguese, and other national languages.

"Over here is the British embassy. Just beyond there a bit is the German embassy. See there. No. To the right. Yes. Slightly obscured by the trees. That is the French embassy. All of the Western governments have embassies here except your government, the United States. Why is that, Mr. Robinson?" He did not wait for my answer. "Your government says, Mr. Robinson, that it will not permit diplomatic relations with our country because of the help we are getting from the Soviet Union. This makes no sense to us because your government has diplomatic relations with the Soviet Union. The United States in fact has diplomatic relations with all of the communist governments of Eastern Europe but will have none with us, a developing country that presents no threat to U.S. interests. After all, Chevron, an American company, pumps our oil. We are truly mystified by America, Mr. Robinson."

He paused, appearing to calculate whether he had said too much to strangers. Abandoning caution, he added, "Is it because we are Africans?"

"Yes. I believe that, in part, is the reason," I said slowly but with conviction.

We were quiet for a time, looking out over the city, alone in our thoughts. Then our Angolan escort said, "Our government is saving this land here for the American embassy. Perhaps one day . . ."

Angola's bloody civil war had begun shortly after a fourteen-year armed rebellion against Portugal led to independence on November 11, 1975. The United States, South Africa, and much of western Europe had supported Portugal's defense of its colonial empire, leaving Africans throughout southern Africa with little choice but to seek military support from Warsaw Pact countries and humanitarian assistance from the liberal democracies of Scandinavia. When Portugal retreated, the United States under the guiding hand of Secretary of State Henry Kissinger threw its military support behind the Angolan guerrilla leader Jonas Savimbi, who with the further support of white minority-ruled South Africa was intent on overthrowing the new and widely recognized government in Luanda, now assisted in its defense by Cuban forces.

I do not intend in this narrative to plow the heartless dry ground of Kissingerian realpolitik, its principal proponent's stunning insensitivity to the pain of others, or his well-documented capacity for remote savagery. But might it not be a meritorious idea to have those who would underwrite slaughter go and survey the grisly results, if not be required to stand, face to the sky, under a rain of ordnance that they, the revered cowards, provided? Human beings—men, women, children, Angolans, Africans, black people, some who knew what the war was about and a large majority who did not—had died throughout Angola by the thousands, and were still dying.

We could not leave Luanda by road for fear of ambush by the soldiers America and South Africa had armed for Savimbi.

Ibrahim and I flew to the provincial capital of Huambo on an Angolan Airlines Boeing 737. With us were journalists from the *Washington Post,* National Public Radio, the *New York Times,* and CNN. The plane provided for our use was nearly empty. We took off after dawn and climbed steeply to a safe altitude. Approaching Huambo, the Angolan copilot emerged from the cockpit and told us, "To avoid antiaircraft fire we are going to have to make a steep dive to the runway." Then, the harrowing plunge.

The besieged city was in shambles. There were few undamaged buildings. Chunks of masonry littered the streets. We had a day-long round of meetings with local government officials who served tea and behaved as if we were not in the middle of a war zone. As the discussions wore on, I noticed through the sashless window a child hobbling along on one leg and a stick crutch. Following my line of sight, the local official said, "Land mines. They are everywhere. Some are from America. Some are from the Soviet Union."

The day before, we had visited an orphanage of hundreds of war orphans, more than a third of whom were land mine amputees. We saw more of the same at an overcrowded rural hospital where medicines were in short supply and the medical staff was overwhelmed.

The morning following a heart-in-the-mouth flight back to Luanda from Huambo, Ibrahim and I went to the British ambassador's residence to meet with Ambassador Michael John Carlisle Glaze, CMG. Glaze's wife stayed through the introductions and pleasantries, departing after tea. The ambassador was engaging, expansive, insightful, and candid. He, the voice of the conservative Margaret Thatcher in Angola, summed up America's cold-shoulder and hot-arms policy toward Luanda as "lunacy."

Later that evening we met at government headquarters with the president of Angola, José Eduardo dos Santos, a soft-spoken man of striking appearance and elegant bearing. I presented a letter signed by thirty-five members of Congress, including seven Republicans, inviting him to visit the United States.

"We will arrange to have you make your case directly to the

American people. You will meet with members of both branches of Congress. Your visit will provoke the news media to convey to the American people what our policies and arms are doing to the Angolan people."

"Will I be meeting with President Bush?" President dos Santos asked.

"We will do our best, but I do not know what the chances are."

While I thought the likelihood of President Bush agreeing to a meeting was small, I strongly believed that the visit would be worthwhile—though in ways I could not easily explain to someone largely unfamiliar with the constitutional mechanics of the American political system. If the visit went well and aroused the American public, we could discredit any further Bush administration sponsorship for Savimbi's killing machine.

"I feel strongly, Mr. President, that we cannot change American policy without your presence. A meeting with President Bush will be sought but we won't know the answer until after you have arrived. In any case, the real value of your visit will not turn on President Bush's decision."

He thought for a while. "Yes. Then I will accept your invitation."

After agreeing on a date for the visit, Ibrahim and I departed the next day for Washington via Paris. We had six weeks to make all the arrangements. We scheduled a tea meeting in the Senate and meetings in the House of Representatives with members of several committees. We began making media calls to NBC's *Today* show, *ABC's Nightline,* and the Sunday morning talk shows. Senator Edward Kennedy and his sister-in-law Ethel Kennedy agreed to host a dinner for President dos Santos at Mrs. Kennedy's home. Invitations were sent out. Nine days before the visit, we had heard nothing from the White House about George Bush's willingness to meet even briefly with Angola's president.

Seven days before José Eduardo dos Santos's scheduled arrival in the United States, I received a call from the Angolan ambassador to the United Nations. The government of Angola had canceled the trip. It was a simple matter of Angolan national pride. President dos Santos could not visit the United States and suffer a public rebuff from an American president who was, alone save South Africa, supporting efforts to violently over-throw Angola's globally recognized government. The hardliners in Luanda had won. Their government's decision was under-standable. The Bush administration's military support for Jonas Savimbi continued. All in the name of Soviet containment.

Within days of my return to the United States, Senator Orrin Hatch, Republican of Utah, wrote to Attorney General Dick Thornburgh urging that I be investigated by the Justice Department. "Mr. Robinson, by his own admission, is actively working to change a stated U.S. foreign policy. . . . Mr. Robinson should not be permitted to propagate Marxist propa-ganda under the cover of academic independence. . . . It is known that the Marxist regime financed Mr. Robinson's trip to Angola."

In fact, my trip had been paid for by the United Church of Christ. Senator Hatch reconsidered his request only after Anthony Lewis wrote in a *New York Times* column: "Even by the standards of extremist politics in this country, the Hatch letter is remarkable. I do not recall a senator charging that it is a crim-inal offense for an American to try to change a stated U.S. for-eign policy. James Madison and the other Framers of the Constitution thought they were creating a system in which citi-zens would do exactly that."

The morning Lewis's column appeared, Senator Hatch called me to apologize.

Hatch's singular obsession, communist containment, was the driving imperative in the formulation of American foreign policy for forty years after the end of World War II. Over this period the lion's share of American foreign assistance to Africa would go to six nominally anticommunist African despots, all uniformly undemocratic, repressive, corrupt. When the United States ended arms flows to Ethiopia's deposed Haile Selassie, the Soviet Union initiated arms flows to Selassie's successor, Mengistu Haile Mariam. Across the border from Ethiopia in Somalia, as the Soviets cut off arms to the ruthless dictator Siad Barre, the United States took over in 1977, pumping into Barre's arsenal and coffers during the next twelve years more than $200 million in arms and $887 million in overall foreign assistance, which enabled Barre to create the rubble of today's Somalia. The results were much the same with the other major American client-leaders of Zaire, Kenya, Sudan, and Liberia. In Zaire the CIA-imposed Mobutu Sese Seko had arguably become the world's wealthiest kleptocrat. During the 1980s the United States provided $500 million in aid to Liberian military dictator Samuel K. Doe, who had overthrown his country's longstanding, if flawed, democracy.

▮ July 1993: Washington, D.C.

On a brilliant early afternoon in July 1993, Nelson Mandela came to TransAfrica's beaux arts limestone building to meet with African-American leaders over lunch. Accompanying the man who would soon become the first black president of South Africa were African National Congress officials Thabo Mbeki, Barbara Masekela, and Lindiwe Mabuza. (Mbeki would later become the deputy president of South Africa and heir apparent to Mandela, Masekela would be appointed ambassador to France, and Mabuza, the ANC's representative to the U.S., would become ambassador to Germany.)

The horseshoe driveway was electric with Secret Service activity as the string of black sedans pulled to a stop.

Awaiting Mandela beneath chandeliers hanging from the ornate ceiling of the Du Bois reception room on the second floor were twenty-two influential African-Americans. Virtually all of them, in one fashion or another, had caused the United States for the first time to oppose in a meaningful way the South African apartheid machinery that had kept Mandela imprisoned for twenty-eight years. Congressman Ron Dellums, chairman of the House Armed Services Committee, had authored the only comprehensive antiapartheid sanctions legislation ever passed by the U.S. House of Representatives. Congresswoman Maxine Waters, even before coming to Washington, had shepherded state sanctions against South Africa through the California legislature. Congressman Charles Rangel, a member of the House

Ways and Means Committee, had seen to it that American corporations investing in South Africa were denied tax credits. John Jacob, president of the National Urban League, Dorothy Height, president of the National Council of Negro Women, and Ben Chavis, executive director of the NAACP, had all placed the issue of apartheid high on their organizations' list of concerns. Edward Lewis, publisher of *Essence,* and Earl G. Graves, publisher of *Black Enterprise,* had given space in their magazines to the issue and money to the cause. Johnnetta Cole, president of Spelman College, had urged college students to join the battle. Activist Sylvia Hill had been relentless in the campaign against apartheid. Vice presidents from Philip Morris and Anheuser-Busch, George Knox and Wayman F. Smith, had won sympathy from their companies and material support for South African democracy as well. Sugar Ray Leonard had given $250,000 to TransAfrica Forum's South Africa educational programs. Jesse Jackson had given years of inspiration. U.S. Civil Rights Commissioner Mary Frances Berry, Congressman Walter Fauntroy, and I had become the first to be arrested at the South African embassy, leading five thousand others across the country to do the same. Attorney Gay McDougall had helped to get us out of jail and would later be principal organizer of the democratic elections that would make Mr. Mandela president. William Lucy, secretary-treasurer of the American Federation of State, County, and Municipal Employees, had delivered cash for our coffers and bodies for picket lines by the thousands.

We were all there awaiting the man who symbolized the cause for which we had successfully fought. Many of us had come to know Mr. Mandela between his release from prison and this July luncheon. Some were meeting him for the first time.

Mandela patiently took time in the foyer to meet each member of TransAfrica's staff, professional, clerical, and custodial.

On the ten or more occasions I had met with Mandela in small or large groups since he was freed in 1990, he had been unfailingly solicitous. Our first meeting had taken place a month after his release from Pollsmoor Prison at his office in Johannesburg. Joining us around the table were TransAfrica's Ibrahim Gassama and four ANC officials including Joe Slovo, an avuncular and formidable longtime member of the ANC's Central Committee. Mandela poured orange juice for all and hosted a discussion that he made a studied effort not to dominate.

Later, in October 1991, I brought the Democracy Now delegation of twenty-three African-Americans, including Arthur Ashe, Quincy Jones, and many of those attending the July luncheon, to Johannesburg in an effort to strengthen American public support for an expedited South African democracy. Mandela arrived early for a morning session. I was called down to meet him in a Carlton Hotel reception room. We had talked alone for fifteen minutes when a black hotel worker came in to tidy up. She was stunned to encounter Nelson Mandela—and more stunned when, being in the presence of a lady, he stood up. Flummoxed, she managed to say, "Good morning, Mr. Mandela," to which Mandela responded, putting her at ease, "I am just fine, thank you, and how are you today?"

Nearest the door of the Du Bois reception room was Sugar Ray Leonard, who had never met Mandela. Upon approaching Leonard, Mandela, a former amateur boxer, dropped into a boxing stance. The assemblage roared.

After lunch for twenty-six around the Zimbabwean wood conference table in the adjoining African World Room, Mandela was effusive in his thanks to the African-American leaders for all they had done to end apartheid. He described at length plans for South Africa's first democratic elections and South Africa's need for multilateral aid and broad programs for housing, education, health care, and economic development. We understood that the antiapartheid efforts we had made were only a step in the right direction. The difficult work of winning a substantial American foreign assistance commitment lay ahead.

Five minutes before the meeting was scheduled to end, Barbara Masekela, sister of South African musician Hugh Masekela, said that the ANC had turned to major American corporate CEOs to raise money in support of the upcoming election efforts. Among others, J. Wayne Fredericks's name was mentioned as prominently associated with this effort. We were offended. Not because the ANC had reached out to corporate America. They should have done so and vigorously. But we were offended that we hadn't been extended the simple courtesy of notice.

"Fifteen years ago, when Americans knew or cared little about apartheid or the African National Congress or even you, Mr. Mandela, the people around this table made South Africa a major issue in America. Whenever I testified before Congress in support of sanctions against the South African government, I was tenaciously opposed in that view by J. Wayne Fredericks and many of those the ANC would now embrace. To seek their support is prudent and desirable. But for us who have heard nothing about this initiative from the ANC is an affront."

Beyond introductions these were my only comments during the meeting. A discussion arranged for one purpose had turned in an entirely different direction.

Someone asked Ms. Masekela: "After all of our efforts, how could you do this?"

"That was then," replied Masekela. "This is now and we must move on."

■ October 1994: Washington, D.C.

The whole matter had become a tangle of ironies. I had seen the early signs and ignored them.

After visiting with Mandela in Johannesburg in 1990, I had been invited by the ANC to attend a business development conference at the Carlton Hotel for the white business community and ANC officials who, presumably, would assume power very soon. My ANC host, an affable young man, had escorted me to all my scheduled appointments downtown and in Soweto. I arrived at the Carlton in late morning with the host and Ibrahim Gassama of my staff. We went up the escalator, heading for the second-floor conference room where the meeting was being held. At the top of the escalator we were stopped by a white South African conference official who told my host that I would not be allowed in, notwithstanding an invitation from the ANC. I turned and prepared to leave, but my host would have none of it and continued the exchange with the conference official.

As their discussion proceeded, Thabo Mbeki emerged from the meeting already under way behind double doors twenty feet from where we were standing. He saw me and came over to speak, whereupon my ANC host explained to him the situation, which was becoming for me more humiliating by the moment.

"I'll take care of it," Mbeki said and disappeared into the meeting.

Five minutes later Mbeki, the future deputy president of the country, returned to tell me, "I am sorry, Randall, we don't control this conference. There is nothing I can do."

As I stood there looking foolish among milling conferees and suffering the refusal of an admission I had neither sought nor particularly wanted, Pauline Baker, a white American foreign policy think-tanker who'd made little to no contribution toward the successful U.S. sanctions effort, came up the escalator, paused to speak and observe what was happening, and walked unimpeded into the meeting.

Following Mandela's inauguration as president in May 1994, a state visit by him to the United States was planned for October of the same year. I called South Africa's ambassador to the United States, Harry Schwarz, to propose a small breakfast for President Mandela at TransAfrica. The breakfast would be a fund-raiser for our educational facility with Mandela as honoree and special guest. Ambassador Schwarz, who was white, had been the last South African ambassador to the U.S. appointed by an apartheid government. Although we had often differed publicly before apartheid's final collapse, Schwarz and I had a reasonably cordial relationship.

He told me that Mandela's schedule for Washington was still being developed and that he would get back to me. A few days later Schwarz informed me that the TransAfrica breakfast had been confirmed by Pretoria for Saturday, October 8, Mandela's last day in Washington. I then set about inviting guests who would be willing to make five-thousand-dollar donations to TransAfrica Forum's Arthur R. Ashe Jr. Foreign Policy Library, a publicly accessible reference library of more than six thousand books on Africa, the Caribbean, Latin America, and U.S. policy toward those areas of the world.

With Mandela's arrival in the United States just days away, the breakfast of twenty guests was fully subscribed. The donations were badly needed to keep TransAfrica's doors open. Traditional corporate funding for TransAfrica had never developed because of our campaign for American corporate disinvestment from the old South Africa that had imprisoned Mandela for decades. Foundations had grown skittish in their support as well, because of the activist stratagems we had used to prod Congress toward meaningful economic sanctions. Six days before the breakfast, all the promised donations had been made and committed to program use.

Ambassador Schwarz called the next day. "Randall, I'm afraid I have bad news. Your breakfast has been canceled. The president wants to leave early. I feel awful about it. I've done everything I can do to have it reinstated but I'm afraid I have not been successful."

I was dumbstruck. I could not fathom what I was being told. The planets seemed to be whirling in new and wild orbits. *Harry Schwarz, who once represented a white minority government in South Africa, is appealing on my behalf to Nelson Mandela, the man I spent the last eighteen years of my life working to free?*

New York mayor David Dinkins and Congresswoman Maxine Waters intervened directly with Mandela upon his arrival in the United States, but to no avail. We returned all the donations, nearly going under.

President Clinton held a state dinner at the White House in Mandela's honor on Wednesday, October 4. I declined the President's invitation to attend.

The following evening, Mandela called me at my hotel in Nashville, where I had given a speech at Vanderbilt. He told me he was sorry about what had happened but offered no further explanation.

My voice was low and tremulous. "I am angry and deeply hurt. I have never before asked you for anything. Absolutely nothing. And you would do this. If it were not for my organization and its efforts, you might still be in prison."

If this story were atypical, there would be no cause for concern. Certainly, my bruised sensibilities are of small consequence. But there is a troubling pattern here of discourtesy and indifference practiced by South Africa's new leaders toward old friends. The new South Africa very much needs substantial American assistance in renovating the social and physical infrastructures of South Africa's black community. Once there was an army of Americans eager to push our government in a helpful direction. Now, that well-meaning force has been all but dissolved—puzzlingly, by the hand of the ANC itself.

This troubling and puzzling trend was affirmed in the spring 1997 series of articles written for the *Johannesburg Star* by Moeletsi Mbeki, prominent South African journalist and brother to Mandela's heir apparent, Thabo Mbeki, South Africa's deputy president:

> One of the important silent revolutions that took place in American society after World War II which was to South Africa's advantage, was the rise in power and influence of the black population in that country. It was because of this growing power of the African-American community that the U.S. government was ultimately forced to implement sanctions against the apartheid regime and also talk to the ANC in the 1980s.
>
> Since coming to power, ANC leaders have virtually cut off all contact with TransAfrica, the black American lobby that was established by the Congressional Black Caucus in the 1970s to advance the cause of African and Caribbean countries in America's corridors of power. It was TransAfrica that spearheaded the demonstrations that lead to the Comprehensive Anti-Apartheid Act of 1986.
>
> The ANC government is engaged almost exclusively with the American Establishment and its multinational corporations. Links with the U.S. government and with large American corporations are important but ultimately agreements with these two players are unlikely to survive for long if significant sections of American public opinion oppose them. South Africa thus needs to cultivate sympathetic constituencies in the U.S. and not just depend on the good intentions of whoever happens to be in the White House. This is a lesson that Israel long learned and uses it to good effect to protect itself against dictates from successive U.S. administrations whatever their party.

▌March 20, 1997: Cape Town, South Africa

I had neither seen nor spoken to President Mandela in two and a half years when Bill Cosby called in early February to invite Hazel and me to accompany Camille, his wife, and him on a trip to South Africa, where he was slated to give several performances in mid-March that would benefit the Robben Island museum project. Any reservations we had about going (and they were not inconsiderable) were overcome by our affection for Bill and Camille. So here we were.

President Mandela sat in the living room of his Cape Town residence on a long sofa between our small daughter Khalea, who had been beckoned by the president to sit next to him, and Bill. Camille, her daughter Ensa, and her mother, Mrs. Hanks, sat in flanking armchairs. Hazel and I sat on a sofa across from the president. The discussion that ensued was warm. Bill was at his ease-putting best. The president was charming and gracious. Later, speaking to the press assembled on the lawn, he was effusive about the public-spiritedness of the Cosbys and the value of my antiapartheid work during his people's long struggle for freedom. He spoke along the same lines and at greater length during a dinner that evening on Robben Island attended by one hundred guests, including Hillary Rodham Clinton, her daughter, Chelsea, UN Secretary-General Kofi Annan, and U.S. Ambassador James Joseph.

Badly healed wounds had been salved. Yet I had little in the way of new insight into the forces that had driven the ANC and its erstwhile American friends asunder to begin with. The paranoid in me suspected it, in part, to have been the work of shadowy meddlesome intelligence operatives sponsored by God only knows whom. History is littered with "self-destructed" causes and alliances. A word here. A dollar there. Spooks hard at their nasty global sub-rosa table game.

The larger reason for disaffection, however, was more likely our underlying ignorance about each other beyond the antiapartheid cause that obscured for a time all else. With victory came power, along with undiscussed and sometimes mutually antagonistic expectations, tension, suspicion, and eventual disillusionment.

Pain is personal. Those with injured feelings invariably regard themselves as specially singled out. We were not. The ANC had offended old friends in every corner of the globe. Indeed, with much the same callousness it had alienated a significant segment of its own constituency in South Africa. During our campaign here for American sanctions, little had we realized that the ANC was comprised of at least three groups: those like Mandela who were detained in South Africa as political prisoners; those who languished in exile; and the much larger number who made up the mass democratic movement on the ground in South Africa, including hundreds of thousands of trade unionists and nongovernmental organization members. From these ranks came the votes that elected a new postapartheid ANC government led by the former political prisoners and exiles.

Virtually the moment the ANC became the government, it moved to collaborate with the United States and other Western donor governments in cutting off aid to nongovernmental organizations and redirecting it to the new government. Many NGOs shriveled and died. The very trade union members who had provided an indispensable pressure for change now chafed under an ANC government that consulted seriously on policy matters only with Western governments and large corporations. Trade union members who had joined the new parliament began to resign in frustration. The Congress of South African Trade Unions, a longstanding ANC ally and the largest trade union federation in South Africa, even planned a strike for May 1997 in protest of ANC-sponsored legislation in Parliament.

At the same time that the ANC was scuttling its original supporters abroad, tensions at home threatened to cleave the former exiles and political prisoners now in power from the mass democratic movement that had delivered them to that power.

It all seems so gratuitously self-defeating. Why would a new government, inexperienced in both foreign relations and domestic management, spurn its friends willy-nilly at home and abroad? I have uncovered only parts of the answer. In an unguarded moment on the verge of assuming high office, a former exile told a prominent African-American antiapartheid leader: "Once we take power, we will conduct our relations with the West only on a state-to-state basis." Imprisoned, banished, and driven underground, South Africa's new leaders had virtually no understanding of how American political society worked. They knew little of the important and often powerful role in America of constituency organizations in policy development. Put simply, for them, government was power, major corporations were power, and it was with the biggest of governments and the largest of corporations that they wished to associate. Their erstwhile nongovernment friends abroad only reminded them of their centuries-long nightmare of powerlessness and exclusion at home. Into the white Western official doors of Valhalla they have rushed for transference therapy. The malady is one that African-Americans would easily recognize.

State-to-state parity, however, is not possible for South Africa with the United States. South Africa is only a regional power whose policy formulations have already been visibly circumscribed by Washington. As Moeletsi Mbeki put it: "The U.S. is a superpower and therefore has agendas that are far more important to itself than its friendship with South Africa. In fact friendship with South Africa, in American eyes, means fitting South Africa into these agendas rather than the opposite, that is, fitting its love for South Africa into its global agendas."

The sooner this sobering insight dawns on South Africa's new leaders, the brighter their country's future will be.

PART SIX

Haiti Redeemed

The clouds cleared. The cowards fled.
Their Titid had come home at last.
And we were there with him and them,
Anonymous in a concert of freedom's celebration.

The scene of hundreds of thousands of Haitians on October 15, 1994, at the National Palace on the occasion of the return of President Jean-Bertrand Aristide and the restoration of democracy.

■ April 1994: TransAfrica Headquarters

I am in the nineteenth day of the hunger strike I have undertaken to protest American treatment of refugees fleeing Haiti.

The army there, together with paramilitary thugs called FRAPH, has murdered upwards of five thousand civilians—men, women, children.

It is estimated that 350,000 Haitians are hiding in the interior.

Another 50,000 have fled onto the vast and capricious sea in overcrowded, rickety boats. Half of them will drown. But they continue to flee because the odds at sea are better than staying home and facing certain death at the hands of Haiti's brutal military.

I voted for President Clinton in 1992. I thought I had discerned a capacity for decency and compassion in the man beneath the candidate. I was wrong. In the campaign Mr. Clinton called President Bush's policy of returning fleeing refugees to Haiti "inhumane." Now President Clinton is doing the same and with even greater efficiency. He has cordoned Haiti with American military vessels whose crew members are scooping up the desperate refugees like so much pond scum. The President knows from American intelligence reports that many, if not most, of the repatriated refugees either "disappear" or suffer summary execution by an army our country trained and armed during the Cold War—and which President Bush continued to train even after the military overthrow of Haiti's nascent democracy. The bloody coup left as its immediate aftermath six hundred dead and Haiti's first democratically elected president, Jean-Bertrand Aristide, exiled to a tiny apartment on Seventh Street not far from where I lie now.

I am in the basement of the TransAfrica building. Hazel and Khalea have only just left for the home I've not seen in three weeks. I live now in a concrete, windowless room from which it is difficult to distinguish night from day. Twenty days ago I vowed publicly not to eat until President Clinton changes our policy and agrees to provide safe haven to those Haitians who are found, upon screening, to have fled Haiti with "a well-founded fear of persecution." This is the language of international law by which all members of the family of nations are bound. I have only asked the President to keep his original word and comply with the law. I am prepared to die if necessary.

I have lost thus far twelve pounds. I am weak and having difficulty turning coherent thoughts into comprehensible sentences. Thus I speak more slowly than normal. I am also behind in my liquids. This has caused my blood to thicken and my heart to work harder to pump it. Yesterday evening my pulse reached 108. For the first time my doctor, James Davis, appeared alarmed.

No one is here now. I am alone in the basement of a fifteen-thousand-square-foot building. The only sound comes from the gurgling water pipes that run overhead.

The periods of monastic quiet have been the most difficult for me. I have nothing to do save read, think, and regard the cold blank ugliness of my cell.

I must try not to be discouraged, but controlling my spirits through the long empty weekends has become increasingly difficult. I have no sign that in the end my act of conscience will sway the President. As if taking leave of himself, the President, as reported in the *New York Times,* says of me: "I understand and respect what he's doing, and we ought to change our policy." But then he adds somewhat cryptically, "He ought to stay out there." I do not know what he means by this.

There have been other signs of encouragement, however. Congressional Black Caucus members, led by Ronald Dellums, have begun committing acts of civil disobedience at the White House. Fellow House member Joseph Kennedy has joined them. Seven congressmen have thus far been arrested.

Senators Chris Dodd, Tom Harkin, and Paul Wellstone have come to visit, as have Congresswoman Maxine Waters, Danny Glover, Jonathan Demme, KRS-One, Earl Graves, and delegations of Haitian Americans. Dick Gregory brought literature on fasting. Quincy Jones has sent flowers. From around the world, consulates of Haiti's deposed democratic government have flooded our building with bouquets. Jesse Jackson called yesterday from South Africa. Hazel and Khalea are here every day. Jeanie and my two older children, Anike and Jabari, come regularly. Every Friday there is a candlelight demonstration of support on the R Street sidewalk outside. Khalea marches with them under the watchful eye of our deputy director, Maryse Mills. Khalea likes to walk with the candle. She believes it is helping her friend President Aristide and the people of his country. She does not know that her father has stopped eating. The media have now made of the fast a national story.

Many who visit seem to intuit the kind of support I need to balance my spirits. James Healy, an activist priest, has a talent for this.

I am thinking too much this evening about why the fast can't work and will end in my death. The flowers that line the tops of a row of file cabinets have begun to look funereal. I am recalling what the storied eighty-year-old dancer Katherine Dunham told me by telephone during the first week of the fast: "I wish I'd talked to you before you started this, Randall."

"Why?"

"Because it won't work. I tried it and it didn't work and it won't work for you either."

This depresses me but I am resilient. I will keep my word and see this through. The President's national security advisor, Anthony Lake, has called several times. I have known and thought well of Lake for a number of years. And while I have reason to believe he thinks equally well of me, it is likely that his calls are inspired more by political exigency than personal concern for my health. I spoke to Lake of my intentions three days before I began. He tried to dissuade me. "Randall, the policy is being reconsidered now. Give us two weeks."

"Tony, the administration has had two years and you're still sending refugees back."

The policy has from the beginning been indefensibly discriminatory. Cubans plucked out of the ocean didn't need to be fleeing in fright from anything. They were all brought to Florida and within a year became eligible for citizenship. At the same time that America welcomed Cubans, it was sealing Haitians into the death chamber of their island.

We at first tried to fight the Haiti policy battle in much the same way we had won sanctions against apartheid. We would pursue again a two-track strategy of public demonstrations and pressure for legislation that would lead to the restoration of Haitian democracy. I believed strongly that the refugee issue was the key to overall success. If we could bring the United States to screen and shelter endangered Haitian refugees, the White House would then, and only then, vigorously seek the downfall of Haiti's military dictatorship, solving the problem at its root.

It was plain enough that the last thing the United States wanted was a large influx of black Haitian refugees. We would make their exclusion politically difficult to publicly explain and defend.

On September 9, 1992, we had organized with the NAACP a White House protest of the Bush administration's policy of automatic repatriation of Haitians. By then some 27,000 who had fled since the September 1991 military coup had been forcibly returned by the Coast Guard. More than a thousand demonstrators turned out. Among them were D.C. mayor Sharon Pratt Kelly, Congressman Charles Rangel, Hyman Bookbinder, retired president of the American Jewish Committee, and Katherine Dunham. We had made T-shirts for each marcher bearing a silhouette map of the United States with the legend HAITIANS LOCKED OUT BECAUSE THEY ARE BLACK. More than a hundred of us were arrested, Arthur Ashe and I among them. Arthur, then ill with AIDS, said to the *Washington Post*, "I'm outraged. The Haitian refugees are entitled to a fair hearing just to see if they are indeed political refugees." The story made national news, and candidate William Jefferson Clinton excoriated the Bush policy of indiscriminate repatriation.

I have recently noticed a shrinkage of my limbs. The biggest loss is from my thighs. This bothers me and not only for reasons of vanity. My meager limbs are a constant reminder of the seriousness of my course. I have been advised to lie on the bed as much as possible. That way my body fat will burn off slowly. My friend Dick Gregory has even advised against the use of deodorant so as not to introduce toxins into my system. As I must meet endlessly with supporters and journalists to have any chance of success, I have declined, in this one instance, Dick's advice.

Because of the increasing publicity, strange people have begun to ring the front doorbell at all hours of the night. We have hired Mr. Hicks, a uniformed guard from a security firm. He arrives every night at eleven and stays somewhere on the floors above until seven in the morning.

President Aristide was here yesterday. We visited and held a press conference together two floors up in the Du Bois Room. He has become a dear friend of the family. He loves children. Khalea tells us she intends to marry him when she grows up. He is a small man who exudes strength and the courage upon which he must have drawn mightily to dare represent the democratic hopes of Haiti's impoverished millions to the pitiless generals and dissolute hill-living rich. He once survived several assassins' fusillade while standing and looking directly at his assailants.

How different he is from all that is said about him in American papers, where he has been variously described as a power-hungry lunatic and a communist. This public picture of him, which bears not the slightest resemblance to the man I know, is the inventive work of Brian Latelle, CIA Latin America station chief. Latelle claimed in a report circulated in Congress that Aristide had been treated for a mental illness (which he never suffered) at a Canadian hospital (to which he had never been) where he was treated by a certain doctor (who never existed). Of course the report was thoroughly disproved, but by then the thoroughly intended damage had been done.

From the beginning the American foreign policy establishment has not liked Jean-Bertrand Aristide, who all too cheekily for our taste elected early on not to become just another poor country's U.S. marionette. This is his lone sin and it has earned him the CIA's ire, which was virulent enough to scare away from Aristide's inauguration every Caribbean prime minister save Michael Manley of Jamaica.

It was Manley, my close friend of fifteen years, who interceded for me with Aristide shortly after he was elected president in December 1990 and seven months before he was overthrown by the military and driven into exile. Michael Manley was one of the greatest hemispheric political leaders of our era: a rare blend of intellectual candlepower, oratorical skill, political courage, humility, and integrity. There was no one I had ever known whose opinion I respected more than his. I asked:

"Michael, I'd like to have Aristide come up to Washington and address our annual dinner, but I don't know him. What do you think about the idea, and would you talk to him about the usefulness of coming?"

"I think it is a wonderful idea, Randall. I'll call him and talk to him about TransAfrica's work in Washington. He doesn't know many people in the United States and, given the powder-keg condition of Haiti now, he's going to need friends in Washington to offset the awful things that are being said about him in America." Manley's statement within months would prove to have been prescient. "I talked to Aristide only days ago. He is trying to find sleeping cots for the military. Might they be donated by the United States from army surplus?"

"I don't know, but I can try to find out."

I reflected on what little I knew about Haiti.

Former Haitian slaves, having soundly defeated a French army of sixty thousand troops commanded by a brother-in-law of French emperor Napoleon Bonaparte, triumphantly asserted their independence on January 1, 1804. They renamed the country, known as Saint-Dominique under French colonial rule, Haiti, its Arawak Indian name before Christopher Columbus arrived on December 4, 1492, to call the island Hispaniola in honor of Spain. France had lost its richest colony in the New World, and with it went Napoleon's dream of empire. On the heels of his humiliating defeat, Napoleon sold France's major American holding, the Louisiana Territory, to the U.S. under Thomas Jefferson for fifteen million dollars.

The revolt of the Haitian slaves had made the purchase possible. Haitian military hero Henri Christophe had fought alongside George Washington's troops at Savannah during the American Revolutionary War. But if Haiti expected friendship from the United States, it received a painfully opposite response. Fearing that the successful Haitian slave rebellion would embolden slaves in the South to revolt, successive U.S. presidents sustained for sixty-five years an economic embargo against Haiti that would end only with the abolition of slavery in America.

Concerned about German designs on the island, the United States occupied Haiti during World War I. Later, the Cold War produced American training and arms for the military killing machine that menaced Haiti up to, during, and beyond its first seven months of democracy in 186 years of independence.

This was the daunting environment in which Aristide, a charismatic young Catholic priest, found himself when he filed last, in a field of eleven, to run for the presidency in 1990. Marc Bazin, a former World Bank official, was the candidate supported by the United States. With no campaign resources to speak of and a late start, Aristide won seventy percent of the vote. Fourteen months later the exiled Aristide and I met for the first time in his modest Washington apartment.

"I can think of little else but what is happening to the Haitian people," said Aristide. "Every morning the streets of Port-au-Prince are littered with the bodies of those suspected of supporting democracy."

The morning before I began the hunger strike, I had flown to New York to appear on the *Phil Donahue Show* with Susan Sarandon, Harry Belafonte, and a young Haitian woman who had been horribly disfigured. FRAPH thugs had come to her home in the Port-au-Prince neighborhood of Cité Soleil looking for her husband, who was suspected of democratic sympathies. The husband escaped through a rear window. The thugs turned their machetes on his wife, severing an arm at the elbow and carving deeply into her face from hairline to neck. She was left for dead, but miraculously survived and fled into the sea.

That evening, Aristide joined Hazel and Khalea and me for dinner at our home in Washington. We had noticed on previous occasions at our home that he ate almost nothing, which we thought might have been the result either of unpalatable fare or general abstemiousness. It would be years before he would tell me that he thought it insensitive of him to eat more than a little, given the conditions of terror and hunger that prevailed in his country. When Ethel Kennedy asked him to dance after the wedding of her son Congressman Joseph Kennedy, Aristide quietly and politely explained to Mrs. Kennedy that dancing would be, for him, inappropriate for the same reason. But he would dance happily, he added pleasantly, when Haiti was once more free and democratic.

It is 10:00 P.M. Mr. Hicks will be here in an hour. I have been thinking of food. Although the hunger pangs stopped after the first week of my fast, I miss very much the act of eating, especially at dinnertime. It is a conditioned expectation that surprises me. Hazel told me before she left that she had talked to Kweisi Mfume, chairman of the Congressional Black Caucus, about a letter she had heard was circulating for signatures from black members of Congress. From what we could learn, the letter from the congresspersons would praise my fast and close by asking that I end it. Hazel told Mfume that I would not stop the fast until Clinton changed the refugee policy and that those concerned could help best by writing instead to President Clinton urging a change of policy.

I worry about how Mama is accepting what I am doing. She seems composed on the telephone, but I worry still. A church colleague told her just yesterday, "You have lost one son and now you are losing the other one."

I hear something down the hall. A light knocking sound. I am wearing a faded blue crew-neck cotton pullover with jeans and athletic socks. After putting on my slippers, I pad down the dark narrow basement hall in the direction of the knocking sound. It is coming from the metal fire door that leads up a flight of concrete steps from a storm drain to New Hampshire Avenue. The door, an emergency exit, is nearly impossible to see from the street at night and is almost never opened.

The knock comes again. I do not open the door. Clearly, if the caller's business were legitimate, he'd approach the glass double doors on the building's front, the R Street entrance, and ring the bell.

The caller can't have heard my slippered footfalls. I wait.

Now the caller is on the steps climbing to New Hampshire Avenue.

I wait a minute more, release the bolt and pull the door toward me. It is warped and, in my weakened state, difficult to move. The fire department in a late night false alarm months before had to jam it to gain entry. Now the door cannot be opened without considerable effort followed by the sound of metal scraping concrete.

I look up the dark steps and see nothing. As I step back to close and bolt the door, I notice on the sill a small plain white envelope. I pick it up and see that it is sealed. It bears my typed name but no address or postage stamp. I take the unopened envelope down the hall to my room, where I place it carefully on the bed and look at it for a long while before picking it up to estimate the thickness of its contents.

During the antiapartheid campaign I received many death threats by phone and mail, all anonymous. Several, I recall, were from a woman who would call my home once a week for several months and say, sotto voce, "You are a dead man." But I have received no such threats during the fast.

I consider waiting to consult Mr. Hicks, then decide in a large irrational rush to open the envelope. Inside is a short letter on a piece of unletterheaded plain white bond. The letter is dated April 30, 1994, today's date. It is from Morton Halperin, a special assistant to the President for national security. He asks if I would agree to a visit tomorrow afternoon, Sunday, May 1, by him and my old law school classmate Samuel Berger, now the deputy national security advisor. He gives his home telephone number and asks that I call him without concern for the lateness of the hour.

"Mort?"

"Yes?"

"This is Randall. You dropped off a letter for me an hour ago. Can you and Sandy come at four tomorrow?"

"Yes, we will be there at four."

I call Hazel to tell her what has happened and ask her to enlist a sitter for Khalea tomorrow afternoon so that she can join me in the meeting with Halperin and Berger.

▪

Mr. Hicks has arrived. I perform my ablutions, put on pajamas, and climb into bed.

Earlier in the evening Dr. Davis came to weigh me and check my heart, pulse, blood pressure, neurological signs. "The real danger arrives when the body begins to burn vital organ tissue. The damage then could be irreversible."

"Have I reached that point yet?"

"I don't know. We can't do an ultrasound on your heart here. So there are some signs I can't take from a routine examination."

"How close to the line do you think I am?"

"Close. If you go on for more than another week, you could be in serious trouble."

I do not fall asleep. I am wondering what message Halperin and Berger will deliver tomorrow. I think of the months of fruitless entreaty that eventually left me with no alternative to the undeniably drastic tack I am now on.

Certainly Ron Dellums has been superb. At the same time that TransAfrica placed a *New York Times* ad signed by seventy-five prominent African-Americans who opposed Haiti's dictatorship, Dellums introduced a bill, just as the fast began, that would, if enacted, reverse the President's noxious refugee repatriation policy. Aristide, in our press conference here yesterday, called Clinton's treatment of Haitian refugees racist. I am told that White House officials are furious. But, really, about what? Aristide only told the truth. It is this penchant of his that set our government's frustrated puppeteers against him to begin with.

The Dellums bill is quite comprehensive, banning all trade

with the Haitian dictatorship, calling for seizure of the Haitian military's assets in the United States, and requiring that the administration make real efforts to restore democracy. Hazel now works for the House Armed Services Committee as a policy advisor to Chairman Dellums. It was in this capacity that she drafted the bill at the chairman's instruction. The problem, however, remains: Legislation at the best of times moves at a glacial pace and the administration continues to frustrate our every effort to see the awful problem solved.

I do not know how much fault the President must bear here. But if wise delegation of authority is the standard, the President has performed miserably. He has given the whole of his Haiti policy over to Lawrence Pezzullo of the State Department to manage. Pezzullo's dubious record as an American official in Nicaragua during the Somoza dictatorship led none of us to believe that the restoration of democracy in Haiti would be for him a primary objective.

Months before I made the decision to fast, exasperated Democratic members of Congress summoned Pezzullo to a members-only briefing in a meeting room in the U.S. Capitol building. Attendees included Maxine Waters, Charles Rangel, and John Conyers. Congressman Joseph Kennedy chaired the informal discussion that proceeded unrestricted by the normal rules and conventions of hearing-room courtesy.

In his bearing Pezzullo is very unlike what one would expect to find in a diplomat. He is a disheveled man who speaks with unpolished syntax in a gravelly voice. The members had summoned him to express concern about the administration's failure to produce results in Haiti. The military thugs had reneged on the Governors Island Agreement, which required of General Raoul Cedras and his henchmen the surrender of power and the restoration of democracy. To the members at the meeting, the President and Pezzullo and the U.S. appeared to be doing nothing. The military was still very firmly in power. Refugees were still being returned to them by the U.S. And the elected president of Haiti was still waiting on Seventh Street.

Pezzullo's presentation to the members of Congress seemed to reflect little preparation, giving the impression that he regarded their interest as something of an intrusive annoyance. This attitude may have caused him not to grasp even slightly the members' concerns about the painful lot of ordinary Haitians and their inherent right to have the president of their choice. The Haitian voters and the deposed president for whom they had voted were quite peripheral to Pezzullo's special plan for Haiti. He made clear his view that Aristide, along with the 1990 election that lifted him to the presidency, should be forgotten about. The United States would seek to have Haiti run by an amalgam of interest groups that would include far rightists, politicians sweepingly rejected by the Haitian electorate, the military, and the handful of wealthy Haitians who supported its coup.

The angry members of Congress tore into him with a vengeance rarely seen in Capitol Hill colloquies. Perhaps Congressman Rangel captured best their indignation:

"Mr. Pezzullo, I know that the President does not know what is going on in his Haiti policy. I have enough faith in the President to know he does not know. For if he knew what a mess was being made of his Haiti policy . . ."

It was becoming clear by then to me and a substantial section of Congress that not only did Clinton's general Haiti policy have to be jettisoned but Lawrence Pezzullo with it.

▪

I wonder what Mort and Sandy will say. It must be related to the call I received a week ago from Tony Lake. He asked if I would meet with him at a neutral place. I told him I would not leave my building during the fast. We set an appointment to meet here. But then, fearing that he would be seen at TransAfrica by journalists, he canceled on the day of the meeting.

Now I remember the calls from Lake as I look across at Halperin and Berger, seated in straight-back stackable chairs at the foot of my bed. Hazel sits in a chair beside the bed and to my left. We talk for an hour. Hazel and I say little. We listen for a message that does not come. They are not here to talk. They are here to look at me. To estimate my nearness to death. There are awkward silences I elect not to fill. Halperin looks more comfortable than Berger, whose face can't seem to decide whether it is in a meeting or at a funeral.

"Randall, we'll have some answers on the issues you're concerned about within two weeks," says Berger toward the end of the hour.

"Sandy, I could be dead in two weeks."

On Monday, day twenty-one of my fast, Mary Frances Berry comes to visit me. "I've just left the White House and something's beginning to happen. My impression is they'd like me to serve as an unofficial intermediary. How do you feel about it?"

"I think it's a good idea."

"I assume that your position has not changed."

"No. The administration has to end the automatic repatriation, and screen for legitimate political refugees, and provide shelter to those fleeing for valid reasons. When they do these things I will end the fast, but not until. My other concerns about the speedy restoration of democracy I will continue to press."

"I'll come back to see you as soon as I know something."

On Thursday, day 24, I am taken by ambulance to Providence Hospital in upper Northeast Washington. My pulse is dangerously elevated. My heart is laboring. I am suffering from severe dehydration. An IV of fluids is started. Hazel is at my bedside. Jesse Jackson has come to pray for me. Dr. Davis has gone downstairs to join Susan Taylor, editor-in-chief of *Essence* magazine, and Bianca Jagger in a crowded press briefing on my condition. I have now lost almost twenty pounds. I am very weak. Providence is a Catholic hospital. Crucifixes are affixed to every wall. I am afraid. But only Hazel, I think, sees that I am.

In the afternoon an ultrasound test reveals that my heart has not yet been permanently damaged. A *New York Times* photographer takes my picture as I lie in bed. The picture appears the next morning in *USA Today*. I look moribund and it unsettles me. I must call Mama.

I am released from the hospital on Friday afternoon after receiving five quarts of fluid. My pulse and heartbeat have fallen to a safe level.

Mary Frances Berry comes to my congested room at

TransAfrica to see me on Friday. "You should expect a call from the White House Saturday."

"You mean tomorrow?"

"Yes."

On Saturday, in the early evening, Tony Lake calls to tell me that the President has ended the policy of automatic repatriation. Haitian refugees will be screened, I am told. The mechanics for the screening process are being worked out now. The U.N. High Commissioner for Refugees will be involved. I am further told by Lake that William H. Gray III, a former congressman and currently president of the United Negro College Fund, will be introduced in the morning by the President from the White House Rose Garden as his special advisor with responsibility for implementing the President's revamped Haiti policy. This means that Lawrence Pezzullo has been fired.

I put my hand over the receiver and say to Hazel, "Darling, we have won. We . . . have . . . won . . ."

Lake is waiting for my response.

"I am very glad to hear all that you have described. When will this be made public?"

He tells me that Berger will appear on NBC's *Meet the Press* in the morning and asks if I would agree to appear on the show with Berger in separate segments. Before hanging up, Lake tells me that the President has invited me to accompany Vice President Al Gore to South Africa as a member of the official U.S. delegation to Nelson Mandela's presidential inauguration. He says that the delegation will depart tomorrow evening from Andrews Air Force Base. I decline by telling Lake that I am quite weak and in no condition to travel.

Sunday morning on *Meet the Press* I announce the end of my twenty-seven-day fast. Hazel comes to take me home. I have missed much of spring, the season of recurring natural miracles. The daffodils and crocuses have withered and given way to azalea blossoms of red, white, and lavender. The air is warm. The leaves are still small and new with the brilliant satin green of mid-spring. It is exhilarating to be alive and out of doors.

At home Hazel starts me back to vigor with a bowl of chicken broth. The warm fluid feels odd on my stomach. I am nagged by mild feelings of guilt about eating, as if the administration's capitulation has yet to register. Hazel and I talk about why President Clinton chose Bill Gray, a longtime friend of mine and the congressman for whom Hazel worked as foreign policy advisor upon leaving TransAfrica. Was he named because he was black? If the new policy initiative should go awry, will the President scapegoat Gray and find cover from me and other critical blacks behind the color of the new Haiti advisor's skin? Perhaps I am being unfair. But I do not trust these people. We have won an important round, but is the victory illusory? Have we been hoodwinked? Does someone know something I don't know? I do know one thing. Gray is a brilliant politician who knows how to land on his feet.

Gray in fact called me before Lake to tell me he would be named. I said I was pleased with the President's choice.

"Randall, I am going to have to get up to speed quickly on Haiti issues. I don't know Aristide but I want to work with him." Already this signaled a marked change. Pezzullo had met with Aristide often enough but "he never listened to or heeded a thing I said," Aristide had told me.

Gray has an uncanny natural talent for getting a result. He knows wheat from chaff and instinctively separates the two quite nicely. He cares about how the black community will judge him and knows that it will be naturally suspicious of the President's appointment. He is too savvy to become a crossfire target. He will reach out. He has already asked himself, I am certain, the same questions that I raise. Like, *Am I being set up?*

Racism seeps into the most rarefied of chambers and Gray is no stranger to it. When he was running to become chairman of the House Budget Committee in 1984 and seeking support from his House colleagues, he was told by a white member what he would hear from more than a few others: "I'd like to support you, but the chairman of the Budget Committee has complicated responsibilities and the job requires complex skills." Not even thinly veiled was the sentiment. He had won the post in any case.

"Randall, we will need to work together to pull this off."

"I will vouch for you, Bill, to Aristide. We must as quickly as possible build a bridge of trust between the two of you that does not yet exist between Aristide and anyone in the administration."

"That will be helpful. Before I forget to tell you, Haitians picked up on the open seas will be taken for screening to the U.S.S. *Comfort,* a hospital ship that will be moored in the harbor of Kingston, Jamaica. We're developing the screening procedures now. One thing I will insist upon is that the refugees, many of whom have been drifting at sea for days, get a chance to rest on the *Comfort* before the questioning begins."

■ Summer 1994: Washington, D.C.

The set was thick with tension. We were waiting out a commercial break. The show's host, CNN's Frank Sesno, was listening through his headphones to voices from the control booth. Senator John McCain, a Republican from Arizona whom I'd never met, stared across at me. I returned his stare. Our instant dislike for each other was palpable and intense. The topic of the segment just taped was a proposed plan to send American troops to Haiti to restore democracy. The subject itself was scarcely more than a precipitant for a highly charged and larger catharsis.

Senator McCain, who had supported President Reagan's military intervention in Grenada in a spirit of "anticommunism," opposed the sending of U.S. forces to Haiti, citing the absence of any "strategic interests." I had pressed the point in the segment that the Haitian army, which the United States had trained and armed during the Cold War, had run amok, overthrown the democratically elected Jean-Bertrand Aristide, and killed five thousand Haitian civilians in the three years following the coup. We had some responsibility, I argued, to disable the killing machine we had constructed and loosed on the people of Haiti. "Surely, Senator, there must be something in the world worthy of American opposition beyond communism."

He glared at me and described both my failure to appreciate the dangers of communism and the price of his personal struggle against communism, which included seven years he had spent in a North Vietnamese tiger cage.

I was as livid as he. "I bet if the Haitian victims were white and not black, if white people were being hacked and shot to death by the thousands, your position would be different."

"I knew you would say that. I knew you would say that. I knew it," he choked out.

Blacks and whites understand almost nothing of each other in America.

Who's to say there are none, but I have never happened across a black person who felt as passionately about Vietnam and communism as Senator McCain did.

Clearly, as an economic system, communism has not worked, does not work, and likely will never work. Yet its mere suggestion, for some, can roil the emotions and fever the blood. Not for blacks. Historically, our pain has been sourced closer by. No communist tossed a single African into the hold of a slave ship. No communist ran a plantation or segregated a school or red-lined an entire neighborhood or invested in apartheid or rained drugs on a black inner-city community or humiliated my mother and father or threw me in the back of a U.S. Army pickup truck.

Senator McCain felt, with reason, that I undervalued his pre-occupying hatred for communism. With equal reason, I felt that he cared not a whit about the thousands of black victims of an American-sponsored killing machine in Haiti.

■ Summer 1994: Kingston, Jamaica, and Washington, D.C.

I am climbing the ladder that runs diagonally up the hull of the *Comfort*. The ship, a floating building, rises five stories out of the water. It is so enormous that once you're on the football-field-size deck, no motion can be felt underfoot. There are tents on deck to shelter the refugees upon their arrival. In the ship's gray interior are the processing stations through which the refugees must pass before a decision can be rendered. The U.S. Army men and women here have been responsive to my questions and are unfailingly courteous. I have found the military much more attractive from the outside, from a civilian's perspective. The young UNHCR officials appear idealistic and vigilant in their monitoring of the screening process. I am concerned, however, about a somewhat dissipated official from the State Department. Up on deck, he has somewhat sappily told me that he sees no reason to allow a rest period for the exhausted refugees no matter what the guidelines require. I share this with Gray by phone before I leave Kingston. Gray is furious. "We'll see about that," he tells me.

All through the late spring and summer of 1994, Haiti's ruling troika of General Raoul Cedras, General Phillippe Biamby, and police chief Joseph-Michel François has been slow to recognize the unmistakable signs of their dictatorship's inexorable demise. By May 21 the United Nations had toughened sanctions, stanching the flow of all goods into Haiti save food and human-itarian assistance items. Rape, a crime once virtually unknown in Haiti, has become an increasingly routine practice of soldiers who are growing more vicious and desperate by the day. Political killings escalate as the junta orders UN and Organization of American States human rights monitors to leave the country by July 13. Only two weeks earlier, more than one thousand Haitian refugees were intercepted by the Coast Guard, overwhelming the screening facilities of the Immigration and Naturalization Service. Guantanamo Bay is added to the *Comfort* as a processing facility. Still, shelter space for the new tides of fleeing people fills faster than the United States can find countries to accept them. The problem is exacerbated when Guillermo Endara, president of Panama, withdraws his commitment to provide safe haven in his country for the outflowing refugees.

The United States asks the Haitian military rulers to accept exile in France or Spain. The dictators refuse. On July 19 American officials consult UN officials on a resolution that would authorize a military intervention. By July 31 the resolution is adopted.

By mid-August President Clinton has approved the timetable for sending American troops into Haiti. The date for multinational intervention is set for September 19, at 12:01 A.M.

"Randall, President Clinton is not prepared to go forward with the intervention until President Aristide makes clear whether he supports or opposes it." This from William Gray in a Sunday afternoon call to me at home. "Aristide has balked on signing a letter of support. We must have a letter from him to move. One sentence would be sufficient."

"Hazel and I are having lunch tomorrow with Aristide and Mildred Truillot, his legal advisor. We'll talk to him then."

At lunch the next day in the dining room of Aristide's small apartment the four of us talk of nothing of consequence until the table has been cleared and the waiter has left the apartment. This precaution makes little sense inasmuch as the apartment is loaded with electronic listening devices.

"Randall, my constitution forbids me to expressly authorize a military intervention of Haiti," said President Aristide.

While no one present wants an intervention, we all know that Haiti's murderous rulers will not surrender power until forced to.

"I'm afraid there is no choice. Without an intervention, you will remain in exile indefinitely and Haitians at home will continue to live in terror. We have to come to terms with that. President Clinton wants assurance that you will not publicly criticize the intervention once it is undertaken. There has to be a way to craft a letter that satisfies his concern and at the same time does not have you violate the Haitian constitution. I think it is urgent that you work this out with Bill Gray as soon as humanly possible."

In the days ahead acceptable language is worked out.

September 19 arrives. President Clinton is demonstrating great political courage and resolve. He enjoys nothing close to majority support in either house of Congress for an intervention, but he proceeds in any case when his negotiators, former president Jimmy Carter, General Colin Powell, and Senator Sam Nunn, fail in Port-au-Prince to gain from the dictators a capitulation. At 5:45 P.M. the Pentagon orders American troops into Haiti. Sixty-one planes carrying paratroopers take off from Pope Air Force Base in North Carolina and Homestead Air Force Base in New Jersey. With the planes en route, President Clinton issues at 7:00 P.M. a thirty-minute ultimatum. Finally, the Haitian military rulers agree to step down.

■

From May 8, at the very moment President Clinton announced his decision to screen fleeing refugees, Haiti's military dictators were doomed to accept exile or be crushed by a multinational intervention force led by the U.S. The President had good reason to believe that he needed the electoral votes of Florida to be reelected. Overwhelmingly, Floridians were opposed to an influx of Haitians. Cubans were welcome, Haitians were not. I knew from the beginning that if I could persuade the President to screen the fleeing Haitians, the U.S. would soon run out of space for them at Guantanamo. Then the President would have to choose between risking the loss of Florida and military intervention in Haiti. His decision was predictable.

Ultimately, the refugees had won freedom for themselves and for Haiti by fleeing it.

Fall 1994: Capitol Hill

Some time after the multinational force peacefully entered Haiti on September 19, Congressman Benjamin Gilman, ranking Republican member of the House Armed Services Committee, introduced a resolution calling for the immediate withdrawal of American troops. At the same time Congressman Lee Hamilton, chairman of the House Foreign Affairs Committee, and Robert Torricelli, chairman of the House Subcommittee on the Western Hemisphere, introduced a resolution calling for a withdrawal deadline. President Clinton and the Armed Services Committee chairman, Ron Dellums, believed it unwise either to withdraw prematurely or to indicate to an enemy (in this case the murderous Haitian military) in advance the date of any withdrawal. In this spirit, Chairman Dellums and Congressmen John Murtha, Alcee Hastings, and Norm Dicks introduced a resolution allowing the president latitude with respect to troop withdrawal. The various resolutions were set for House floor debate on October 6. Inasmuch as Chairman Dellums had theretofore been the leading congressional voice on Haiti, had sponsored the only comprehensive legislative proposal on the issue (the Governors Island Reinforcement Act), and further chaired the committee of House jurisdiction over military matters, he became the consensus House leadership choice to manage the floor debate on his resolution.

As the members assembled in the well of the House chamber that day and Chairman Dellums was readying himself to manage the floor debate, John Murtha, a Democrat from Pennsylvania and junior to Dellums in seniority and rank, approached him and said, "I'm managing the bill because you need a white person managing it. You can't have this look like a black thing."

The normally even-tempered Dellums exploded. "Are you out of your mind? Do you mean to tell me that after twenty-four years in this body, in spite of the fact that I am chairman of the House Armed Services Committee, although everybody in this chamber knows I have prime responsibility for ushering a two-hundred-sixty-four-billion-dollar defense authorization through this House and to the president's desk—when you look at me, all you see is a black face? I'm no foot-shuffling, hand-rubbing . . ." As this exchange took place on the floor of the House of Representatives of the United States Congress, staff members scattered in every direction. When Chairman Dellums was done, Congressman Murtha flushed and moved away. Dellums proceeded to manage this resolution, which shortly thereafter carried the House by a large margin.

October 15, 1994, Restoration Day: Port-au-Prince, Haiti

We had flown for three hours in the retrofitted Air Force Boeing 707 bearing on its fuselage the familiar legend UNITED STATES OF AMERICA. Earlier we had waited on the tarmac at Andrews Air Force Base for the arrival of President Jean-Bertrand Aristide and Secretary of State Warren Christopher. Dressed in summer clothes, we shivered in the postdawn October chill, but no one complained. Aboard were members of Congress including Senators Tom Harkin and Christopher Dodd and Representatives Charles Rangel, Major Owens, and Joseph Kennedy. Jesse Jackson traveled with us, as did authors Amy Wilentz and Taylor Branch.

Hazel and I stood in the forward cabin talking to President Aristide and Mildred Truillot while Secretary Christopher talked five feet away to Samuel Berger, the deputy national security advisor. Aristide was looking beyond me and out a window. His expression changed and he moved closer to the window. As the plane approached landfall, his eyes watered. He turned toward the three of us and got out only the word "home" before his voice caught. He had lived in exile for one thousand one hundred eleven days and had finally come home to Haiti. It seemed the most improbable of outcomes, first that he would live at all, and then that he would live to see again the country where so many had perished seeking the simplest of freedoms. So many whom he had known, had struggled and suffered with.

I looked around the forward cabin. It occurred to me that a few in the forward cabin and perhaps more than a few aboard virtually hated Aristide. It was a feeling broadly shared throughout the branches of America's faceless foreign policy bureaucracy. He appeared to own himself, a quality never liked by American officials in Third World leaders. There was no trace in his character of simpering gratefulness. He was a brilliant man who knew and rather liked who he was. Whole and self-contained. Unflaggingly unwilling to sell what his poor constituents owned in common of their country to North American and local corporate privateers for pittances. For him independence meant something more than a flag, an anthem, and a ragtag band. For these sentiments he was detested in Washington. That he had won seventy percent of the vote, in a fair presidential election with a ninety-percent turnout, in the eyes of American officialdom counted for little. Had not the flanks of his bravery been so relentlessly defended by the majority of those flying with us today, the miracle of his return would never have occurred. It had been the tireless stout hearts aboard that had made all the loud, public fuss about honoring democracy's verdict. The spotlit bureaucrats had little choice but to go along. Hypocrisy has its value.

Indeed, no one questioned that the vast majority of the Haitian people loved Aristide. How dearly they had paid for their democracy and their Titid's return. They had turned out in droves to vote for him in 1990, although just three years before the military had turned polling places into lakes of blood.

▪

Throughout the 1970s and 1980s, the repressed and disenfranchised Haitian poor founded across their mountainous country literacy groups, cooperatives, and peasant associations. Thus the beginnings of the political party Lavalas, Creole for "flood," were germinated. The humble poor believed that individually they were mere drops that together could make a flood that would ultimately wash away corruption and tyranny.

In the front ranks of this movement were young Catholic priests—leaders of Ti Legliz, Creole for "little church" as opposed to the "big church," the Vatican's Catholic church in Haiti whose bishops had been nominated by the ruthless dictator François "Papa Doc" Duvalier. The official Catholic church in Haiti had become a pillar of Duvalierist domination and had been vehement in its opposition to Lavalas and the "little church" push for democracy. The Vatican had even become the only state in the world to recognize the military dictators who had overthrown Aristide three years before.

On the tarmac below, awaiting the return of his president, was Father Antoine Adrien, the aging priest who had become a fearless symbol of hope and leadership for the young "little church" priests like Aristide, William Smarth, and Jean-Marie Vincent, who had on one of many attempts against Aristide's life thrown himself between Aristide and his assailant. Father Vincent would not be waiting below for his president. He had been assassinated two months before.

There had been so many killings. Big or small, no democracy adherent escaped attention. The military had forbidden anyone even to possess Aristide's picture. When caught by soldiers stapling one to a public billboard, Claudie Musseau had been forced to take it down with his teeth and eat it before being killed on the spot. In 1991 George Izmery, a wealthy Middle Eastern merchant who supported the drive for democracy, was dragged from his store and shot to death. In 1993 his brother Antoine was shot dead by barefaced soldiers while attending a memorial service for those who had been killed in an army massacre three years earlier. Congressman Alcee Hastings of Florida (who had, on a Florida Beach, happened upon a boatload of dead Haitian refugees including a pregnant woman) had had dinner with Aristide's American-educated justice minister, Guy Mallory, only weeks before he was gunned down in 1993 on a Port-au-Prince sidewalk in broad daylight.

So much blood had been shed at the hands of a power-mad military that the United States had trained and equipped. But these facts alone had not been compelling enough to make a great many important Americans care. After my fast, and while

Aristide waited on Seventh Street, Congressman Porter Goss, a former CIA officer, proposed in innocuous language an amendment to a defense authorization bill that would have had the United States wash its hands of the whole matter by dumping Aristide with the exiled members of his government and eighty thousand refugees on the Haitian island of Ile de Gonave, a mosquito-infested parcel of land with no infrastructure and no natural defenses against a Haitian military that had promised Aristide's death should he return. The dumping might well have been carried out had Congressman Ron Dellums not achieved through a parliamentary maneuver twenty-one days later a House revote that defeated the Goss effort.

■

All save Aristide and Secretary Christopher had deplaned down the mobile staircase to the tarmac. Waiting at the foot of the staircase were Robert Malval, Aristide's prime minister, and General Dupréval, who had become commander in chief of the army after General Cedras and company had decamped for Panama. Standing beside them was a set of identical twin boys of seven years. Besides General Dupréval, the only evidence of the Haitian army to be seen was the small military band standing near the terminal building. The army had gone to ground in the face of an international intervention force whose tents could be seen everywhere from the air. As we were descending earlier across Port-au-Prince, Haitians on the ground had spotted the aircraft bearing Aristide and begun waving, shouting, and chasing it through the streets toward the airport.

We had waited fifteen minutes before President Aristide, wearing the red and blue Haitian presidential sash, and Secretary Christopher stepped out onto the staircase platform.

The crowd erupted with a roar. Aristide smiled and waved. I had a fleeting feeling of foreboding as the memory of the tragic airport homecoming of the Philippines' Benigno Aquino came to mind. I looked at General Dupréval, who had been in every sense very much an army man. His flat square face betrayed nothing as Aristide began to descend. At the foot of the steps Aristide was warmly greeted by Malval and presented with flowers by the twins, who are believed in Haitian culture to bring good luck. Aristide then approached General Dupréval, opened his arms, and embraced him.

After working their way through a long receiving line, Aristide and Christopher boarded the first of eleven U. S. Army helicopters laid on to take us to the grounds of the National Palace, where Aristide would address the nation.

The National Palace is a grand, gleaming white, exquisitely designed structure in the center of Port-au-Prince. From my vantage point on the guest platform behind and to the right of President Aristide, Haitian celebrants jammed the streets beyond the palace grounds' wrought-iron fence as far as the eye could see. Hundreds and hundreds of thousands. A single dove was released into the air in memory of the five thousand who had been killed by the army and its adjuncts. American soldiers, some of whom were Haitian Americans, mingled with a people who for once welcomed their presence. On the platform with hundreds of diplomats and dignitaries, Mildred Truillot, a Haitian American lawyer who would later became Mrs. Aristide, waved the Haitian flag with the rapture of a child. In turn Aristide, known affectionately to Haitian millions as Titid, stood at the podium to receive a long and thunderous welcome. He spoke largely in Creole. Mildred translated for Hazel and me. That most non-Haitians there hadn't understood more than a few words of the president's speech made little difference. The very spirit of the occasion was intoxicating. Amy Wilentz, author of a wonderfully poignant book about the Haitian travail entitled *Rainy Season,* found the day so stirring that she cried as Warren Christopher spoke.

In the end, it was a day unlike any I had ever experienced or likely ever would again. As our helicopter lifted off from the grounds and rose into the warm late afternoon air, we looked down to a million waving upturned hands bidding us farewell.

PART SEVEN

Of Tyranny and Accommodation

Things are never what they seem. In any struggle over policy out-comes, we all know the tools of contest: position, publicity, money, celebrity, fear, and vulnerability. Damn the mesmerizers and the drug of oratory. Damn us all who, lost in battle, obfuscate and dis-tort. Damn the millions who believe dogmas without a clue as to why. Damn the demagogues who cast us all on the road to hell. Damn the whites who compel our scarred black souls to ram-parts, watching only outward toward them. The enemy within and the enemy without, the former more difficult to identify than the latter. Not only are these enemies (black and white) not mutually exclusive, they exist very much interdependently.

■ 1990s: Of Nigeria

The two influential Nigerians had completed the formal part of their meeting with me at my office in Washington. The one I had developed some relationship with, the senior of the two, asked his younger colleague if he would wait outside in the reception area. Appearing to have expected the dismissal, the younger Nigerian closed the double office doors quietly behind him.

The Nigerian cleared his throat and adjusted his position on the tan leather couch. "Randall, we've always been honest and straight with each other, have we not?"

"Yes."

"I have been asked by someone in the Nigerian government to explore a matter with you. Do you need money?"

"Yes. TransAfrica is in dire financial straits and I don't know how much longer I can keep the wolves at bay."

The Nigerian looked at me uncomfortably across the glass coffee table and said nothing for a while.

This was new terrain. For months we had talked only about my efforts to push Nigeria's military toward democratic reform.

"There are those in Nigeria who want to know how much it would cost to keep you quiet. The offer could go as high as a million dollars."

Silence. His message hung in the air. He had always talked in spirited bursts. This was different.

More silence.

"My friend, you know I cannot do that."

The Nigerian looked relieved.

"Why me?" I was truly incredulous. In twenty-five years of human rights advocacy, I had never been offered a bribe. Never expected to be offered a bribe. Not to mention a million dollars.

"After Ken Saro Wiwa was executed, the United States and European countries all withdrew their ambassadors from Nigeria, stating that the diplomats would not return until real progress was made toward human rights and democracy objectives." He had recovered his energy of speech. "Well, after only three months and no such progress, all the European ambassadors are back in Abuja. Cash payments were made to Europeans in and out of government. In Nigeria anything and anyone can be bought."

Nigeria's military dictator, Sani Abacha, had sound basis for this belief. Ten billion dollars a year in oil export income flowed through his hands. Much of it he regularly diverted to what he called euphemistically his "extrabudgetary accounts" in Germany, Switzerland, and Lebanon—billions salted away abroad in private numbered accounts. Much of the rest he used to buy enough army loyalty to hang on. He pacified civilian government officials and a corrupt business community with oil-industry-related contracts.

Generals have been in power for twenty-seven of Nigeria's thirty-seven years of independence. Since oil was discovered in the 1970s, Nigeria has exported low-sulphur crude valued in excess of $210 billion. Yet the country is broke, with only enough foreign reserves to buy two months of imports and an annual per capita income of $250 (Haiti's is $260), down from $1,000 in 1980. After the regular theft debit there is little money left for schools, roads, hospitals.

Nigeria is a moral, spiritual, political, and public relations disaster for the black world. With one hundred million people, it is the world's most populous black country. With its nearly bottomless oil and natural gas reserves, it should be one of the world's wealthiest countries. Instead it has become a swamp of inefficiency and metastasized corruption. A small clutch of amoral generals and gluttonous businessmen have camped meanly on a population of honest, hardworking, creative, long-suffering people.

White racists sift hither and yon for scraps of evidence to support specious claims of black inferiority. They must feel giddy to have struck the mother lode in Sani Abacha. Almost nothing works in Nigeria outside the machineries of kleptocracy and repression.

We black people have so little control over how we are perceived, even by ourselves. We neither own nor influence a single global information system. We scream our good news to deaf ears. Look at the miraculous democratic progress across southern Africa! Look at Botswana's culture of political openness and prudent economic management! Look at the Caribbean's twelve-nation chain of stable middle-income English-speaking democracies whose people equal or exceed Americans in literacy! Look at the phoenix of Uganda! Look, goddammit, at the Dance Theater of Harlem! Look!

No. Says Republican congressman Porter Goss: "Haiti does not have a good track record dealing in the long term with democracy." The reasons are "cultural, historic, ethnic, and racial." Jesus! Is he simply stupid? Does he think Yugoslavia and Albania are black? Does he think Barbados and Jamaica are white? Does he not know that Haiti was shoved into its two-hundred-year nightmare by the United States and Europe as punishment for its successful slave revolt against Napoleon Bonaparte? Does he not know his comment is racist? Does anyone know that he made it, and if they do, do they care?

No. As further evidence of our powerlessness, like it or not, they make us all look at the Nigerias. And we must not look away. We must not deny or rationalize. We must not defend or explain. Beyond the sordid events, we in the black world must understand it for what it is: a crossroads war of values. If Nigeria cannot be resurrected, Africa is doomed for at least a century. Nigeria is our mirror of sorts. In it can be seen a large, talented, and decent civil society working tirelessly to establish beachheads of democratic behavior. Lawyers, scientists, writers, disenfranchised voters, and the gone-to-ground former officeholders they once elected—all pursuing at significant risk the cultivation of a democratic culture: a culture of forbearance, tolerance, civility; a culture of national consensus-based decision making; a culture of honest commercial relations. A culture of zeal to spur economic and spiritual productivity that could propel the African world to global parity.

Also seen in the mirror are the black enemies of the black world and black progress: the brutal and rapacious Nigerian generals who govern to steal and steal to govern. They talk of elections with no real commitment to hold them. They talk of democracy with no notion of the freedoms implied. Their parameters for governance are set at the fore and aft opportunity-points for self-enrichment: power achieved not to render public service but only to steal as much as possible for as long as possible.

We should feel a righteous rage as they cart off the material birthright of all Nigerians and sully in the doing the image of all Africa's progeny.

The generals are so well beyond accountability as to make hypocrisy unnecessary. As a rule, societies, economies, governments (even authoritarian ones) prosper only when there are threshold requirements for ethical behavior encoded in the culture. Such values do not exist in Nigerian political culture. Normative values have been and continue to be the values of official pilferage.

God! Almost everywhere we continue to pay for slavery.

Subjugated and humiliated for centuries, psyches profoundly damaged, we lost a belief in our very adequacy. What slavery had begun, colonialism sustained. Few remember (sadly even we, the modern victims) Africa in the glory of its antiquity when its societies and empires rivaled and often exceeded those of Europe. The glittering achievements of ancient Kush, Songhay, and Egypt crushed under the weight of slavery and colonial subjugation. Totemized to the very bottom of the world's socioeconomic pole, we learned with the assistance of white masters first to hate ourselves and then to turn on ourselves. In Nigeria the postcolonial modern white masters wear the suits of multinational oil company executives.

Ninety-five percent of Nigeria's foreign exchange revenues are earned through the export of oil. Half of those earnings are produced by Royal Dutch Shell, followed by Mobil, Texaco, Exxon, and Agip Petroleum. These companies place under the control of one man, General Sani Abacha, oil export revenues in excess of $10 billion a year. Through the revolving door. Cash flooding in from the United States and Western Europe and out to Abacha's family and colleagues.

Watching this circus of graft-driven tyranny from the sky-boxes of a metaphorical modern Roman coliseum are the very prosperous American, Dutch, British, French, and Italian oil company partners of the generals. With thumbs pointed decidedly down, they never intervene on behalf of the victims. In 1993, when the people of oil-rich Ogoniland protested Shell's destruction of their environment, Shell invited in the Nigerian military to put down the protest. More than two thousand people were killed, and some sixty villages leveled.

The leader of the movement to protect Ogoniland's environment was the writer Ken Saro Wiwa, against whom the government brought what appeared to be specious murder charges. We may never know whether the charges held any water or not. Ken Saro Wiwa was tried by a three-man court on which one of Abacha's generals sat. Bribes to government witnesses were broadly confessed. Exculpatory evidence was routinely disallowed. No claims to fairness of judicial procedure were offered by the government.

The expected guilty verdict was announced. No appeal was permitted. Mr. Saro Wiwa was hanged with nine other activists on November 10, 1995. Before the executions Owens Wiwa, a medical doctor, met with a Royal Dutch Shell executive, imploring the company to intervene to save his brother's life. Owens Wiwa was told that Shell would consider intervening only if his brother ceased his protest of Shell's environmentally damaging activities in Ogoniland. Owens told the executive that his brother would never do that. In that case, the Shell official told Owens, the company would do nothing for his brother.

Ken Saro Wiwa had mounted a threat to the generals' oil income stream and paid for it with his life.

The war of values rages across the African world. With little or no material support from a United States that has funded its Cold War client dictators for the last thirty years, African nations of their own volition are moving, if haltingly, toward multiparty democracy. It is a trend that Nigeria's military rulers have tried feverishly to check. Nigeria played a pivotal role in toppling the elected government of its neighbor Niger. A similar but unsuccessful attempt was made to overturn the West African government of Guinea-Conakry.

After the coup in Niger, the tiny coastal democracy of Benin, with its population of 5.5 million, found itself surrounded by unfriendly and undemocratic regimes, with Nigeria on one border and on another Togo, led by President Gnassingbé Eyadema, who had ruled with an iron fist for three decades with the support of France.

As Benin's presidential election scheduled for March 3, 1996, approached, the country's democratically elected president, Nicephore D. Soglo, found himself in Nigeria's crosshairs. Intolerant of a gathering democratic trend, General Abacha threw his support (and money) behind retired general Matthieu Kerekou, who had run Benin before Soglo for seventeen ruinous years.

Benin's small economy is almost completely dependent upon its larger neighbor, Nigeria. Aware of his regional power, General Abacha launched a double-barreled salvo. He funded Kerekou's campaign while closing Nigeria's border with Benin. Benin's economy plummeted instantly, as did Soglo's popular support. General Kerekou paid homage in Abuja to General Abacha shortly after his victory. On the day he left Abuja, Nigeria reopened its border with Benin.

Even in war-ravaged Liberia, Nigeria's rapacious generals have passed up no chance at the trough. Nigerian soldiers make up the larger part of the West African multinational peacekeeping force operating in Liberia. For these services, Nigeria's treasury was billed millions more than the actual cost. The billing was not supported by auditable books. It is estimated that for every one dollar actually spent by the military on Liberian peacekeeping, four dollars were diverted to numbered accounts abroad.

■

It was a warm late spring day in 1995. I opened my fourth-floor Dupont Circle office window to catch the breeze.

"Robinson! Mind your own business and stay out of Nigeria's!"

Down below, a placard-bearing crowd of at least a hundred people circled in front of our building. The buses that had brought them in the wee hours from New York City carried New Jersey plates and were parked across from the demonstrators on New Hampshire Avenue.

This was one of many demonstrations conducted at TransAfrica's headquarters by mercenaries whom the Nigerian mission to the United Nations gave a stipend of up to $300 per person for a day's work.

Then followed full-page $60,000-a-throw ads in the *New York Times* lodging ad hominem attacks against me. The ads were signed by little-known Nigerian organizations that couldn't possibly afford such outlays, by organizations that did not exist, and by some that did but had given no consent to be listed. There was never much doubt that the Nigerian government had begun to defend itself with a very well funded American campaign. Roy Innis, president of CORE, began to ferry large numbers of African-American journalists and ministers to Nigeria, all at the Nigerian government's expense. A cash-strapped NAACP was given $10,000 by General Abacha. The money was quickly returned.

In June 1995 Gwendolyn Baker, president of the United States Committee for UNICEF and an African-American, informed me by letter that I had been chosen to receive a human rights award from the committee. The award would be presented, she wrote, in the UN General Assembly with Secretary-General Boutros Boutros-Ghali in attendance. Such was the tradition of presentation, I later learned, for the committee's annual citation.

When Nigeria's ambassador to the United Nations, Ibrahim Gambari, learned of the committee's planned award, he urged that the choice be rescinded, failing which he would take the matter to the Secretary-General. Ms. Baker stood firm and the award was presented, though not in the General Assembly, as was the custom, but in a UN social function room. The Secretary-General did not attend. There is rank irony in this episode, given Ambassador Gambari's previous hardy support for my antiapartheid work.

More than sixty prominent African-American leaders, including twenty-six members of the Congressional Black Caucus and the heads of the NAACP, the National Urban League, the Southern Christian Leadership Council, and the National Council of Negro Women, asked President Clinton in a letter of December 1995 to freeze Nigerian government assets in the United States and to organize a multilateral oil embargo. The oil companies lobbied the White House furiously against any Nigerian sanctions. TransAfrica organized daily demonstrations at the Nigerian embassy in Washington with demonstrators costumed as grim reapers with scythes bearing the message NIGERIA IS DYING.

The black community's response to my activist work on Rhodesia, South Africa, Namibia, and Haiti had been, at least to my ear, unalloyed praise. Those campaigns enjoyed an easy resonance here. South Africa, and to a lesser extent Rhodesia and Namibia, jibed well with American racial conflict rhythms. African-Americans viscerally understood apartheid and its regional variants. The American treatment of fleeing Haitian refugees tapped into the same residual black anger.

The response to Nigeria has been different. Nigeria's crisis has developed in a distant, less known place. Its victimized people have created no firestorm of resistance. Both victim and victimizer are black. White Americans in large part don't care. African-Americans, without our usual race-button energy and anger, have condemned the generals through our leaders' voices but not with the old all-consuming antiapartheid vigor. Perhaps we're fighting this one with more detachment because we ashamedly doubt whether a society as systemically corrupt as Nigeria's can ever be made to work. To put a finer point on it, where has any society of failed core values been made to work?

For that matter, aren't Americans addressing fundamental societal problems just as unsuccessfully at home? American progress of any kind, recently, is wholly and deceivingly technological. This provides an electronic disguise for what really ails us—social rot deep within.

Fifty years is a blip in the life of a society. I never saw a gun in all my public-school days begun fifty years ago. Today one in eight American junior high and high school students carries a weapon to school. More alarming, there is no crescendo of outcry from Americans, who are either numbed or scared witless. Political leaders (who largely aren't leaders at all—that takes courage) largely don't address American society's real problems. Solutions would require real leadership and massive public and private investments of energy and capital at all levels in programs to salvage our nation's youth. Planning prisons for those still in diapers and approving prohibitively expensive and unnecessary military hardware are much more to the liking of American society's contemporary political leaders. And so we drift, anesthetized by television, whose executives beam back to us and the whole world our social rot while laying claim to social responsibility by rating the rot they produce and show us.

What is going on? Is the world dying? One billion of the world's people survive on less than a dollar a day. The figure will reach 1.7 billion by the end of the century. Monks in rapidly industrializing Thailand are raping and robbing people.

These problems, then, are hardly peculiar to Nigeria. Name a society that has renovated itself after a meltdown of its core values.

If I sound like a pessimist, I assure you I am not. I consider myself a thoughtful realist. Nigeria will have its democracy despite the de facto opposition of the generals' multinational corporate kindred spirits and the indifference of the industrialized world. The generals will end up where tyrants invariably do, either dead or chased out of office. The decent and courageous people of Nigeria together with their friends abroad will see to that.

Rebuilding society is another and an infinitely more difficult matter. How to do it? Societies remain *viable* largely by dint of collective forbearance. Law must be broadly more observed than enforced. Constitutions come and go. In thirty-six years of independence, Nigeria has written for itself three democratic constitutions. For one reason or another, all have failed. In the power sectors of the army, government, and business, the country has never achieved the requisite forbearance long enough to germinate and grow a democratic culture of law observance. Law, in *viable* political societies, is not an uncomfortable overlay but rather a mass expression of the very social values that caused such societies to cohere in the first place. Law is but one face to a social contract proffered, accepted, and observed in *viable* societies by critical-mass numbers, particularly among influential elites throughout the various power corridors.

In working societies, police and other law enforcement agencies serve only as representatives for law-observing majorities with writ and instruction to deter and contain illegal and, importantly, antisocial behavior. When illegal behavior is no longer aberrant but mainstream, society weakens. When the principal violators of law and constitution are members of government and its law enforcement agencies, society becomes dysfunctional.

This is the current state of Nigeria. All the earmarks of a thoroughgoing police state are there. The police and military are not agents of the citizenry but rather terrorizers arrayed against it. Due process means nothing. Torture is commonplace. That the government leaders steal grandly is not disputed, even by those (a few of whom are prominent African-Americans) who would defend or explain the government.

No doubt, many white Americans and Europeans rejoice at the sight of Nigeria's spectacle of bad governance. To their enduring credit, the large majority of America's African-American leadership have not ducked or dissembled. They have looked a painful dictatorship in the eye and condemned it roundly and publicly.

A handful of others took a different course, including two members of the Congressional Black Caucus (Senator Carol Moseley Braun and Congressman William Jefferson) and Minister Louis Farrakhan, who at a March 1996 National Newspaper Publishers Association luncheon following a trip to Nigeria said that General Abacha merited exemption from criticism inasmuch as Abacha's critics, I among them, had not criticized Abacha's predecessor, General Babangida, who ruled for a longer period than General Abacha. The logic of his point escaped me. We should have condemned Babangida and we were quite justifiably condemning General Abacha, who, in any case, ran a decidedly crueler show than his predecessor and had been the real power behind several previous military coups, including General Babangida's.

Farrakhan went further, saying that General Abacha should be allowed three years for democratic restoration in addition to the two and a half years he had ruled to that point. His patience was ironic. In October 1995 Farrakhan called me to ask if I would meet with a follower of his who was a Nigerian former military officer. I agreed. During the meeting the former military officer said to me, "I want to carry out a coup against General Abacha and I need guns and resources."

"Why are you telling me this?"

"I was hoping you could connect me with people in the Clinton administration and the CIA."

I was dumbfounded. "I don't know anybody in the CIA and that's not what we do at TransAfrica. There's no way I would be in favor of CIA sponsorship of another military coup. Democracy should be restored by use of public strategies."

From the beginning of our effort on Nigeria, I had supported the imposition of a multilateral oil embargo and a freezing of the generals' assets in the United States and Europe. Nothing short of such tough punitive measures would ever incline the generals to relinquish power. By letter, black leaders had warned President Clinton that if he did not move with dispatch, Nigeria could erupt into civil war, drawing much of west and central Africa into its vortex.

While in Haiti in January 1996 for the wedding of President Jean-Bertrand Aristide, I spoke with National Security Advisor Anthony Lake about Nigeria at President Aristide's home in Tabarre. I asked him when the United States would come forward with a package of meaningful sanctions. He told me that sanctions were in the offing. By March 1996 President Clinton had proposed a package of multilateral sanctions to the heads of state of Canada and Europe. The sanctions included a program for freezing some Nigerian assets and a limited prohibition of new investment, but no oil embargo. The oil companies' fierce lobbying had paid off. Canada, as expected, quickly agreed to support the package. Britain balked. The rest were slow to answer.

The Clinton White House through this period was having a difficult time finding African support for any sanctions against Nigeria. Nelson Mandela, president of South Africa, had called for sanctions following the November execution of Ken Saro Wiwa, and South African officials were annoyed when Mandela received no support from the U.S. for his call. Now Mandela, under pressure from other African leaders, was in full retreat, even going so far as to bar prodemocracy Nigerians attempting to meet in South Africa in April 1996 from entering the country.

General Abacha appeared to be having some success in his effort to interpose Africa, indeed to interpose as much of the black world as he could manipulate to his defense, between Nigeria and the never terribly purposeful pressure from the white industrialized nations of North America and Europe. If he could divert attention from the assorted villainies of his autocratic regime, if he could recast it as race theater—them against us, global black folk victimized anew by white colonialists, slavers, and racists—if he could punch black folks' race defense buttons, he could buy time. (He couldn't win, of course. Tyrants never do. But they never learn, either.) Viscera on. Minds off. Down through time. It never fails. Demagogues cum tyrants *do* know this.

The question rumbled through African capitals and came squarely home to Mandela and South Africa. Are you one of us or one of them now? Is South Africa still a part of Africa or has it become a satellite of Europe?

Countless unwitting African-American clergy, journalists, and local elected officials streamed through the Nigerian capital of Abuja in Mercedes-Benz limousines afloat on General Abacha's lavish sponsorship. "Nigeria has been defamed. Nigeria has been misunderstood," they were told over formal dinners. "We must be allowed to solve our own problems in our way. Europe is Europe. Africa is Africa."

In this war of values, it is very often hard to know where the front is. As the Allied diversions at Calais had fooled Hitler,

Abacha was now doing much the same to us. In any war of principles he had the distinct advantage of shamelessness.

If I am to be attacked by blacks, he must have thought, let those blacks be connected in their criticism to the very white nations that have been the black world's age-old enemies. Nail Mandela and my African-American critics to that cross and see how well they do.

How better could General Abacha sustain a successful deflection of black world criticism than by offering the diversion of a pernicious white world that does not understand Nigeria and cares nothing for its fate? His shelter works only because it is constructed on a foundation of truth. After all, was it not Europe and the United States that enslaved millions of my people's forebears, decimating Africa in the process? Was it not white world colonialism that rode roughshod over traditional African governance systems for achieving social cohesion and conflict resolution? Are these not the same white folk, from Stanley and Livingstone to Schweitzer and van Riebeeck, who from the moment of their lamented arrival have had no respect for Africans, their various histories, languages, cultures, mores? Are these not the white industrialized countries that smothered African independence under a mountain of debt, building roads and bridges Africa neither wanted nor needed? Are these not the whites who today lecture Africa that democracy can only mean the precise kind practiced at Westminster or theorized by Madison?

Cleverly, in the calculus of tyrants like General Abacha, the white world in the sight of blacks can be made to seem damned when it does and damned when it doesn't. Those who deserve to be damned are of course, those who defend, undergird, and invest in an enterprise they know clearly enough to be criminal and cruel—the skybox corporate neocolonialists. But those who warrant no censure, those with the capacity and willingness to penalize the generals, are as stuck to the mean record of their white world antecedents as we are to the enormous suffering of their black victims.

This explains why President Clinton needed African support for his sanctions package. It also explains President Mandela's retreat. General Abacha's strategy of turning what should have been a straightforward human rights issue into a racial square-off appeared to have produced some success. History casts very long shadows. The race line etched in pain and humiliation is very hard to cross.

■

For a moment, if only for intellectual exercise, let us in unison wrench ourselves from the diversion and look squarely at the objective and indisputable facts of Nigeria's tragic decline. I need not say again that it is undemocratic. In many quarters the term "democracy" itself is freighted with the baggage of foreign imposition. Suffice it to say that Nigeria's hundred million people are ruled wholly without their consent or participation. This runs directly against the grain of African precolonial governance traditions. The society is inarguably among the world's most corrupt. With the courts increasingly powerless, Nigerian citizens are in virtually every way lacking any rights. The country has crumpled into itself. It cannot attract outside general economic investment. It cannot entice home tens of thousands of highly trained Nigerians scattered across the globe. It cannot develop. On its current course, it can only pursue its slow, inexorable slide downward, consuming in its wake much of Africa's unremarked but significant progress.

Beyond posing a general danger to Africa's very future, Nigeria puts at risk incipient reform elsewhere. These promising new starts in smaller African countries threaten Africa's colossus more by example and power of idea than by any tangible menace.

Mali, landlocked and sandy, is one of the world's twenty poorest countries. A former French colony and home of an ancient learning center at Timbuktu, this West African country of eight million had until 1992 endured thirty-five years of military dictatorship. Scarcely four years after its first free elections brought to power President Alpha Oumar Konaré, Mali has undergone a signal transformation presenting a largely unnoticed salutary augury for Africa.

A multiparty system has replaced a constrictive single-party machinery. Twenty newspapers have supplanted a former state monopoly. The economy has been growing at a rate of six percent. The five-year conflict between Tuareg nomad rebels and the Malian army has ended.

Unvisited in recent years by a single high-level American official, Mali is one of many small bright lights shining across Africa. Where Nigeria executes political dissidents, Malia's president opposes capital punishment on principle across the board. Where Nigeria shuts down publishing houses and arrests journalists wholesale, a free press thrives in Mali. Where oil-rich and graft-ridden Nigeria is virtually bankrupt, tiny resource-poor Mali is managing its economy on an upward trajectory.

Standards are all. Where do we set the bar? From the ranks of black leaders globally, what must we expect and demand of ourselves? From Nigeria to Mali, from Washington, D.C., to Kingston, Jamaica, how rigorously must we come to evaluate our leadership performance and values of governance? Have we in the Nigerias of the world become so inured to gross official malfeasance that we've lost all capacity for disgust? The battle lines are drawn by the questions. Winning the values war makes the black world's recovery not only possible but probable. From the vantage point of a new constructive and critical self-awareness, all other important recoveries, economic and political, can occur in train. The Caribbean's democratic leaders have always understood this. The broadening ranks of Africa's enlightened new leadership have come to understand it as well. It is this vision, this crystallizing hope, this glimpse of a rising future that Nigeria's kleptocratic rulers are dedicated to crushing.

◼ Mid 1990s: Of Rwanda

In December 1993, I had lunch at the White House with a high-ranking Clinton administration foreign policy official. "Randall, if we don't do something soon about Rwanda, it's going to blow sky-high. I don't know how much time we have but it can't be very much."

I was trying to adjust to his sense of urgency. My hands had been full with the campaign going forward against the military dictatorship in Haiti. I hadn't been following Rwanda on a day-to-day basis.

"I'm having trouble getting this thing up on the screen around here. Ghanaian peacekeepers are training to intervene in Rwanda, but they've got to have some of our armored personnel carriers available to them through the United Nations. The arrangements are moving at a snail's pace. If we don't get something done soon, we're gonna all have hell to pay. Do you think you can get some media attention for this?"

It is broadly understood throughout the U.S. foreign policy establishment that almost no one in the upper reaches cares much about Africa or the Caribbean. This is self-evident even at times when a vigorous response is demonstrably in the interest of the United States. That great neurologist in the sky bangs the Africa policy knee at the State Department and absolutely nothing happens. Zilch. Pervasive indifference. The interior reflex mechanism is not merely defective. It is dead. Perhaps worse. Death implies foregoing life. And there was never even that.

The foreign policy machine appears to operate on a reward and punishment basis. The reward is often the absence of punishment. In order to manipulate the policy apparatus toward one outcome or another, the person or organization or constituency wishing to work the levers must have the capacity to develop pressure. This pressure may assume any or all of several forms, from the financial to a concerted focusing of public opinion. The serious and implacable pressure generated without exertion and applied in monochromatic club discussions daily, nightly, late-nightly, courses silently and effortlessly through every chamber of the Policy House. This inside-the-house pressure is essentially the exclusive preserve of well-placed, well-heeled white Americans formed in columns headed by captains of industry, scions of wealthy families, and their ilk. These are the people who believe political influence to be their birthright—those, that is, who give the idea a moment's thought.

It is this silently coursing white establishment consensus that has shaped, since time immemorial, definitions of what U.S. national interests have been, are, and will be. They own the country and with it the right to decide what is right for it and us and the rest of the world.

The Policy House knew about the looming disaster in Rwanda and didn't care. The rest of us might have cared but didn't get told.

"Randall," my White House host continued, "we're now bogged down with the United Nations haggling over the lease terms for the armored personnel carriers. We're even debating the color the things will be painted. I'm trying to move this thing. But I don't know. We need some pressure on this from the outside."

I could see his point. What I could not easily see was how to generate public pressure quickly when less than one percent of the American public even knew Rwanda existed.

Rwanda had been saddled with a mean history and a corrupt and vengeful president in Juvenal Habyarimana. From the beginning in the late 1880s Germany, the original colonial power, had favored Rwanda's minority Tutsi people over its majority Hutus. The Tutsis, who had centuries ago migrated down from around Ethiopia into Rwanda and the neighboring area of Burundi, were tall people with relatively keen features. The Hutus were generally much shorter with broader features. In a place where Aryans were not an available choice, the Germans practiced the racism of relativity.

Whatever modest opportunities existed to be awarded the indigenous people under a colonial regime were made available to the Tutsis. Positions in civil service, opportunities for higher education abroad, and jobs of any consequence throughout the colonial system were given almost exclusively to Tutsis. As a qualification for school places, minimum height requirements were set, locking out virtually all Hutus.

No doubt there were preexisting ethnic tensions between Tutsis and Hutus. Rwanda and Burundi were, even then, Africa's most densely populated countries. A living was hard to win from the mountainous terrain. The simple economics of survival had early on given rise to mutual mistrust. Discriminatory German colonial management policies served only to exacerbate these tensions.

Germany lost its African colonies with its defeat in World War I. Belgium took over in Rwanda and Burundi and left in place the discriminatory structures. When Belgium granted Rwanda and Burundi their independence on July 1, 1962, the deeply resented minority Tutsis found themselves running everything worth running—the government, the army, and all other systems of real authority.

Juvenal Habyarimana, a Hutu, became Rwanda's president after a coup on July 5, 1973. If an ethnically riven Rwanda needed a visionary and conciliatory leader of character, solid traits, forbearance, and wisdom, it would not get its man in Juvenal Habyarimana. He was a corrupt demagogue bent on Hutu revenge against the hated Tutsis. Soon he would begin to train Hutu militia with a clearly stated mission of genocide. Arms had been supplied to him by France and apartheid South Africa. The Bush administration gave him a modest amount of military assistance as well. His program for mass slaughter of the Tutsis was undisguised. Invitations to the killing party had been broadcast on the radio in the capital, Kigali. We knew. Our Policy House knew exactly what President Habyarimana was up to. It didn't seem to matter.

"If we don't get these peacekeepers in there soon, it's going to be bad, very bad," my White House host told me, "but it's moving very slowly here."

On April 6, 1994, President Habyarimana and the Hutu president of Burundi, Cyprien Ntaryamira, were killed in a plane crash. Virtually no one believed the crash was the result of pilot error or mechanical failure. Following the plane crash, some 500,000 Rwandans were hacked, shot, and bludgeoned to death in the bloody genocidal convulsions that rolled across the country leaving hardly a family untouched.

■

In public life, you are only who you appear to be. Who you really are is seldom known to anyone save the person with whom you share your life. I have been nakedly honest only before Hazel. She alone has seen the idealistic boy within, struggling to keep the middle-aged man decent in public effort where only the victories count. Why do we do what we do with our lives, in any case? It is so much easier to know in youth before anyone is watching. Those years of uninformed certainty when moral conviction, in and of itself, is enough to inflate a young man's sail. Before the taint of tactics. Before learning how to win. Before an ego large enough now for public advocacy smothers the child who believes purely and naively.

I am happy only at home with Hazel and my family. I garden, but only flowers. I am not a practical man. If there were but two personality types, actuaries and romantics, I would be forever in the company of the latter. I love music, virtually all kinds. I hear with the heart. Gospel carries me home through the black ages. McCoy Tyner offends. Rachmaninoff invented melodies so beautiful that they merit a place among the natural wonders. Stravinsky grates. William Grant Still, the wonderful black composer of the early 1900s from Mississippi who had such apparent influence on George Gershwin, has been largely forgotten, sadly even by African-Americans. Anita Baker renders me for the span of her song a better person.

I think that I must be what is called a shy extrovert. I never remember anyone's name a moment after being introduced. I try to listen to the name but I simply cannot. The whole business is unnatural. Were I not paid to do it, I would never again make a public speech. I loathe it. Not so much the speaking, but the time just before. Were it not a requirement of my job, I would never do another television interview, particularly the remote kind to camera. I don't relish talking to strangers, but I prefer even them to a black camera lens.

I have neither needed nor wanted the company of people save the few I love and who love me. In sum, I am poorly suited for the work that I have done for the last eighteen years.

My work requires the raising of a great deal of money. I am not wealthy but I have many wealthy friends. Because they are my friends, I don't like to ask them for money. Most people with money are strangers to me, but as I've already said, I don't relish talking to strangers. It must be fairly obvious by now that I am not a very good fund-raiser. Fortunately, some like Edward Lewis, Danny Glover, Bill Cosby, Martin Payson, Earl Graves, and Sugar Ray Leonard have given me money despite my deficiencies. I ask myself—or is it the dying child within asking—*Why can't virtue of message be enough to carry the day?* Remember, in public battle over public policy, you are only who you seem to be. Who you really are is irrelevant.

It is axiomatic. The message goes nowhere without a messenger. Further, the message almost never expands beyond the stature or manipulative creativity of the messenger. If the message is the warhead, a talent for public manipulation and salesmanship is the essential delivery system. The messenger exists only as he seems to. If he does not seem to, he does not exist. Nor does the message. A tree falls in the forest and all that.

Which brings us to the sine qua non for effective outside-the-Policy-House advocacy: a gift for self-promotion, a gift used or, more appropriately, misused to its fullest by those self-seeking souls unburdened by any restraint of shame. This is not to disparage self-promotion, especially when it is an inadvertent by-product of a public effort to alter wrongheaded public policy. We have seat belts in our cars, and consumer safety standards generally, because of the public advocacy of Ralph Nader, whose formidable public stature has carried in its trail a salutary and major public policy influence.

My academic friends and the foundations that fund their painstaking research appear to understand none of this. For forty years of apartheid, the tenured opponents of that system won grants, did research, wrote monographs and books, gave testimony ad nauseam before Congress. All to no effect. American policy toward South Africa had been and remained one of de facto public and private embrace. Few if any members of Congress felt compelled to read or listen to anything the academic community had to say. Only when a campaign of massive civil disobedience was packaged for public participation in late 1984 did American policy begin to turn around.

This is not the preferred way to make or influence foreign policy. But in America, if you are outside the Policy House, a position to which virtually all blacks have been relegated, it is the only way to have impact. We have won most of the battles in which I have fought. But the price has been dear and I am tired and diminished by the process. In all the years of meeting with presidents, secretaries of state, national security advisors, U.S. trade representatives, and members of Congress, I cannot recall a single change of policy course that resulted from any of the hundreds of discussions, the thousands of letters, the scores of presentations to perfunctory nods and courteous closings. Like water off a duck's back. It never ever meant a damn thing.

In 1989 I arranged a meeting between the leadership of the U.S. House of Representatives and national black leaders to discuss the crisis in Angola. The meeting was held in the Speaker's office on the House side of the Capitol Building. There were ten members of our delegation, including Jesse Jackson, Dorothy Height, president of the National Council of Negro Women, and William Lucy, president of the Coalition of Black Trade Unionists. Across the room seated on a sofa and waiting to hear our concerns were the Speaker, Thomas Foley, the majority leader, Richard Gephardt, and the deputy majority whip, David Bonior. Their black colleague William H. Gray, the majority whip, was invited to attend but declined.

I thanked the House leaders for receiving us and told them that for too long the southwest African country of Angola had been a killing field with the highest per capita amputee rate in the world. The size of Texas, Angola had not known peace since African forces there began a military struggle for independence in 1961 against Portuguese colonialism almost five hundred years in force. The war against Portugal barely concluded, civil war had broken out in 1975, the two sides becoming Cold War proxies of the United States and the Soviet Union. As I've pointed out earlier, the side the United States chose set us at odds with the government of President José Eduardo dos Santos, a government that had been recognized around the world, even by the conservative British government of Margaret Thatcher, not to mention the virtual entirety of Africa. Under the stewardship of Henry Kissinger we lamentably elected to militarily support the rebel Jonas Savimbi, leader of UNITA, in his efforts to overthrow the government in Luanda. The move also made the United States a de facto ally of the apartheid regime then very much in control in South Africa.

"Mr. Speaker," I said, "of Angola's nine million people, nearly a half million have died in a war that grinds on and on. We need your vigorous opposition to any continued U.S. arming of Jonas Savimbi. He is destroying Angola. He is not a democrat. His human rights record is deplorable. It has even been documented by a noted British author that Savimbi presided over the public burning of one entire family at his headquarters in Jamba. Please move to cut off assistance to him and press the Bush administration to recognize the Angolan government."

I stopped.

We waited for his reply.

Nothing. He looked at us blankly.

We waited longer.

I tried to read his expression. Certainly no hostility there. Had he heard what I'd said? I couldn't be sure. He didn't seem opposed to my request. He didn't look vaguely curious or befuddled. Comatose. He looked comatose. Benignly and completely indifferent to the concerns we had come to press upon him. If he uttered a word in what remained of our meeting, I cannot remember it.

■ Early 1996: Washington, D.C., and Miami

On March 1, 1996, Congresswoman Maxine Waters and I held a meeting of African-American leaders and Caribbean ambassadors with Mickey Kantor, the U.S. trade representative, to discuss the growing threats to vital markets abroad for Caribbean agricultural exports. In attendance, among others, were the Jamaican and Saint Lucian ambassadors to the United States, Drs. Richard Bernal and Joseph E. Edmunds, Donald Payne, who now chaired the Congressional Black Caucus, Wade Henderson, director of the Washington office of the NAACP, and Bill Lucy.

When Caribbean islands lose markets for their produce, their economies are damaged. Unemployment spikes. Foreign currency reserves erode. Social services and infrastructure deteriorate. Democratic institutions weaken. Large- and medium-sized islands with diversified or even partially diversified economies (Jamaica, for example) take a battering but somehow survive. When tiny islands like Dominica lose markets for their bananas, their economies simply collapse. Bananas or sugar are virtually all they have to sell. And when their fragile economies implode, the fall of democracy follows.

Exacerbating economies-of-scale problems that drive up the per-unit cost of production, farmers on the tiny volcanic islands of the Caribbean grow their bananas vertically on terraced patches sculpted from the mountainous terrain making up much of the available arable land. It's an expensive banana to grow.

Chiquita Brands grows its bananas on the broad flat expanses of countries like Mexico, Honduras, and Guatemala. The banana is cheaper to grow and ordinarily would be cheaper to sell than any the small-island Caribbean farmers could even hope to produce.

A modest access to European markets has been afforded by former European metropole countries to their former colonies of Africa, the Pacific, and the Caribbean. Of the banana market, the European Union has made available eight percent to Caribbean producers. Owing only to this protected access, Caribbean countries with a scant three percent of the world banana market precariously cling to viability.

Non-ACP (African, Caribbean, and Pacific island) countries together with multinational companies like Chiquita control more than eighty-five percent of the European Union market and ninety percent of the world market.

But Chiquita and the non-ACP countries of Latin America wanted still more and took aim at the special arrangements between the Caribbean banana-producing countries and the European Union. Egged on by Chiquita—and at the apparent suggestion of the United States—Guatemala, Ecuador, Honduras, and Mexico were primed before our March 1 meeting to challenge the special arrangement before the World Trade Organization in an effort to have the Caribbean's market niche struck down.

Our meeting with Mickey Kantor began at 8:00 A.M. First, the Caribbean ambassadors presented their case for continued market access: they explained in detail that the abrogation of the special European arrangement would result in the devastation of their small economies and destabilization of their democratic systems. The African-American participants warned against an American abandonment of stable and friendly regional democracies. After all, it was Eugenia Charles who, as prime minister of the now threatened Dominica, stood with President Ronald Reagan in support of the 1983 American military invasion of Grenada.

We made the further point that the other side of Caribbean economic frailty was the growing grip of the drug industry.

Even before our meeting, the State Department had reported in an official document that farmers in Saint Vincent, fearing lower banana prices, had begun to grow marijuana crops instead. Increasingly, Latin American drug cartel traffickers in the Virgin Islands, Barbados, Trinidad, Saint Kitts, and Jamaica were establishing staging and storage facilities on those islands for drugs that would move from Colombia through the islands and ultimately on to the United States.

Shortly after Michael Manley stepped down from his second term as prime minister of Jamaica, he told me: "Jamaica is only a few years behind Colombia with respect to drug infestation. Other Caribbean islands are in the same fix. Soon the drug industry's reach into our countries will overtake the governments' power to control it. We don't have the resources to deal with this problem. It may be that the United States had better intelligence about drug industry operations in Jamaica than I did when I was prime minister."

On February 7, 1996, on the occasion of the inauguration of President René Préval of Haiti, I spoke in Port-au-Prince with General John Sheehan, commander in chief of the U.S. Atlantic Command. He confirmed to me the seriousness of the drug threat to the stability of the Caribbean. General Sheehan had made a significant contribution to Haiti's democratic transition and remained greatly interested in the stability of the region. An American security assistance package of $50 to $75 million for patrol boats and police training could, General Sheehan thought, adequately equip the Caribbean to defend its island chain from use by drug dealers in Colombia and the United States as a drug road into the American market. No one at the State Department took notice of his proposal.

I said to Mickey Kantor: "If the United States doesn't give these countries in the Caribbean a chance to sell their bananas, they inevitably will sell something else, if only to survive. To do otherwise, the United States will appear to have been bought by the president and principal owner of Chiquita, Carl Lindner, who we all know has contributed recently at least a quarter of a million dollars to the Democratic Party."

Kantor was unfailingly gracious in that self-effacingly informal manner peculiar to American officials. "Carl Lindner's activities and actions have no impact on American trade policy," he said. "We must try to find a way to reconcile what I believe is a discriminatory arrangement with the requirements of GATT in a way that will not harm the economic interests of the Caribbean." He paused and looked at us with penetrating decency. "I recommend," he went on, "that informal meetings be convened with all the parties involved: the European Union, the Caribbean banana-producing countries, the United States, and the Latin American banana-producing countries. Together we can search for a mutually acceptable solution. As long as these discussions are taking place, there will be no application made to the World Trade Organization for a ruling on this matter."

Kantor had been unequivocal. We left the meeting heartened. We had clearly won time if nothing else.

The follow-up all-parties meeting was set for April 9 in Miami at the Belmont Hotel. Elaborate preparation was undertaken for the meeting throughout the Caribbean. The day before the meeting, at great and scarcely affordable expense, Caribbean participants flew into Miami from London, Brussels, and throughout the Caribbean. At the table on meeting day sat the United States, the European Union, the Latin American and Caribbean negotiators. Useful discussions began in the morning and stretched into the late afternoon. Then suddenly, painfully and humiliatingly for the Caribbean participants, the bottom fell out. As they sat hopefully offering proposals for an acceptable solution, it was announced that the United States and the Latin American countries had reduced the discussion to farce by earlier formally referring the matter to the World Trade Organization for a ruling.

In unambiguous language, with an open face and an earnestness of voice and eye, Mickey Kantor had in our March 1 meeting told us a bald-faced lie. The Caribbean ambassadors, relatively new to American political society, had believed him. But so had we battle-weary cynical African-American trench fighters. We too had swallowed his extravagantly embroidered lie.

The following morning, a U.S. trade official involved in the multilateral discussion was seen having breakfast in the Belmont Hotel restaurant with a ubiquitous officer of Chiquita Brand, the company that as United Fruit had in 1954 worked with the CIA to overthrow Guatamala's democratically elected government and wreaked havoc on democratic aspirations and workers' rights throughout Central America.

So what purpose did all our elaborate meetings serve? It's the staged demonstrations that always make the difference. Sacrifice a little coveted dignity. Provoke arrest. Starve nearly to death. Create a short-lived groundswell. Only then do the policy-makers stir and respond. Only after the fire is built, with any media manipulation tactic short of the unseemly, do the talk shows book and the cameras roll. Congress rouses but slowly. News assignment editors present America with a public policy controversy, brand new to most Americans but bitterly old to a selfless and unsung few wearied in the long effort to make polit-ical leaders lead.

It is not pretty but nothing else works. Legislation is put on a fast track. The President publicly engages the issue. Media manipulation is no longer necessary. News organizations run prospective interviews to ground on weekends in remote places. American action of one kind or another is initiated and ripples through the international community. Victory is inevitable. After twenty-eight years, Mandela walks out of prison. After three years, Aristide goes home. Academic grantees and foundation grantors celebrate an outcome to which they made no effective contribution while mildly dis-daining the tactics of those advocates outside the Policy House who did.

No such groundswell was developed for Rwanda. The President was under no pressure to assign it priority. No public accounting would be required from him or Congress no matter the outcome on the ground in Rwanda. After months of desul-tory low-level circular back-room White House discussion, seri-ous prophylactic measures had not been taken.

Rwanda blew up. A half million people died. The American people heard of Rwanda for the first time.

By the time the killing had subsided, the United States had

spent in excess of a billion dollars on relief efforts. Had real attention been paid earlier, the crisis might have been averted, if not altogether then certainly in substantial part.

If democracy, when healthy, is rooted in an enlightened citizenry, ours is in a parlous state. This is particularly so in the way we make policy toward a world of countries we may have heard of but know nothing about or, I suspect, more often have never heard of at all. We don't require world studies in our schools. We generally offer only the romance languages of Europe in public school curricula and teach even those languages in English. Minds incubating in an American school environment know without knowing that if there is a world beyond Europe, it merits small respect and has no history. From this pool of fools emerge those who comprise our national foreign policy leadership.

Some years ago, when he was chairman of the House Subcommittee on Africa, Howard Wolpe told me that he didn't think there were twenty members of Congress who could name five African countries.

The price of this ignorance is dear. Americans end up believing that problems in the world begin only with their learning of them. Even then what little we get to know is media-presented without historical context. We can't then hope to participate constructively in any policy debate.

Our democracy is reduced thereby to the narrow stricture of electoral ritual. A small homogeneous community of anonymous foreign policy professionals acts with impunity and without oversight or responsibility to account. In cases like Rwanda, it acts hardly at all.

And who are these people after all? There is a disquieting opaqueness about them. I see them from time to time across a conference table. They appear interchangeable. They share a fashion of language uncommon to the rest of us: circumspect policyese is what they speak. Balance and pragmatism are encouraged. Passion and conviction are seen as career destructive. Perhaps I am seeing only the race line again but I don't think so. There is that, all right, but something more.

Perhaps it is that they are invisibly powerful and known to us only by their unclassified memoranda and articles in *Foreign Affairs*. They write in value-neutral prose, erecting intellectually formidable arguments for policies that often produce in human terms disastrous results. The results are borne by faraway people they cannot know and do not resemble.

They must be smart or seem to. Credentials help. But who really are these people?

As Ronald Reagan's assistant secretary of state for Africa, Chester Crocker obstructed democracy for South Africa hardly less obdurately and even more successfully than George Wallace opposed the integration of the University of Alabama. Haiti's relief from military tyranny was delayed by the not merely inept but vile diplomacy of the State Department's Lawrence Pezzullo. George Bush's assistant secretary of state for Africa, Herman Cohen, is now collecting representation fees from the very African countries whose interests he formerly held in callous disregard. With any competence and half a heart, these men might have served objectives that are well within even their own set forth definitions of American interests: the promotion of democracy in Africa or the Caribbean or wherever. None did. Ever.

Though time has proven them tragically wrong, they have suffered no reproof. Within foreign policy circles, what are Africa and the Caribbean to bruise anyway? In any case, it is they who will write the history.

Should I confess anger? In my line of work, emotion is a disability. Well, I am angry. Angry that I and others like me have had not only to contest tyrants abroad but first to overcome the tyrants' first line of defense found in our own U.S. Department of State. Angry that so many have had to work so hard to cause our nation to do the right and decent thing. Angry that a good and decent white policy official in the White House could not win attention from his colleagues a few doors down the hall for the looming disaster that became the holocaust of Rwanda.

December 1996–April 1997: Dominica, Saint Lucia, and Washington, D.C.

Terry Telemaque, appearing weary, emerges from the dense thicket onto a narrow muddy path. He is carrying a large cluster of bananas on his head. It is hot and steamy amid the banana plants that carpet his small patch in the hills of Dominica. It is only slightly cooler on the path. His skin is dark. His hair is flecked with gray. He is in his early forties but looks older. His knowing eyes are those of a worn, defenseless man struggling against the large and pitiless forces of his impending destruction. His T-shirt is torn and stained with sweat.

Terry is approached by Congresswoman Maxine Waters, who has come to his country to talk to small banana farmers like him. He tells her his story.

"If they [Chiquita] squeeze us out, we will be the ones that suffer. We have no alternative. We have no factory. We have nothing to turn to.

"If somebody [U.S.] say they love somebody, you shouldn't only say you love them. You should try to help them and prepare for them. Don't try to do them cruelty. Some big men are trying to do us cruelty because when you take away a man's daily bread, you take away my livelihood. You send me on common crime. You send me to steal. You force me to drugs."

Waters and the members of her delegation have heard variants of Telemaque's wrenching story earlier that day and the day before in Saint Lucia, where small banana farmer Patrick Joseph told them:

"We are trying to fight Chiquita who wants our market share. We might have to sell them our bananas so we can eat for two months, knowing well that at the end they are going to destroy us if they capture our market share. We might have to plant marijuana knowing that before you can harvest that crop the police might come and arrest you and put you in jail. But you are alive. The idea is to stay alive. You will do what it takes to keep you and your family alive."

U.S. economic assistance to the Caribbean has been falling steadily for years. A member of the Waters delegation asks if an increase in foreign aid would make a difference. Randy Rodney of the Dominica Association of Evangelical Churches is unequivocal in his response.

"Ladies and gentlemen, we need trade. We need income from work done. We need industry. We are not looking for handouts but rather an honest way to earn a living. Please try your utmost to assist us by using your offices and influence wherever it matters, and may the Lord bless you all."

■

The narrow legal issue before the WTO panel in Geneva was whether the European Union's trade regime that guaranteed access to Europe's markets for Caribbean bananas violated WTO trade rules. What was more seriously at stake was the economic survival of at least four countries (Dominica, Saint Lucia, Grenada, and Saint Vincent) that earned more than half of their national income from the sale of bananas. Europe was their only market. Because Caribbean bananas were so much more expensive to grow than those from Central America, the Caribbean banana industry required, for survival, protected access to its eight-percent slice of Europe's market. Bananas, the only fruit that can be viably grown year round in the Caribbean, were literally all that these countries had to sell—at least legally. They asked to be allowed to present their case before the panel. The U.S. trade representative objected.

On March 19, 1997, the WTO dispute panel issued a four-hundred-page report upholding the complaint brought by the United States and four Latin American countries in which Chiquita grows its bananas.

The United States had dealt a lethal blow to four tiny black democracies it claimed as friends. And for the larger and more economically diverse island of Jamaica, the decision was the second half of a one-two punch. As a result of the North American Free Trade Agreement (NAFTA) reached by the U.S., Mexico, and Canada, apparel and textile factories in Jamaica had already been shutting and rapidly locating to the now tariff-free export-friendly environment of Mexico. Even before the WTO handed down its ruling, the World Bank had estimated that companies producing more than a third of the $12.5 billion in goods exported annually to the United States from the Caribbean could relocate their factories to Mexico under the existing U.S. trade rules.

▪

Time magazine (March 31, 1997) published a story about Chiquita's head, Carl Lindner, written by Michael Weisskopf:

Lindner wanted U.S. trade Representative Mickey Kantor to help him pry open European markets, which rely on various tariffs and trade barriers effectively to shut out Lindner's bananas. Though hundreds of companies ask Washington to investigate unfair trade practices, the U.S. Trade Representative accepts only about 14 cases each year. Even fewer are taken to Geneva for resolution by the World Trade Organization. And only rarely do such cases make the cut when hardly any U.S. jobs are at stake; Chiquita employs most of its 45,000 workers in Honduras and Guatemala. And yet Kantor took the case. . . . On April 12, 1996, the day after Kantor asked the WTO to examine Chiquita's griev-ance, Lindner and his top executives began funneling more than $500,000 to [Democratic party coffers in] about two dozen states from Florida to California, campaign officials told TIME.

Carl Lindner, already with nineteen percent of the European market, was well on his way to driving tens of thousands of Caribbean banana farmers out of business altogether.

■

"I think you should know that we could be jailed for three months and fined five thousand dollars," I said.

Silence. Daryl Leathers of TransAfrica's staff was at the wheel of the Ryder sixteen-foot flatbed truck. Between Daryl and me was Ken Cook, who headed the Environmental Working Group, a Washington-based public policy organization.

"Daryl, pull over for a couple of minutes. We don't want to get there before the press does."

"Okay."

"Are our people behind us?"

Daryl checked his mirror. "Yeah, both cars are there."

Ken flipped open his cell phone. "The press is there now. We'd better move."

"Daryl, you and one of Ken's guys will be on the flatbed unloading the boxes. Ken, you and three others line up on me to pass the boxes. I'll dump them on the steps."

"Which car is Debbie in?" Deborah Harrod of TransAfrica and Jackie Savitz of the Working Group would hold the fifteen-by-four-foot sign.

"Debbie is in the second car."

"Don't forget, Daryl, if the police rush us, push all of the boxes off the truck before they can do anything."

There were ten network television cameramen and newspaper photographers on the sidewalk as we approached the site on Seventeenth Street across from the Old Executive Office Building and a quarter block from the White House.

"Are you all ready?"

"Yes."

"Let's move, then. We may have less than a minute to do this."

Within five minutes, we had dumped two thousand pounds of bananas on the steps of the United States trade representative's building. The sign read CHIQUITA BOUGHT CLINTON AND CLINTON SOLD OUT THE CARIBBEAN.

We had committed a crime in broad daylight witnessed by as many as a hundred people, but the police, out in force, made no move to deter or arrest us. USTR officials obviously wanted no public attention drawn to a trade issue about which Americans knew nothing.

■

On the front page of the *Washington Post* (April 16, 1997) was a long story about a forty-four-year-old drunk driver who had been sentenced to five months in jail. There was no mention anywhere in the paper of the ton of bananas that had blocked access to a federal building a stone's throw from the Oval Office. The *Boston Globe* ran a picture of the banana pile—and noted in the caption that we were protesting the elimination of trade preferences for Africa. *Newsweek* magazine got it right in a detailed two-page story. CNN carried the story on its national and world networks. The other networks made their footage available to the local affiliates, where it was shown in every major market save Chicago. In our efforts to dramatize an issue the Clinton administration had taken pains to paper over, we had made a good, if not spectacular, beginning.

Later in the day I spoke on the subject to the Democratic Caucus of the House of Representatives. On the panel with me were two officials from the United States trade representative's office who said neutrally that the administration only wanted to address a trade rule violation and had no intention of hurting the Caribbean. Marcy Kaptur, a congresswoman from Ohio, wanted to know how anyone could expect the Caribbean to survive if it lost its only banana market. "While you people are doing the bidding of a private business like Chiquita, you never think of the consequences for people on the ground—men, women, and children—small farmers with families. What's to happen to them?"

"We are prepared to talk to the Caribbean—" began the U.S. trade official.

Over the years, I have grown to detest these facile, well-educated, tax-supported shills for the insatiably acquisitive, venal rich.

PART EIGHT

Plantation Redux

Black athletes, artists, and other celebrities generally know that in many very real ways America remains for blacks a huge planta-tion on which the black community has neither the capacity to know (much less reward) its authentic champions nor any real ability to punish its heretics. Only those who remain immediately of, or in, the black community can be constrained to account to it—those who need its votes, patronage, or retail dollars. Those blacks who swim out into mainstream career America are restrained thence only by an innate and controlling sense of decency (when present) and by the plantation owner's circus hoops through which ascendant well-behaved black stars of one ilk or another—artists, athletes, politicians, journalists, generals, cabinet officers, judges—can jump to glory, fame, and often untold wealth without any objective need to ever go "home" again.

Blacks are obviously no longer slaves, nor are we confined by law to this or that neighborhood of the plantation. We have toward the end of the twentieth century progressed to the status of trusty. We can move about as we please or, more accurately, as we can afford. But we have transmitted intergenerationally and exponen-tially all of the stubborn social disabilities born of slavery. No one cares up at the Big House, though. For we are "free."

We control nothing. For the mainstream, we write books but are not publishers, appear in movies but finance few, graduate from but endow no colleges, vote for but never control the President, buy from but own only one of the Fortune 500 companies, pay taxes but have little say over their use, withstand the propagation of vile media images of ourselves but control few of the machineries for image manufacture, observe the rise of black public figures but, with few exceptions, have little ability to punish or reward those who rise from our midst.

■ October 16, 1995: Washington, D.C.

The size of the assemblage strains belief. More than one million African-American men have assembled on the Mall in Washington, D.C. It is the largest demonstration of any kind in Washington history.

Of 248 million Americans, 30 million are African-Americans. Of 30 million African-Americans, 10 million are male and above the age of fifteen. If these 1990 U.S. census figures are even vaguely accurate, this would mean that roughly one in every ten African-American males above the age of fifteen has arrived to be counted on this clear fall afternoon.

Only one person could have convened such an enormous meeting of black men: Louis Farrakhan. My guess is that he is the only American who could put together a gathering of this size, period. Not Ralph Reed. Not Jesse Jackson or Michael Jackson. Not Phyllis Schlafly and Pat Buchanan pulling together. Not Billy Graham. Not Bill Clinton. Not anyone. Why?

Louis Farrakhan stayed at home. He never crossed the compromise line into white mainstream politics with its horsetrading, deal making, language trimming. He tended full-time the banked furies of black inner-city despair. Love him or loathe him, he, more than any other, presents the best public measure of the burgeoning black anger and roiling disaffection that grind away like hot geological plates under the happy big white lawn of mainstream America. He has made himself the steward of the teeming black forgotten.

I am not a Farrakhan devotee. He is demagogic. He is far too comfortable in the company of tyrants abroad. He is gratuitously offensive to nonobeisant blacks, whites generally, and Jews particularly. He is flawed. (But what else could he be?) Yet he does have courage and the mettle for leadership. He has said to white America what white America has said to black America since Reconstruction: Go screw yourselves.

He was given a Hobson's choice and he ignored it. Thus he is locked out of official Washington. The man who brought more than a million black men to the Mall has no measurable policy influence with Congress or the White House. But, in a studiously ignored general black community, Farrakhan's exclusion is his coin.

■ The City of Privilege

The twenty-foot bronze bas-relief city gate opened slightly.

Terms of admission were offered. The terms were seen to be insulting.

With his forces numbering the vast majority of African-Americans, Farrakhan elected to remain outside the walls of the great city Privilege, capital of the American State of Mind.

A comparatively small number of African-Americans operate, with varying degrees of success, inside the great white city of Privilege. I would fall into this group.

Before negotiating what neighborhoods they will be allowed to live in and what jobs they will hold, black entrants to the city are told that they must accept in toto the parameters set by the city's masters for national, state, and local policy discussion. Running afoul of these nonnegotiable parameters, they are told, could result first in political loneliness and ultimately in expulsion from Privilege.

The blacks in Privilege greatly fear expulsion. If Hobson's choice is little or nothing, the black residents of Privilege feel it is their duty to stay and fight hard for little. More than expulsion, however, they fear Vernon Jordan disease, a degenerative condition among blacks in Privilege that results in a loss of any memory of what they came to Privilege to accomplish and, further, any memory of the millions camped outside the gate with Louis Farrakhan. I do not worry about contracting this disease. I am told by my physician that it afflicts only those blacks who both wish feverishly and after careful screening are allowed to be close to the President socially. Inasmuch as the mere mention of Vernon Jordan disease violates a Privilege city ordinance, I am likely to be fined heavily by the foundations and corporations charged with the responsibility of enforcing this little-known ordinance.

Now an example of how black residents of Privilege might contravene the policy-discussion parameters.

Blacks who have college degrees, wear suits, and work in offices are not allowed to publicly say the word "reparations." Japanese Americans who live in Privilege may say it but not their African-American counterparts. This is very strange. Japanese Americans were unjustly interned for a few years during World War II. The work load was light. They were dispossessed of their property but not of their history, language, culture, and family members. In contrast, African-Americans were "interned" without compensation and with hard labor for hundreds of years. These forebears of the Vernon Jordan disease victims, the other black residents of Privilege, and the millions camped against the city gate were dispossessed of everything—property, history, language, culture, and family.

Japanese Americans said the word "reparations" publicly and repeatedly. They said it in newspapers, at public meetings, in the courts, and to thoughtful white people generally. Happily, Japanese Americans won their reparations.

Congressman John Conyers, a black member of the House of Representatives from Detroit and a courageous resident of Privilege, must have been emboldened by the Japanese American success. After all, the reparations case for the descendants of black slaves was patently stronger than that presented successfully by the Japanese. But . . .

Congressman Conyers did not know that Regulation 407, section 2(b), promulgated under the National Serious Discussion Restriction Act of 1962, disallowed for blacks the "airing or presentation of any set of grievances or casual circumstances that may be seen to have led to a painful present social condition if the original grievances or casual circumstances occurred more than two days before the painful present social condition became manifest."

Congressman Conyers was summoned to appear for sentencing before the Administrator for Public Policy Discussion, who also doubled as editor of the *Privilege Post.*

The administrator, Hirum Firum, was seventy-two years old with white wavy hair and walleyes. He was a scion of an old and wealthy Privilege family.

Administrator Firum arranged his ruddy face in a thoughtful expression and commenced with the reading of his opinion. "I have determined that your recent public remarks were silly as defined by law and in egregious violation of the public policy discussion parameters set out under Regulation 407. Your sins are further compounded by irrelevance as the term is defined under the It's All Forgotten Act of 1865. Listed among your egregious public pronouncements are that Africans were transported to Privilege as slaves, possessed as chattel property, exploited under abominable work conditions for centuries, and finally dismissed into a social and economic abyss without compensation for services rendered or restitution of any kind for injuries inflicted, psychic, social, or economic. You have further claimed that fifteen to thirty million Africans perished in 'the middle passage,' a denudation from which Africa is yet to recover. You have gone on to suggest, hysterically, that postemancipation general conditions of prejudice and discrimination have exacerbated the already woeful plight of blacks in a way that would explain the disparity between whites and blacks in income, test scores, and crime rates."

Administrator Firum paused to sip water from a glass on the table before him. Congressman Conyers sat impassive and alone in an armless chair five feet in front of the table.

Firum continued, "Pursuant to the Discussion Restriction Act and the It's All Forgotten Act of 1865 by which our nation and my newspaper are bound, I am expunging from the public record all your statements about the cumulative social and economic consequences of slavery and discrimination. I take this action not only in the national interest but in the interest of the black community of Privilege. The less they know about what happened to them, the less they will use it as a crutch." Firum looked up at Conyers, who was stolidly staring at the wall behind the administrator. "Congressman, I trust that the blacks of Privilege will quickly forget the nonsense you've been filling their heads with. After all, the government of Privilege cannot guarantee equality of success but only equality of opportunity, starting now. Or soon. Probably. In any case we will let bygones be bygones. My newspaper and others will divert attention from this unpleasantness with major coverage of the wedding of Menace Rodman, the black lady basketball star. Now *she* is a success your people should take a look at. Menace is a real role model! Negative Films Limited is doing a movie on her life starring Whoopi Goldberg."

Firum stopped abruptly. He had lost his place.

Congressman Conyers stared past him.

"As for reparations, Congressman, even if you had a case, we couldn't figure out how much to pay and to whom. You know. It all happened so long ago. The Japanese thing was easier. Kinda near and neat, you know." Firum chuckled at his witticism but was quickly sobered by Conyers's unblinking stare. "I am sentencing you to thirty days as a laughingstock to be served in Pillory No. 1776 in front of the Colin Powell Public Library on Booker T. Road at Gotcha. This will discourage the black citizens of Privilege from trying to provoke public discussion on issues outside our carefully set parameters. We can't control those hordes outside the city walls with that Farrakhan. But who listens to them anyhow?"

Over the next thirty days, thousands of whites visited Privilege's black community for the first time to see the pilloried congressman. They came mostly out of curiosity. Some appeared embarrassed. Others looked blankly at the stoic congressman's face poking through the pillory. A few laughed. There were only a handful of blacks to be seen. All had forgotten what his crime was and why he had committed the crime they had forgotten.

Congressman Conyers never caught sight of the most prominent black citizen of Privilege to visit the site of his bondage. The visitor rode by slowly, watching from the backseat of a long black sedan, wearing sunglasses. He was a shining star of the recent Republican National Convention and the most successful product of the GOP's Take Off Meteorically program which was known popularly as TOM. The whites of Privilege admired the new black star on the rise. More than a few Privilege blacks loved him too. But that was because whites thought so highly of him.

The handsome young former football hero, Congressman J. C. Watts, told his driver to move on before he could be recognized. His celebrity was becoming a burden. This new fame was largely the result of a stirring convention address in which he extolled to Privilege's poor people (who were not present, and who included more whites than blacks) the inestimable value of the loss of the meager welfare benefits on which the poor depended for food and housing. "You will have your dignity," the mocha-colored congressman said to the cheering throng, more than a quarter of whom were millionaires.

Upon leaving the dais, charged with adrenaline, the congressman was confronted by a network television journalist.

"Congressman, why don't we cut off aid to Israel, wealthy farmers, and corporate bailout recipients? How about a little dignity for the rich? Don't they deserve to have dignity as much as the poor?"

Congressman Watts was caught off guard. The camera was jutting at his face. "You can't have it all. If the poor have nothing else they will have at least their dignity. The rich will have no dignity but they will still be rich."

He thought it was a bad answer, poorly constructed, in large part because he didn't believe a word of it. But such was the price of black success in Privilege.

■

If there is really no such city with statutes limiting the speech and behavior of African-Americans, the city of Privilege very-much exists in the hearts, minds, and habits of Americans white and black, rich and poor, powerful and powerless.

African-Americans can speak but they cannot make themselves heard unless they say acceptable things and present no threat to the settled order. More than a few U.S. cavalrymen of the late 1800s believed that "the only good Indian is a dead Indian." One hundred years later, more than a few powerful Americans in business, media, government, education, religion, and virtually all other identifiable areas of civic function believe that the only good black is a black who "goes along to get along."

Virtually all black political, research, and civil rights organizations that operate in the United States—including my own organization, TransAfrica—are dependent upon grants from white American individuals and institutions. Thus African-American organizations are not "owned" by those whose message the organizations are perceived to convey.

TransAfrica was conceived in September 1976 in the home of C. Payne Lucas, the founder and president of Africare, which receives grants from private donors, corporations, foundations, and the U.S. government. The quarter-century-old organization, headquartered in Washington, D.C., has done seminal and invaluable development work across Africa. It is the only major African-American bridge to Africa in the development field.

C. Payne Lucas was one of four incorporators of TransAfrica in 1977. He sat on TransAfrica's original board of directors. When Ronald Reagan won the presidency in 1980 and immediately began to construct a de facto alliance with the white supremacist regime in South Africa, as I've described earlier, TransAfrica tenaciously opposed this emerging friendship. Fearing a loss of program support from the new administration, C. Payne Lucas resigned from TransAfrica's board of directors. I understood. I thought he did the only thing he could do, and we remained friends.

This story of black vulnerability has myriad chapters. The actor who speaks racially objectionable lines because he can find no other work. The politician who joins the Republican party "because the line for blacks is shorter over there." The African president who devalues his country's currency, driving food prices sky-high for his impoverished people, because the United States and the International Monetary Fund have pressured him to do it. The Caribbean president who sells off to

North American fire-sale bidders his country's parastatal institutions (as well as his country's independence) because an aid-providing U.S. has ordered him to "privatize" his tiny island nation's economy. Resource-starved black college presidents who honor a ninety-three-year-old South Carolina U.S. senator for being a rabid segregationist for only the first seventy years of his life. Black Republicans who sing the praises of their party's president after he has instructed his State of the Union speechwriter to "put something in for the jigs."

As a group, African-Americans have virtually no power or influence. Those like Colin Powell, who appear to have mainstream power, enjoy the appearance of power only as long as their circumscribed influence is not directed toward fundamentally altering social and economic conditions for a black community whence they sprang, at home and abroad. To make the point more broadly, blacks at rarefied levels can maintain altitude only as long as they accept, without unseemly exception, a national policy agenda to which they have made no real shaping contribution.

Two of the best placed, and most influential blacks in the country are Vernon Jordan and Colin Powell. During the Haitian crisis, as I've detailed, Haiti's brutal U.S.-trained army killed 5,000 prodemocracy civilians and chased 350,000 into internal hiding and another 50,000 into the open sea. When these men, women, and children, fleeing for their lives in jerry-built boats, were rounded up by U.S. vessels and returned to Haiti, President Clinton knew well that the practice was resulting in the mass deaths of innocent Haitians. Neither Powell nor Jordan raised any public objection to the forced repatriation policy. Jordan, I was later informed, was annoyed with *me* for publicly stating that the President, his friend, had become "complicit in the killing of fleeing innocent black Haitians."

Jesse Jackson and members of the Congressional Black Caucus like Donald Payne, Ron Dellums, Maxine Waters, and Major Owens did criticize the President and did so relentlessly. But their seats were further from the throne. Distance from the top for blacks varies directly with the discomfort one occasions for those who run things.

In the late seventies after a meeting with President Jimmy Carter on the subject of U.S. policy toward white-ruled Rhodesia, Ron Brown told M. Carl Holman, then president of the National Urban Coalition, that I had spoken too forcefully to the President on the continued need for American sanctions against Rhodesia, thus putting at risk any future access for me to the Oval Office. I had not been strident or impolite but simply firm in my view that any American retreat from multilaterally applied sanctions would set back the transition to democracy and lengthen the civil war that by then had claimed tens of thousands of lives. Later Ron Brown would become a registered lobbyist for the Haitian military dictatorship of Jean-Claude Duvalier before being named secretary of commerce in the first term of President Clinton.

This is not to disparage those blacks who elect to meet the unspoken requirements set out by white power brokers for higher-level black political success. Their choices are indeed as defensible as those of the brittle "race nationalists" who compromise nothing and therefore, in mainstream America, accomplish nothing.

The intent here is to examine why talented blacks feel constrained to choose, and to examine as well those blacks who manage to negotiate with honor the shoals of a racist and privilege-protective national political power society.

Ron Dellums, highly visible in his public advocacy, not only played a major role in shepherding through Congress the sanctions legislation that hastened the end of apartheid in South Africa but also became the first African-American chairman of the House Armed Services Committee. The former federal appeals court judge Leon Higginbotham, in his opposition to the appointment of Clarence Thomas to the Supreme Court, was not so neutered by the weight of white society honors that he couldn't think first about the impediment to black progress that Justice Thomas would doggedly pose.

Arthur Ashe, Bill Cosby, Danny Glover, Maya Angelou, Ray Leonard, Robert Guillaume, Alice Walker, and Stevie Wonder are just a handful of the artists and athletes who have supported black causes around the world and sustained careers simultaneously.

There are literally hundreds of thousands of more anonymous blacks who participate vigorously in a range of social causes. They raise and give money, write letters, show up for rallies, testify before Congress, travel to hot spots, attend meetings with policymakers, and speak out publicly. They do these things because they believe in their essential rightness and not because they feel pressure from the general black community.

Arthur Ashe, a member of TransAfrica Forum's board of directors and cochair of Artists and Athletes Against Apartheid, had great difficulty persuading black athletes to join the anti-apartheid campaign. Most were effectively cut off from the black community by white agents who warned them that they would be putting their endorsement prospects at great risk should they associate with any undertaking that was even vaguely controversial.

In 1990 Harvey Gantt, a black former mayor of Charlotte and North Carolina's Democratic candidate for the U.S. Senate, had at least an even chance to unseat Jesse Helms, racial bigotry's elected standard bearer. When Michael Jordan, a godlike figure in North Carolina, was asked to endorse Gantt's candidacy, he declined, explaining that "Republicans buy shoes too." Winning narrowly, Helms moved on in 1994 to become chairman of the Senate Foreign Relations Committee, from which post he has done incalculable damage to the interests of Africa, the Caribbean, and the developing world in general. Jordan's involvement might have made the difference for Gantt and removed from power a man who makes little secret of his malignant hostility to black interests, here and abroad.

Keith Richberg, a black writer at the *Washington Post*, visited a number of African countries and wrote a series of articles in 1995 that disparaged Africa beyond anything I could recognize from my years of rewarding travel to more than twenty countries across that continent. His painfully negative renderings appeared to bolster his career at the *Post.*

On the other hand, few, I suspect, realize how dedicated Bryant Gumbel was to black causes during his long stint as host of NBC's *Today* show. A few years ago Gumbel assembled the *Today* show staff and asked if anyone could identify the continent from which the show had never broadcasted. None could.

"Africa," Gumbel said. "We've yet to go to Africa." His staff was stunned.

By dint of Bryant Gumbel's tenacity, the *Today* show in November 1992 originated for one week from Harare, Zimbabwe. This live broadcast from Africa was a first for American television. As a result Americans got to learn more about Africa—its peoples, politics, cultures, and arresting landscapes—than they'd ever theretofore had any opportunity for.

▪ Spring 1997: Of Zaire/Congo

When White House press secretary Michael McCurry announced in April, "Mobutuism is about to become a creature of history," the thirty-two-year reign of Mobutu Sese Seko as ruler of Zaire was entering its last days—but no thanks to the United States.

Laurent Kabila, a surviving loyalist of the once-and-future Congo's first prime minister, Patrice Lumumba, and leader of the Alliance of Democratic Forces for the Liberation of Congo-Zaire, had by then secured the eastern half of the country and controlled virtually all of the country's revenue centers. Mobutu, ill with prostate cancer and reportedly financially strained after squandering five billion dollars looted from Zaire's treasury, thrashed about desperately in Kinshasa, the capital, for a miracle that might save his regime. After more than three decades of undisguised plunder, routine human rights abuse, and ruinous governance, he had tragicomically called (while pinned against death's proverbial door) for a cease-fire and national democratic elections.

For the whole of his country's postcolonial existence Mobutu had been hated and feared by his people. Now he was simply hated. His old Cold War enforcers—the Americans, the Belgians, and the French—had not shown up with the cavalry as they had so often done in the brutal past. The Cold War had ended and so had Mobutu's usefulness to the West. Ever the antiseptic if forgetful broker, the United States was working through South Africa and the United Nations to arrange a cease-fire. American officials, who for so many years publicly credited Mobutu with holding his nation of 250 ethnic groups together, still earnestly submitted that they feared instability more than anything else.

The aging kleptocrat must have been incredulous when told by Washington that he should slip quietly into exile—and that he would not be welcome in the United States. How shabby of the American ingrates. Despite the billions in U.S. aid and the two military rescues by Jimmy Carter, France, Belgium, and Morocco, he deserved better than this. He had ferried arms for Washington into Angola. He had given American businessmen the run of his country's precious resources, including a sweetheart deal struck with the American holy man Pat Robertson. He had been for thirty-two years Washington's bulwark against the spread of communism in Africa.

The men in the Oval Office always knew his methods. They knew he had to eliminate a few people. They knew he took a little for himself off the top. They knew he was no democrat, else he couldn't have been their man for so long in central Africa.

Indeed they knew and knew well. They knew that "their man's" personal wealth had come to equal Zaire's staggering national debt. They knew he was murdering his country and his people. They knew he had stolen the education money, the health care money, the road repair money, the telephone system money, and, less wisely as it turned out, the military payroll money. They knew all this and supported him anyway, more *because* of what they knew than in spite of it.

George Bush knew it and selected Mobutu as the first African head of state to be invited by his administration for an official visit to Washington, hailing the Zairian president as one of the United States' "oldest" and "most valued" friends in Africa.

It was never easy to be a friend of the United States and of one's own people at the same time, particularly when one's people were black. Indeed the feat was virtually impossible to accomplish during the Cold War. In Africa, a profoundly racist American foreign policy establishment had little on its mind beyond communist containment. The aspirations of Africa's people mattered hardly at all. After all, to more than a few American officials, even Africa's leaders were unflatteringly indistinguishable. In a March 1997 interview with Lynne Duke of the *Washington Post,* Chester Crocker said that Mobutu was no worse and no better than other African leaders of his era, thus equating statesmen like Julius Nyerere of Tanzania, Seretse Kharma of Botswana, Léopold Senghor of Senegal, and Kenneth Kaunda of Zambia with Mobutu Sese Seko—which is tantamount to seeing no difference between Franklin Delano Roosevelt and Al Capone. The aforementioned countries have been stable since their independence because they have been led by competent, honest, humane people. The Congo-Zaire is a volatile mess because U.S. State Department policymakers indistinguishable from Mr. Crocker tinkered cynically in the affairs of what could have become one of Africa's most successful nations by imposing on its people so obvious a viper as Mobutu.

"Well, it's no secret around here that the CIA installed Mobutu. The trouble is, there is nothing we can do about that now. If he goes down, who would we put in his place?" Richard Moose, assistant secretary of state for African affairs in the Carter administration said this to me as he packed boxes in his office preparing to leave the State Department in the late 1970s. The *we* in his question jumped out at me. Moose was a decent and likable man. But I don't believe that democracy for Zaire ever occurred to him or to anyone else in his job before the demise of the Soviet Union. American strategic interests in the region were not to be made subject to the vagaries of some democratic electorate. Mobutu was America's man, and that was all there was to it.

I don't know how to write this. How to set my voice. How to select the words. I—we—black people globally—have become so accustomed to not being listened to. The urge is to scream, but this irritates the uninitiated. The lawyer in me subdues and pulls me within the rules, realm, and language of the rationalists who enjoy the perennial advantage in their court of discussion. Emotion is off-putting when unshared, and I have no idea how the exterior side of my anger looks. But what the United States has done to Zaire and much of Africa—done with gloves so as to leave no fingerprints—is unpardonable. Zairians,

Somalis, Liberians, Angolans, Sudanese, Kenyans appear to have destroyed their own societies without accomplices. No news-account fingers point at the American partners who comment coolly and with reasoned detachment on the wreckage they have wrought. Power means in the last analysis never having to say you are sorry—or acknowledge that there is even anything to be sorry *about.*

Americans, black and white, have only gotten to see the mute husks of failed African nation states. The viable states are never showcased for popular consumption. Only the images of human misery. Refugee tides. Distended bellies. Corrupt "big" men. Racist assumptions supported, rationalized, deepened. Never taking notice that so very many of the blameworthy were here—*are* here. But their anonymous faces, smug with career progress, are never seen through the flames.

I never knew Patrice Lumumba. I was nineteen years old and in college when he was assassinated in 1960. I recall reading a news story at the time that went "Leftist Prime Minister Patrice Lumumba was killed yesterday in the former Belgian Congo . . ." or words to that effect. He had been killed by Congolese political enemies, the story said. The United States was not mentioned. The Congo seemed to me an unstable, ungovernable place. This was the general tenor of American press coverage. I knew very little about Africa then, and even less about the Congo. But I liked what Lumumba had to say about what he hoped for his country and his people. I had also seen a picture of Lumumba taken while he was being held just before he was killed. He had an open, decent, intelligent face.

Thirty-two years later, upon reading a scholarly article by Peter J. Schraeder of Loyola University of Chicago, I learned of "President Eisenhower's authorization in 1960 of a covert operation designed to 'permanently' remove Congolese Prime Minister Patrice Lumumba from the political scene." Of course this never became an issue for Eisenhower. He had worn gloves.

One questions, in any case, whether Lumumba was in fact a leftist or communist. Technically communism has to do with state ownership of the means of economic production. American political leaders have often seemed unclear about communism's definition, thinking it the opposite of democracy. The two systems, one economic and the other political, are not necessarily, at least theoretically, incompatible. Such distinctions, however, have never bothered the sermonizing stump demagogues who mix the two notions wackily to mesmerizing effect in mainstream America.

In retrospect I seriously doubt that Lumumba was a communist or anything vaguely resembling one. But acquittal on that charge alone would not have removed him from America's crosshairs. American practice over the years would suggest that it is not really communism that bothers us so much. China, now practicing something called market Leninism, calls itself a communist country, but the American establishment is wild about China. It enjoys most-favored-nation status and the American business sector salivates over the elasticity of its market and the low cost of its labor. Vietnam calls itself a communist country, but Phil Knight of Nike loves it because of the shockingly low wages he gets away with paying to his malnourished workers there. So it appears that self-declarations of communism are not what bother those who work the American power levers.

What politically powerful and wealthy corporate Americans have never tolerated easily are the "communists" who are really not communists at all. Those who would qualify in this category include, among others, Third World leaders who tend to put the concerns of their people before all else in a way that disquiets powerful American business interests. Put another way, much of this is about the big influence of big money. Let American or Western corporations have their way in your country, and all is fine. But when national or host-country leaders question privatization, or unionize, or impose workplace safety standards, or condition corporate access in any way, they run afoul of big business. At one time or another Nelson Mandela, Jean-Bertrand Aristide, and Michael Manley of Jamaica were called communists by American political and business leaders. None ever was.

The absence of democracy has seldom discouraged relations with Washington and has more often than not been viewed favorably by the business sector. Indonesia is a useful example. It offers a stable military dictatorship, a rapidly expanding market, and tolerable investment conditions. Despite its deplorable human rights record, Indonesia remains palatable to the Clinton administration and attractive to American investors. General Sani Abacha owes his Nigerian military dictatorship to American, British, Dutch, and French oil companies that operate unfettered either by their own governments or by Nigeria's. Black South Africans appreciate well that if their country had had oil resources, we might never have accomplished the imposition of American economic sanctions over the opposition of a powerful multinational oil lobby.

The Congolese independence movement was led in 1960 from two camps. The one including Patrice Lumumba called for "authentic" independence in the Congo's political and economic spheres as well as nonalignment in its global relations. The more conservative group, favored by multinational companies in the Congo, included Joseph Kasavubu, the Congo's first president, and Colonel Joseph Mobutu, later to be known as Mobutu Sese Seko. Thus was Lumumba branded a "communist" and his death warrant signed.

Five years later Mobutu would be installed by the CIA in a coup d'état and become America's man in Zaire. President John F. Kennedy noted: "General, if it hadn't been for you, the whole thing would have collapsed and the communists would have taken over." Of course, there were no communists—only Africans who took their hard-won independence all too literally.

Shortly after Mobutu's assumption of power, an old friend who had been Kinshasa CIA station chief during the 1960s, Lawrence Devlin, would return to Zaire as the representative of Maurice Tempelsman, an influential American businessman with diamond trade investments in Zaire and access to the Oval Office.

In addition to diamonds Zaire had substantial deposits of copper, tin, zinc, cobalt, silver, and gold. American and French and Belgian investors found the doors to the vault now open. The corrupt doorkeeper Mobutu—their man, the State Department's man, France's man, Belgium's man—was in iron-fisted control.

He was everyone's man but Zaire's.

While his various depredations were draining the treasury, bankrupting the country, and contaminating the values of at least a generation of Zairians, Mobutu did little to cause the United States to consider reducing its military and economic support through the 1970s and 1980s. As Carter's secretary of state Cyrus Vance explained in his memoir, *Hard Choices: Critical Years in America's Foreign Policy,* "None of us wished to face the uncertain consequences that might flow from the collapse of his regime and the subsequent disintegration of Zaire into unstable segments open to radical penetration." Not, at least, until after he had lost his usefulness with the demise of the Soviet Union.

In the early 1990s, more than twenty-five years after installing and maintaining Mobutu in power, the United States began to call for democratic national elections, throwing its support in organizing the elections behind Kengo wa Dondo, Mobutu's prime minister of the moment. Neither Kengo nor his revolving-door successors lasted. By early 1997, Laurent Kabila's rebel army, moving rapidly across a country the size of the United States east of the Mississippi River, had taken every major city save the capital of Kinshasa, then paused only long enough to permit a bloodless capitulation. His army's progress might have been faster had any of the paid-for roads been built by the crumbling regime.

It is too early to calculate the damage that Mobutu's cancerous example of leadership did to Congo's prospects for long-term stability. My guess is that this potentially wealthy country will take decades to repair itself, even should it be blessed with honest, principled, and competent leadership. The country's infrastructure is in unspeakable disrepair. Its customs of commerce have been badly corrupted. Its long-suffering, ethnically riven people now face the question of whether they can even cohere as a nation.

No one is more responsible for the battered state of the country than President Mobutu and the large class of crooked associates he cultivated through the years. But he could have done none of this without powerful patrons in Washington, Paris, and

Brussels. In the last analysis, their acts are no less reprehensible, their character no less wanting, their soft hands no less soiled.

Gloves notwithstanding.

■ May 1997: Washington, D.C.

Father Griffin has died at the age of eighty-seven. The former Tuskegee airman lived an exemplary life, giving love to Mama and affection to her children, thousands to Johnson C. Smith University, the small black college he attended in Charlotte, North Carolina, and a model for living to any who caught steady sight of him. He is buried at Arlington National Cemetery. General Benjamin O. Davis Jr., the highest ranking black officer of his era, attends the interment ceremony and tells Mama that Father Griffin helped countless black soldiers during his time as an army chaplain. General Davis was at one time a very famous American. Father Griffin never once mentioned to me that he even knew him.

For now, Mama wants to remain in Norfolk. Jeanie has started divinity school at American University and is doing very well. Jewell continues to pursue work in the theater. Jabari is attending Howard University and Anike is teaching high school.

In June Hazel and I will celebrate our tenth wedding anniversary. It was more than fourteen years ago that we saw first a sign of what we together might become.

I think of Max every day.

I have been back to Haiti three times since President Aristide's return, on one occasion for his marriage to Mildred Truillot, and on another to head a group of observers to monitor the parliamentary elections of June 1995. Our group included the chairman of the Congressional Black Caucus, Donald

Payne, the actor Danny Glover, the labor leader Bill Lucy, the Harvard Law professor Charles Ogletree, and Gay McDougall, who had organized South Africa's nearly flawless elections. On the ground in Haiti, the group coordinated its deployment around the country with Ambassador Colin Granderson, a distinguished Trinidadian national who headed the OAS/UN Civilian Mission to Haiti. We had arrived only a day before the elections, but Granderson's observers, numbering in the hundreds, had been deployed around Haiti for months. On election day our group visited 120 polling stations around the country and witnessed nothing more irregular than a late opening or two. Granderson's legions visited thousands of stations and saw little to give serious concern.

That evening in Port-au-Prince, at the Villa Creole Hotel, I happened upon Robert Pastor of the Carter Center. "Is the Carter Center monitoring the elections?" I asked.

"No. I'm here alone. I just thought I'd come down and look around."

Weeks later I learned from a *New York Times* editorial and prominently placed article that the Carter Center had reported the elections to have been plagued by fraud and irregularity. The report relied upon by the *Times* had been prepared by the one-man team of Robert Pastor, who after a few days in a country of seven million presumed to know quite enough to counter the assessment of an OAS/UN team of hundreds that had blanketed the country with trained observers for months before and after the elections.

The moral? It has always been painfully clear to African-Americans. If you wish to persuade influential white Americans of anything, whether praiseworthy or outrageous, start by getting a white American to present the tale. This is what Congressman Murtha had labored to tell an incredulous Congressman Dellums.

Some months after returning from Haiti, Hazel and I attended a parent-teacher conference at Khalea's school. Khalea attends Beauvoir, a highly rated private school situated on the well-manicured lush grounds of the Washington Cathedral. She had tested as a gifted child, and we were not surprised to learn that she was doing well in class. Everyone associated with the Beauvoir family was warm and friendly. Andrea Bowrie, Khalea's teacher that year, was no exception. As our successful conference drew to a close, Hazel thought to clarify a matter that had only just occurred to her.

"What does this 'time out' mean?" Hazel asked.

"Children are placed in time out for disciplinary reasons," explained Andrea Bowrie. "They go to a corner alone and remain apart from the class and quiet for a period of time."

"Khalea tells us that all of the black girls in her class have been put in time out and none of the white girls. Is this true?" Hazel asked.

There were three black girls in the class in addition to Khalea. One was Vanessa, whose mother, Gayle Williams, sat on the Beauvoir governing board. Kristin was the daughter of Jack White, a columnist for *Time* magazine. Erica was the daughter of Judge Eric Washington of the D.C. Superior Court. They were well-behaved girls. Kristin was so quiet, I'd not have known her voice, although she came to our home often to play with Khalea.

"Yes, that is true," said Ms. Bowrie.

"How can that be so?" Hazel asked, more mystified than upset. "I know these girls and they are well mannered. Yet all of them have been isolated from the class and not one of the white girls has been disciplined in the same way. Doesn't that seem odd to you?"

"No," replied Bowrie. "Studies show that black parents rear their children to be more aggressive."

Later, there would be profuse apologies from the school, copious tears from the teacher. But the damage was done, mirroring in its particular and personal way the problems we face on a global scale.

Where does a black soul go to rest?

I would not be surprised if much of what I have written here is met by whites with defensiveness, if not incredulity. Our society has not been obliged to think critically and constructively about its racial dilemma for many years. If I have appeared angry, that anger in all likelihood understates the well-masked temper of blacks generally. I don't know what Asians and Hispanics think because I know no Asians or Hispanics well enough. This is intrinsic to the problem. We are, in America, now sealed off from each other in well-defended racial camps with negligible inter-group knowledge or communication. Our nation's white leaders have elected, consciously or unconsciously, to ignore the deepening national racial crisis. In so doing, they have set us all on a course toward disaster.

Somewhere near the halfway mark of the twenty-first century, Asian, Hispanic, and African-Americans will combine to make white Americans a minority.

Better we face the painful problem now than the conflagration looming ahead.

■ SOURCES ■

Associated Press. "Blacks Jailed After Sit-In At Pretoria Mission in U.S." *International Herald Tribune* (Paris), November 23, 1984.

Balch, Emily Greene (ed.). *Occupied Haiti.* New York: Negro Universities Press, 1927 (reprint 1969).

Barber, Ben. "Republican Haiti-watchers Say Vote Fell Short of Clinton Goal." *Washington Times,* January 26, 1996.

Blustein, Paul. "Carribean Could Wonder Where the Yellow Went." *Washington Post*, March 19, 1997, p. C9.

Bredemeir, Kenneth. "Fauntroy Arrested in Embassy." *Washington Post,* November 22, 1984, p. A1.

Brummer, Stefaans. "South Africa Takes a Step Back From Putting Nigeria in the Hot Seat." *Christian Science Monitor,* April 22, 1996.

Buckley, Stephen. "Mali: Tuned In And Democratic." *Washington Post,* March 24, 1996, p. A27.

"Burying Mobutuism." *New York Times,* April 13,1997, p. 14E.

Chege, Michael. "Remembering Africa; Foreign Affairs." *America and the World,* 1991/92, p. 146.

Claiborne, William. "South Africa's Quiet Revolution." *Washington Post,* January 14, 1990, p. B1

Clough, Michael. *Free at Last?: U.S. Policy Toward Africa and the End of the Cold War.* New York: Council on Foreign Relations, 1992.

Cohen, Richard. "Obliged to Lead." *Washington Post,* May 3, 1994, p. A23.

Danaher, Kevin. *In Whose Interest? A Guide to U.S.–South Africa Relations.* Washington, D.C.: Institute for Policy Studies, 1984.

Davidson, Basil. *The Black Man's Burden: Africa and the Curse of the Nation-State.* New York: Times Books, 1992.

de Jenquierec, Guy. "WTO Puts Skids Under Banana Regime." *Financial Times* (London).

Duke, Lynne. "An Ally in Africa, But What Price?" *Washington Post,* April 1, 1997.

——. "Zaire's Mobutu Rejects Resignation Demand." *Washington Post,* April 13, 1997, p. A 23.

Eminent Persons Group. "The US and Chiquita at the WTO." Report, December 2–6, 1996.

Fick, Carolyn E. *The Making of Haiti: The Saint Domingue Revolution from Below.* Knoxville: The University of Tennessee Press, 1990.

Frankel, Glenn. "Nigeria Mixes Oil and Money." *Washington Post,* November 24, 1996, p. C 1.

Franklin, John Hope, and Alfred A. Moss, Jr. *From Slavery to Freedom: A History of Negro Americans,* seventh edition. New York: McGraw-Hill, 1994.

Fredericks, J. Wayne. Statement to the U.S. House of Representatives Subcommittee on Africa, on U.S. private investment in South Africa. July 12, 1978.

French, Howard W. "An African Anomaly: Election Up for Grabs." *New York Times,* March 2, 1996.

——. "A Three-Cornered Struggle to Redraw Zaire's Political Map." *New York Times,* April 13, 1997, p. 12.

——. "Mobutu Imposes Military Rule in Zaire." *New York Times,* April 10, 1997, p. A12.

Herbert, Bob. "Colin's Dream." *New York Times,* August 19, 1996, p. A13.

Hornsby, Alton, *Chronology of African-American History: Significant Events and People from 1619 to The Present.* Detroit: Gale Research, 1991.

James, C. L. R. *The Black Jacobins: Toussaint L'Ouverture and the San*

Domingo Revolution. New York: Dial, 1938 (reprint New York: Vintage, 1989).

Jordan, Gregory. "Publications Focusing on Africa Disappear." *New York Times,* November 18, 1996, p. D10.

Kennedy, Randall. *Blacks at Harvard.* New York University Press, 1993.

Kranish, Michael. "Antiapartheid Pioneer Is on a New Crusade." Boston Globe, April 27, 1994, p. 1.

Leslie, Winsome J. *Zaire: Continuity and Political Change in an Oppressive State.* Boulder, Colo.: Westview, 1993.

Lewis, Anthony. "The Savimbi Smear." *New York Times,* October 5, 1989.

Mazrui, Ali A. *The Africans: A Triple Heritage.* Boston: Little, Brown, 1986.

Mbeki, Moeletsi. "South Africa and the U.S." *Johannesburg Star*, April 1, 1997.

Moffett, George D. "US Sanctions Get Credit For Anti-apartheid Role." *Christian Science Monitor,* July 2, 1991, p. 7.

Mokoena, Kenneth (ed.). *South Africa and the United States: the Declassified History.* New York: New Press, 1993.

Morris, Roger. *Uncertain Greatness: Henry Kissinger and American Foreign Policy.* New York: Harper & Row, 1977.

Murray, Frank J. "6 House Members Arrested in Protest." *Washington Times,* April 22, 1994, p. A1.

Musters, Brooke. "After 5 Convictions, One Drunk Driver Gets 5 Months' Jail Time." *Washington Post,* April 16, 1997, p. A1.

Mutibwa, Phares. *Uganda since Independence.* Lawrenceville, N.J.: Africa World Press, 1992.

Mydans, Seth. "Hellbent on Progress, Thais Sidestep Priesthood." *New York Times,* March 11, 1996.

Payne, Douglas W. "Barbados and the OECS: Leadership in the Caribbean." Working papers, Center for Strategic and International Studies, September 25, 1996, p. 1.

"PC Fritz in Switzerland." *The Rising Tide* 1, no. 3 (March/April 1994).

Ploski, Harry A., and James Williams (eds.). *The Negro Almanac: A Reference Work on the African-American.* Detroit: Gale Research, 1989.

Rasmussen, R. Kent, and Steven C. Rubert. *Historical Dictionary of Zimbabwe.* Metuchen, N.J.: Scarecrow, 1990.

Remnick, David. "Facing Off at the South African Embassy." *Washington Post,* February 5, 1985, p. E1.

Ridenour, David. *Senator Hatch Calls for Justice Department Investigation of Robinson and TransAfrica: Illegal Funding Alleged.* The National Center for Public Policy Research, October 3, 1989.

Ritchie, Joe. "U.S. Details Terms for Closer South African Ties." *Washington Post,* May 29, 1981.

Rohter, Larry. "Promoting a Trade Partnership with the Caribbean Basin Region." *New York Times,* January 30, 1997.

———. "Uncle Sam and Guatemala: Whew! That War's Over. Ready for Another." *New York Times,* January 5, 1997.

Safire, William. "Bananagate." *New York Times,* March 26, 1997.

Schraeder, Peter J. "Bureaucratic Influence in U.S.-Zairian Special Relationship." *TransAfrica Forum* 9, no. 3 (Fall 1992): 31–56 (reprint New Brunswick, N.J.: Transaction Periodicals Consortium, Rutgers University, November 1992).

Shepherd, George W., Jr. (ed.). *Effective Sanctions on South Africa.* Westport, Conn.: Praeger, 1991.

Stockwell, John. *In Search of Enemies: A CIA Story.* New York: W. W. Norton, 1978.

Thompson, Leonard Monteath. *A History of South Africa.* New Haven, Conn.: Yale University Press, 1990.

TransAfrica. *TransAfrica News Report Special Edition: New U.S. Policy on South Africa—State Department Documents Uncover Developing Alliance.* Washington, D.C.: TransAfrica, August 1981.

TransAfrica Forum. *A Retrospective: Blacks in U.S. Foreign Policy.* Washington, D.C.: TransAfrica Forum, 1987.

Toussaint-L'ouverture. *Toussaint L'Ouverture: Biography and Autobiography.* Boston: James Redpath, 1863 (reprint North Stratford, N.H.: Ayer, 1991)

United Nations Development Programme. *Human Development Report 1996.* New York: Oxford University Press, 1996.

U.S. Department of State. *International Narcotics Control Strategy Report.* March 1996.

Uwechue, Ralph (ed.). *Africa Who's Who,* second edition. London: Africa Books, 1991.

Weisskopf, Michael. "The Busy Back-Door Men." *Time,* March 31, 1997, p. 40.

Willame, J. C., et al. *Zaire: Predicament and Prospects—A Report to the Minority Rights Group (USA). Peaceworks* 11, (Washington, D.C.: United States Institute of Peace, January 1997).

Williams, Eric. *From Columbus to Castro: The History of the Caribbean.* London: Andre Deutsch, 1970 (reprint New York: Vintage, 1984).

Wilson, Woodrow. "Reconstruction in the Southern States." *Atlantic Monthly,* January 1901.

World Bank. *World Development Report 1996.* New York: Oxford University Press, 1996.

Index